Imperial Bedlam

Medicine and Society
Andrew Scull, Editor

This series examines the development of medical knowledge and psychiatric practice from historical and sociological perspectives. The books contribute to a scholarly and critical reflection on the nature and role of medicine and psychiatry in modern societies.

Imperial Bedlam

Institutions of Madness
in Colonial Southwest Nigeria

Jonathan Sadowsky

UNIVERSITY OF CALIFORNIA PRESS

Berkeley / Los Angeles / London

University of California Press
Berkeley and Los Angeles, California
University of California Press, Ltd.
London, England

Library of Congress Cataloging-in-Publication Data
Sadowsky, Jonathan Hal.
    Imperial bedlam : institutions of madness in colonial southwest
Nigeria / Jonathan Sadowsky.
        p.   cm. — (Medicine and society ; 10)
    Originally presented as the author's thesis (doctoral—Johns
Hopkins University, 1993).
    Includes bibliographical references and index.
    ISBN 0-520-21616-4 (alk. paper)
        1. Psychiatric hospitals—Nigeria—History.   2. Mentally ill—
Care—Nigeria—History.   3. Mental illness—Treatment—Nigeria—
History.   4. Psychiatry—Nigeria—History.   5. Imperialism—Health
aspects—Nigeria—History.   6. Nigeria—Colonial influence—
Health aspects—History.   7. Nigeria—Colonization—Health
aspects—History.   I. Title.   II. Series.
        [DNLM: 1. Hospitals, Psychiatric—history—Nigeria.
2. Colonialism—Nigeria.   WI ME6490 v. 10 1999 / WM 27 HN5
S126i 1999]
    RC451.N5S23   1999
    362.2'1'09669—dc21
    DNLM/DLC
    for Library of Congress   99-10222
                                                                          CIP

Manufactured in the United States of America

08   07   06   05   04   03   02   01   00   99   10   9   8   7   6   5   4   3   2   1

The paper used in this publication meets the minimum requirements of ANSI/NISO
Z39.48-1992 (R 1997) (*Permanence of Paper*).

Contents

Preface

This project had its origins in a graduate school African history seminar in the spring of 1988, when I first read Megan Vaughan's article on the Zomba lunatic asylum in colonial Nyasaland. I thought that the article raised so many interesting questions—about madness, and about colonialism—that more extended treatments of the subject were called for.

That summer, I discovered in Nigeria's National Archives in Ibadan a number of documents pertaining to colonial asylums, and a central question formed: How did colonial institutions determine whom to confine? The inmates numbered in the hundreds, and although this is not a terribly large number in such a populous country, two factors did make the confinement process especially curious. One was that many in the colonial government recognized that cultural differences made the designation of insanity in Nigerians difficult for them. The second was that the government had very little interest in confining people, given that this represented an expense. They considered therapeutic goals extravagant, and whereas any government has social control needs, it was not clear why asylums were needed in addition to prisons.

The project seemed significant in three respects. First, the asylums provided a case study of a colonial institution and the formation of a colonial social policy. The second developed from the discovery of patient records, which provided a way to examine the social process of determining insanity in a context of cultural difference and political domination. Third, analysis of psychiatric writings by British alienists, as psychiatrists were then known, instantiated the role of social factors in the production of knowledge.

I conducted the majority of the research in Nigeria between January 1990 and April 1991. The data are mostly archival, drawn from Nigeria's National Archives in Ibadan and case files from the Aro Mental Hospital in Abeokuta, to which the hospital graciously allowed me access. To get a stronger sense of the wider social field in which the asylums had been operating I, with the assistance of the Dr. Samuel Osunwole of the Institute of African Studies at the University of Ibadan, also conducted a number of interviews with traditional healers. This study, though, has not been conceived primarily as an investigation of Yoruba medicine. This is a subject that has received, and continues to receive, much deserved attention; to pursue it in its complexity and make a new contribution is beyond the scope of my main interest, the asylums. There is certainly a great deal more ethnomedical and ethnopsychiatric work to be done, and I hope to convince future researchers in this area of the value of a historical approach.

Mental illness is a notably private matter in any society I have lived in or studied. For this reason, my desire to be a tenacious researcher sometimes conflicted with the recognition that there were borders that should be respected. I did not, for example, pursue the families or descendants of inmates in cases where that might have been possible. This, I thought, might have brought attention to the families in inappropriate ways.

One of the greatest dangers in historical research is overestimating the significance of one's data. In this case, a particular hazard would have been to intimate that the asylum inmates in colonial Nigeria exemplify a colonial condition. I argue that their experiences cannot be understood except as part of the colonial situation but also that they were not typical or "normal" experiences of colonialism. I also show that in many cases these people were understood as mad by their kin and neighbors and not only by a colonial state. Arguably, asylum inmates were not even representative of the mad generally. Nigerian physician T. A. Lambo, the dean of Nigerian psychiatry, showed in the 1950s that patients treated in more traditional settings differed culturally from those in institutions and had different frames of reference. The asylums were significant in themselves but were exceptional in a number of respects.

Acknowledgments

Three advisors oversaw this study as a dissertation. Gillian Feeley-Harnik provided consistent inspiration as she stressed the intimate connections between the material and mental or spiritual. David William Cohen showed the value of examining the structure of scholarly debates and showing the assumptions common to both sides. Philip Curtin urged the value of placing specific material in comparative context. Sara Berry and Ruth Leys also provided very helpful guidance during the writing.

The research was funded by the Social Science Research Council, which also provided significant intellectual and logistical support. The SSRC also funded a valuable semester at the Columbia University School of Public Health, where I was a Visiting Fellow in the Psychiatric Epidemiology Training Program. At Columbia, I received valuable commentary from Bruce Dohrenwend, Bruce Link, Michael Teitelman, Inge Goldstein, Sharon Schwartz, and Ilan Meyer.

In Nigeria, the Institute for African Studies at the University of Ibadan provided a constructive working environment. Samuel Osunwole provided especially invaluable help. Bolanle Awe and Bayo Adekola also assisted me in important ways.

Many eminent figures in the Nigerian psychiatric professions welcomed and helped me more than I could have wished—I only hope I was not too much of a nuisance. In particular, I thank Tolani Asuni, Olufemi Morakinyo, A. A. Marinho, A. O. Odejide, Isaac Ekuesan, M. Olu Oyebanjo-Akinsola, and I. Dokun-Fatade. Special thanks to T. A. Lambo, the acknowledged father of psychiatry in Nigeria, who showed great patience as I pestered him for information!

For friendship and hospitality in Nigeria, thanks to Simon Heep, Kehinde Duze, Taiwo Duze, Dawn Davis, Dov and Dorit Shacham, Zvi and Rina Dubitsky, Laray Denzer, Debbie Klein, Kola Imasogie, Kareem Musa, David Moffat, David and Helen Williams, Carolyn Keyes Adenaike, Pius Omole, Leon Volterre, and Femi Areola.

In England, Roy Porter, Megan Vaughan, and John Iliffe provided useful advice. Professor Iliffe shared some of his own research notes with me, and my chapter on the nineteenth century is particularly indebted to his generosity.

The writing benefited from a fellowship at the Institute for Advanced Research in the Humanities in Africa, Evanston, Illinois. In Evanston, Ivan Karp provided especially provocative commentary. My ideas were also clarified by participating in the 1995 National Endowment for the Humanities Summer Institute on the Contributions of the History of Medicine to Social History, directed by Barron Lerner and David Rothman.

Alexander Boroffka was generous in sharing his immense store of relevant documentation and provided a critical reading of the text.

Graduate students ideally learn as much from each other as from their supervisors. For support and critique of often extraordinary kinds I would like especially to thank Keith Breckenridge, Tim Burke, Catherine Burns, Garrey Dennie, Marta Elliott, Tamara Giles-Vernick, Carolyn Hamilton, Carlos Madrid, Sarah Madrid, and Rebecca Plant.

During the period when I transformed this project from a dissertation into a monograph, I profited from the advice and encouragement of my colleagues and students in the History Department at Case Western Reserve University. Catherine Kelly, Miriam Levin, Alan Rocke, Ted Steinberg, and Angela Woollacott read virtually all of the text. I was also lucky to have the support of several colleagues in the Anthropology Department expert in psychological anthropology—Thomas Csordas, Atwood Gaines, and Janis Jenkins, whose work in related areas helped me to clarify the approaches I wanted to take. Martha Woodmansee of the English Department has also been a helpful mentor to me.

Karin Barber, Chris Dole, Sander Gilman, Dieter Hollstein, Paul Landau, Philippa Levine, Shula Marks, Ugo Nwokeji, Micah Parzen, Annemarie Strassel, Mark Warren, Christina Welter, and Andrea Westcot, read all or parts of the manuscript and provided helpful criticism and advice.

Special thanks to Laura Steinberg, who was vital in too many ways to list.

A version of chapter 5 appeared in *History of Psychiatry* 7 (1996): 91–112, and a version of chapter 6 appeared in the *Bulletin of the History of Medicine* 71, 1 (Spring 1997): 94–111. I thank these journals for permission to republish them here.

CHAPTER I

Introduction

Despite the development of psychiatry as a scientific discipline over the last 100 years, the fundamental question of what mental illness is, still haunts the profession. . . . No tests have yet been developed to determine objectively the presence or absence of most mental diseases. . . . The criteria for medical diseases are physico-chemical, while the criteria for psychiatric diseases are social and ethical.[1]

David, patient in Yaba Mental Hospital, 1987

In 1987, to celebrate its eightieth year, the Yaba Mental Hospital in Lagos published a pamphlet entitled *From Asylum to Hospital.* The title of the pamphlet celebrated an advance from custody to therapy that was achieved simultaneously with Nigeria's transition to independence. A number of patients wrote contributions to the pamphlet. A patient, David, wrote a short piece entitled "What Is Mental Illness?" that challenged the celebratory note with this sentiment— familiar from the writings of maverick psychiatrists or radical sociologists but more remarkable coming from a hospitalized mental patient.

What follows is a historical inquiry into the proposition David advanced. Though less firmly committed than he to the principle that the criteria for mental illnesses are entirely social rather than biochemical, it pursues the insight that the identification of insanity conveys important social meanings. The focus is on two institutions in southwest Nigeria, the Yaba Lunatic Asylum (later, "Mental Hospital") in Lagos and Aro Mental Hospital in Abeokuta, during the colonial period.

These institutions originated in the late nineteenth century, when residents of southern Nigerian cities were troubled by an apparent swarm of "lunatics" on the streets. Few Nigerians had enthusiasm for asylums, and most preferred their traditional methods of care. Suspicion toward institutionalization is still strong in Nigeria, and workers in the mental hospitals concede that they are sought out only after Nigerians have brought mentally ill people to traditional or religious healers of some kind.[2] But colonial officials and many Africans shared a perception that a growing number of people were not being adequately taken care of by these methods. The colonial government followed British precedent and built large asylums to confine lunatics. Colonial policy, though, held that the asylums should be a last resort. The insane, most government officials felt, were better cared for in their own communities.

This preference followed from the policy of Indirect Rule, a policy associated with Nigeria's first governor, Lord Frederick Lugard. In Nigeria, particularly the north, Lugard developed the practice of ruling via local African rulers, with the aim of preserving "traditional" ways of life.[3] According to the "dual mandate" of Indirect Rule, British presence in Africa served two purposes: financial gain for Britain and the "development" of Africa. The goal of developing Africa was in some ways a transparent rationalization for colonial rule, but the forms that rationale took had real consequences. Asylum policy reveals with some clarity the contradictions caused by the larger policy. The "African way of life" did not appear to include lunatic asylums—yet the hundreds of people confined were outnumbered by those turned away due to lack of space. The asylum, introduced diffidently in the early colonial period, had become an established, even famous, feature of the Nigerian landscape by the time independence came in 1960.

Critical studies of mental pathology in Africa are not new. In fact, they form a cornerstone of the social criticism of Frantz Fanon, possibly the most famous psychiatrist to have done clinical work in Africa. Fanon's experiences working in a colonial mental hospital in Algeria radicalized him, catalyzing one of the most searching critiques of the late colonial social order.[4] In the section on "Colonial War and Mental Disorders" in *The Wretched of the Earth*,[5] Fanon presented case studies of a number of psychiatric patients, both Algerian and French, who had been traumatized by experiences in the revolt.[6] The case histories Fanon presented are extremely vivid and powerful, but there is an inconstancy in the way he interprets them. On the one hand, Fanon stressed the specificity of the situation. These were not just pathologies of colonialism, he showed, but problems particular to an exceedingly violent conflict. His experiences with patients were an important factor in his own politicization, as the futility of trying to produce mental health in individuals in the midst of an anticolonial war became clear to him.[7] At the same time, though, he generalized boldly, expanding from the material into commentary about Africa and indeed the entire colonized world. For Fanon, the "cases" became exemplars of a colonial condition; for example, he states a number of times that colonialism produces mental pathology itself, an intriguing claim, but one which is difficult to establish and which goes beyond Fanon's more readily persuasive argument that colonialism strongly determines the symptoms and content of the pathology.[8] This latter insight is one I pursue in detail.

The study of insanity and psychiatric institutions in colonial Africa is now receiving renewed scrutiny from historians.[9] Vaughan has led the way; her 1983 article in the *Journal of Southern African Studies* showed how the course of a lunatic's confinement could provide a window through which to observe political and cultural conflict, between Africans and Europeans, and within the two communities.[10] Her work also showed that the agenda of European psychiatric historiography cannot be imported without modification. Vaughan observed, for example, that there was no "great confinement" of the insane in Malawi analogous to that made notorious by Michel Foucault.[11]

Vaughan's work has been followed by Jock McCulloch's wide-ranging study of colonial psychiatry. McCulloch has pursued and amplified the insight that colonial psychiatry had only limited insight into the psychology of Africans but provides useful sources for understanding colonial mentality. So far, though, little of the literature on African psychiatric history has given close attention to the patients' representation of illness experience, which has been a high priority in the wider historiography of medicine in recent years.[12] This probably reflects source limitations more than the priorities of researchers but is all the more reason to pay careful attention to what sources are available. The perspectives of patients are elusive quarry in the history of psychiatry for any part of the world and a major concern in what follows.

*Despite the development of psychiatry as a scientific
discipline . . .*

Colonial asylum policy reveals in microcosm the dynamics of the Nigerian colonial state. It also may provide a fresh look at those most spoiled terms in psychiatric history—social control and reform. The historiography of psychiatry has matured to a point where it is no longer possible to describe the history either as one of progress toward ever more benevolent reforms, or toward increasingly sinister forms of social control.[13] The most important stimulus to the anti-hagiographic research on the history of psychiatric institutions was the publication in 1961 of Michel Foucault's arresting study *Madness and Civilization*. The beginning of a remarkable career of unsettling scholarship, *Madness and Civilization* remains a touchstone for historians and anthropologists interested in mental illness and asylums, for whom it has become a ritual to cite Foucault's work early on.[14] Foucault's most famous claim, that the Enlightenment inaugurated a "great confinement" which interrupted a dialogue of reason and madness as the mad were incarcerated, has become popular folklore as well as a subject of scholarly debate.[15]

The studies that followed Foucault's adopted "social control" as a central concept.[16] The large, custodial asylum was seen as only the most dramatic example of how psychiatry and its allied institutions served to enforce the social order. Though recent scholars have not dropped the phrase, it has come to seem at least passé, if not entirely misguided.[17] Elizabeth Lunbeck, in one of the more successful monographs using Foucaultian approaches, distinguishes "social control" from "the point at which knowledge and power fostered the conditions conducive to the realization of both."[18] And in a study of the European insane in India, Waltraud Ernst maintains that "social control" is overdone if used to maintain the impression that complex phenomena can be captured with a catch phrase.[19]

All of these reactions to "social control" approaches are helpful antidotes to its excesses. But psychiatry, whether caring or coercive, exists for the purpose of controlling anomalous behavior and emotion. Historians of psychiatry will only apprehend their subject by combining a sympathetic understanding of the impetus to reform with an appreciation of the drive toward social control. Description of reform need not be uncritically celebratory, and an appreciation of social control—a scapegoated term, which has often been made to carry the blame for reductionist approaches—need not posit uniformly evil institutions. I use the phrase, therefore, with the following qualifications: It should not be taken to imply that control is unidirectional, the result of the conscious intent of sinister doctors. Nor should it imply that therapy and control are mutually exclusive categories. The social pathways to asylums are complex; doctors and administrators have complex agendas and often act only at the end points of paths to treatment initiated by family members and communities.

My approach draws on the sociology of Allen Horwitz, who, instead of equating "control" and "coercive," sees a spectrum of forms of control, ranging from the more custodial and coercive to the more supportive and therapeutic.[20] Horwitz attempts to predict what circumstances will produce what kind of control, arguing that cultural and social distance between the deviant and the responding community encourages a more coercive, custodial approach, as does lack of social status on the part of the deviant. Certainly Horwitz's theory has applicability to Nigeria, where colonial lunatic asylums housed people whose status and cultural difference made them virtual nonentities in the eyes of British administrators, but where therapeutic services were developed increasingly as the institutions became the charge of Nigerians themselves.

The fundamental question of what mental illness is, still haunts the profession. . .

What, though, is a "lunatic," anyway? In most cases, I bracket the question of whether or not anyone was "really" afflicted with a mental illness. A trained healer has enough of a challenge diagnosing an individual in the course of a face-to-face encounter. The evidence on specific cases of confined individuals in Nigeria only provides clues about what behavior led others to believe these people were mad. Diagnoses were usually made over an intricate political and cultural frontier, by colonial clinicians who were using a clinical vocabulary that is now obsolete. We must work with what we know—that these people were *considered* mad—rather than speculating about the validity of these considerations. Since my subject matter will in part be the historical meaning of psychiatric labels, it would be ahistorical to encumber the analysis with reference to "real" mental conditions. On this point, Foucault's *The Archaeology of Knowledge* may be more apposite than his works on madness and incarceration: "We are not trying to find out . . . whether his disturbances were identical with those known to us today. . . . We are not trying to constitute what madness itself might be."[21]

As I read this passage, Foucault is urging against the pursuit of an essence of madness, in favor of historical inquiry into the ways madness has been named, defined, treated, and challenged. This reasoning informs my terminology. I use words such as "insane," "lunatic," and "madness," which have no clinical status, in what follows to denote *social* phenomena: those considered to be insane or lunatic, that which is considered to be madness. They should not be taken to suggest that such designations are valid in any "objective" or supra-situational sense. I add emphatically, though, that this approach does not deny the reality of mental illness. The danger, in fact, of much labeling theory and anti-psychiatry is that it risks trivializing the suffering of the mentally ill. It seems reasonable that to understand something as complex and troubling as madness, we might need biochemical, sociological, and psychodynamic approaches.

> *The criteria for medical diseases are physico-chemical, while the criteria for psychiatric diseases are social and ethical. . .*

Nevertheless, it will be useful to consider some anti-psychiatry and labeling theory because these fields have yielded important social insights, even if one does not accept them in full. Thomas Scheff, who argued that psychiatry, whether it emphasized organic disturbance or trauma and inner conflict, overemphasized the individual, as opposed to the social context, gave labeling theory its most significant expression.[22] He maintained that all members in a society at times engage in "primary deviance," or the nonconformist behavior of a normally conforming person. If others notice primary deviance, the deviant may be labeled as "crazy" or "mentally ill," labels that arouse pity, fear, and stigmatization. The deviant will then be socialized to act out the "crazy" role— and in turn to reinforce the label. Psychiatry, according to this view, is a science that authorizes final and definitive stigmatization. Once in the hands of the psychiatrist, the deviant is subject to imprisonment, injections, electric shocks, and (in the view of Scheff's most anti-psychiatric followers) diabolical abuse. One of the most critical insights of labeling theory is that once you are designated mad, it can be hard to change the minds of those around you, an insight perhaps expressed by one of David's fellow patients in Yaba, who wrote, "The name written cannot be cleaned."[23]

An apt illustration of labeling theory appears in Chinua Achebe's story "The Madman."[24] In the story, an honorable man named Nwibe is bathing in a river when a known madman steals his clothes and runs off. Nwibe does the logical thing and runs after him to retrieve his clothes but is taken for a madman when he is spotted, public nakedness being a well-known indication of madness in many parts of southern Nigeria. As Scheff might have predicted, the label creates the disease, and Nwibe begins to act like a madman, becoming mute and inscrutable. At the end, Nwibe is cured by the intervention of an adept healer, but, the narrator reminds us, "Such a man is marked forever."[25]

While such a rendering may appeal to the ironic sensibilities of a novelist, labeling theory has not made all social scientists happy, and Walter Gove in particular has mounted a sustained critique.[26] Gove notes that labeling theory usually refers to "mental illness" as a blanket term, failing to make the distinction among disorders such as depression and schizophrenia that the psychiatric profession has tried to make precise.[27] Gove also cites the growing evidence for a significant genetic role in the etiology of mental disorders. Much of this evidence comes from concordance rates derived from studies of twins which have shown that for several disorders identical twins have a higher incidence of shared disorder than fraternal ones.[28] In addition to undermining the thesis that mental disorders are caused solely by adversity, such studies have strengthened the position that mental disorders are "real" illnesses and not simply stigmatizing labels. Twin studies, of course, are controversial in any field of behavioral genetics. My own view, briefly, is that twin studies and other genetic evidence provide strong but not conclusive support for a genetic role in etiology. Neither genetic reductionism nor sweeping denials of any genetic role seem to me persuasive; inquiries into why such either/or propositions remain so powerful might be more useful.[29] None of my arguments, though, require either the support of, or the refutation of, biochemical etiologies for insanity. Yoruba societies, in any event, have long recognized the role of heredity in the genesis of mental disorder, and *wère ile*—literally, "madness of the home," or hereditary insanity—is a diagnostic category in itself among some Yoruba healers.[30]

The arguments against labeling theory are not decisive in favor of the psychiatric paradigm. Scheff himself acknowledged from the outset that it would be quite odd if all the clinical and research work of psychiatry failed to produce *any* useful knowledge about insanity. Labeling may not be the sole or primary factor in the origin of mental disorder, but it probably plays a significant role in treatment rates, course of illness, and stigmatization.[31] The labeling approach has produced insights that are especially helpful for a *social* study, such as this one. And there are serious drawbacks to exclusively biomedical approaches; at their most reductive they divorce the afflicted from social context in ways that are deeply depersonalizing.[32] Such a divorce has clinical flaws but also would lead to an arid history. I attend to the voices of the confined and have in some cases reproduced lengthy quotations from them—not from an illusion that these records "speak for themselves," but from a conviction that there are fertile ways of listening to them which enrich historical sensibility.

> *Mental Illness is only too common wherever the human race is found.*
>
> —"J. O.," patient in Yaba[33]

A conceptual challenge related to that raised by labeling theory concerns the application of specific diagnostic categories on a cross-cultural basis. Even if one grants that mental disorders are genuine illnesses, the nosology developed by modern psychiatry has been subject to constant and often bitterly fought revision. Many investigators question whether it is relevant to past epochs or non-Western societies.[34] While the various editions of the American Psychiatric Association's *Diagnostic and Statistical Manual of Mental Disorders* (*DSM*) have been used by Nigerian psychiatrists in their mental hospitals, anthropologists have challenged the Western psychiatric nosology, viewing it as a cultural canon embodying distinct norms of health and behavior and distinct concepts of the body and person.[35]

The recognition that madness is a site of important cultural differences has some history. Vaughan relates that in Nyasaland officials sought the imprimatur of African subjects to verify that the "lunatics" they were confining were in fact mad by local standards.[36] The *Diagnostic and Statistical Manual of Mental Disorders,* for its part, explicitly requires clinicians to be sure that the behavior which brings an individual into treatment is not a normal practice in the patient's culture or subculture. Such a requirement may not always be easy to fulfill, as it assumes fixed and well-defined cultural boundaries and unchanging practices. It also demands that the clinician take the word of representatives of a given cultural group, who, as Vaughan showed, may have their own agendas.

The idea that what is mad in one culture may be sane in another has been exaggerated by proponents and understated by critics. It is a debate that will continue to run into dead ends as long as the question is posed as an either-or; madness appears to be a feature of all known human societies, but one that nevertheless has distinctive features in each. In addition, until recently many of the debates over the relativity of psychiatric disorders employed ahistorical conceptions of culture that are now obsolete in anthropology. One of the arguments I will make in

chapters that follow is that diagnosis was problematic in colonial asylums for historically and politically specific reasons, among which cultural difference was significant but not alone.

Time and Setting

In African and other historical studies, foci are often defined geographically—by village, town, region, country, or continent.
Or else they are defined by nation, or ethnicity, or some other marker
of identity. The central organizing principle in this study is a pair of institutions; from these we can "fan out," investigating the struggles
within the colonial state over the use of asylums, negotiations in colonial society about the definition of insanity, the processes which led
to confinement and release, and the formation of a specific psychiatric
discourse.

While there is an arbitrary element to any narrowing of a historical subject, there are good grounds for choosing these institutions.
Tropical Africa's first mental hospital (Aro) and first psychiatrist (T. A.
Lambo) came from this region; these developments can be understood
as reactions to a social problem that emerged during colonialism.
Lambo's colleague Tolani Asuni had not even planned to become a psychiatrist until it became apparent on his return to Nigeria after medical
training in Dublin that there was a need for psychiatric services.[37]
Lambo's innovative experiments in outpatient community care and the
use of traditional healers in combination with cosmopolitan psychiatry
have made Aro world-famous. Partly as a result of these developments,
in the postcolonial period Nigeria (and especially the southwest) has
been the subject of an unusually developed psychiatric literature.[38] Aro
became the site for a landmark study of both ethnopsychiatry and psychiatric epidemiology, *Psychiatric Disorder Among the Yoruba,* which
was co-authored by Lambo and a team of researchers from Cornell. The
World Health Organization's massive comparative studies on schizophrenia also used the region as one of its catchment areas. I will argue
that the inclusion of a historical perspective is crucial to these important
projects.

It may be useful, particularly for non-Africanist readers, to situate
these institutions more clearly in time and place. Southwest Nigeria is
characterized by rain forest in the south, and savanna toward the north

near Ilorin. The region, along with Nigeria's neighbor Benin, is the home of a group of culturally related peoples collectively referred to as Yoruba.[39] Yoruba speakers number approximately 25 million, composed of about 25 subgroups.[40] Their antecedents have been traced to the region at least to the ninth century A.D.[41] The political structure has been characterized by constitutional monarchs, *obas,* at times grouped by degrees of federation.[42] A notably urban culture, the spiritual center is considered to be the city of Ife, "the cradle" of Yoruba civilization. From the fourteenth century, the original town of Oyo (to the north of the current location) began to dominate politically and militarily, a dominance that peaked in the eighteenth century.[43] The region has been marked for centuries not only by its high degree of urbanization but has had extensive trading and other contacts both with neighboring African peoples and Europeans on the coast.

The European presence grew considerably from the middle of the nineteenth century, starting with the establishment of missions, and a growing presence of traders and government officials in the latter part of the century. The coastal city of Lagos, which became the capital of the colony and the site of the Yaba asylum, was occupied in 1861, decades before the rest of the region came under formal colonial rule in the 1890s.

The decision to build asylums was made almost immediately after formal colonialism was established, and in 1906 the colonial state started operating asylums in Lagos and Calabar. Until the 1930s the colonial assumption was that even these purely custodial institutions might be an extravagance. From the early 1930s, the desirability of a curative mental hospital was advanced, but little action was taken until the 1950s. In some ways, the history of colonial asylum policy represents a history of stasis in the face of a recognized need for change. For the first decades, the government recognized a need for change in the material conditions but took little action. In the later decades of colonial rule, the government recognized a need to introduce treatment, but when therapy was introduced it was done so largely through the initiatives of Nigerians and in concert with Nigeria's transition to independence.

The decision to study insanity is predicated on the idea that its history uncovers a wider social history; this idea follows not from the fallacy that the mad are exemplars of a social context (such as colonialism) but precisely from their anomalous status. The mad are people whose perception of reality is deemed faulty. Their stories can therefore illuminate perceptions of reality and, when their cases are ambiguous, show ways in which perceptions are challenged.

Before demonstrating the social significance of insanity, I enlist the support of Nigerian fiction, in which madness has been a major (one does not want to say "obsessive") theme. Stephen Clingman has argued that madness has been a central theme in South African literature;[44] a similar claim could be made for Nigeria.[45] One evocative passage comes from Amos Tutuola's 1954 novel, *My Life in the Bush of Ghosts:* "But as he was carrying the wood away, dancing and staggering on, he met over a million 'homeless-ghosts' of his kind who were listening to my cry as a radio. Whenever these ghosts met him and listened to my cry which was a lofty music for a few minutes, if they could not bear the music and stand still then the whole of them would start to dance at the same time as a madman."[46] Tutuola's writing is often taken to refer to a fantasy world, a dream removed from social reality.[47] But Tutuola's achievement was precisely to illuminate the dreamlike quality of the social world, as well as the surreal and brutal juxtapositions entailed in cultural transformation.[48] His work is not so much an escape from the social or real world into fantasy as an exploration of their interaction. His lyrical description of "homeless-ghosts" dancing like madmen takes on added historical significance when placed next to the government and psychiatric reports which lamented the increased number of vagrant lunatics on Nigeria's roads and highways in the 1950s, an increase which led some to think there was something like an epidemic of insanity.

But madness was not always considered especially prevalent in the region. We will begin, then, by looking at the depiction of madness in the nineteenth century, a time when madness was considered only moderately prevalent.

CHAPTER 2

The Nineteenth Century

From Pity to Alarm

There is no telling when any of these now harmless idiots may develop into a raving and dangerous maniac.[1]

Lagos *Weekly Record*, 1895

Concepts of madness, and means for treating it, have a complex, if somewhat hidden, history in southwest Nigeria. Not all of the asylum inmates in the southwest were ethnically Yoruba, but based on the patient names left in records, most probably were. The main Yoruba word translated as "madness" or "madman" is *wèrè;* it is synonymous with "foolish or silly person" and appears in Crowther's Yoruba-English dictionary from the nineteenth century. Like their counterparts in other medical cultures, Yoruba healers also have a more specialized lexicon of diagnostic terms. Before discussing these conceptions, the related questions of the sense in which they can be meaningfully discussed as Yoruba, and the antiquity of that identity, should be addressed.

The nature of Yoruba identity has undergone scrutiny in recent years, as scholars have paid closer attention to the "constructedness" of African identities and indeed ethnic identity in general.[2] Some scholarship has stressed the recent creation of Yoruba identity. Peel has emphasized the extent to which local identities, such as Ijesha, were paramount in earlier times and have continued to be deeply meaningful in the colonial and postcolonial periods.[3] In a more problematic argument, David Laitin has claimed that the strength of Yoruba identity is a reflection of colonial hegemony, as it suited colonial administrative convenience.[4] Other historians, such as Asiwaju, have tended rather to stress that before colonial times "Yorubaland constituted a geographical, cultural and historical entity" with a pattern of "cultural uniformity."[5]

A substantial amount of evidence indicates to me that one can speak meaningfully about Yoruba identity before colonialism. Robert Smith, for example, has pointed to the widespread existence, throughout areas now called Yoruba, of a cycle of narratives describing the creation of the world and the foundation of Ife.[6] It may be true, as many have observed, that the word "Yoruba" originally applied to the people of the Oyo Kingdom, and that the use of the term achieved its modern range as a result of the efforts of the Anglican missions in the nineteenth century to standardize orthography.[7] This, however, does not necessarily imply that relations between subgroups such as Egba and Oyo were perceived no differently from relations between Yoruba groups and non-Yoruba polities such as Fulani or Dahomey. In precolonial times, as today, both local and pan-Yoruba identities had significance, which varied situationally.

Underlying the notion that the Yoruba are a colonial creation seems to be the implication that this is not somehow a real, authentic, ethnicity. The argument thus promotes the idea of authenticity in general while denying it to a particular case.[8] For all the value of much of the "invention of tradition" literature, it has often carried an implicit derision of the traditions in question[9] and has too often provided us with a falsely stark choice between "real" and "invented." The challenge is to recognize how the emergence of Yoruba identity has been processual; it could not have the power and meaning it has if it could simply be called a "colonial creation." On the question of variation among the Yoruba, Barber's formulation may be the most useful. Recognizing the diversity of Yoruba local cultures does not, she argues, preclude also recognizing the existence of "family resemblances," in Ludwig Wittgenstein's sense.[10]

The same reasoning applies to Yoruba medical systems, which are not homogeneous or static but do cohere in identifiable ways. Yoruba healing is an empirical practice, not a closed "belief system."[11] One consequence of this empiricism is that it is also a changing system, so it is hazardous to assume that current practices are identical to those of several generations ago. The ethnographic work done on the subject over the past half century or so can, nevertheless, provide some guides to knowledge and practices with some antiquity. Yoruba healers have used a combination of herbal remedies, dynamic ritual, and an eminent form of divination based on the *ifá* oral tradition.[12] Healers relying mainly on herbs are referred to as *ónişègun*. The *ifá* divination system is especially complex, its practitioners—*babaláwos*—learning a vast number of verses that are consulted at critical life junctures. The healing occupations in Yoruba societies are professionalized, in the sense that the practitioners belong to societies that attest to the competency of their members. Medical knowledge and practice are also often passed on within families. Although there seems to be no question that Yoruba nosologies have traditionally made a distinction between madness and other ailments, Yoruba conceptions of health and illness are holistic in the sense that well-being is considered to refer to mental and bodily state.[13] Many Yoruba are also pluralistic, seeking help in distress from Muslim and Christian healers, as well as from those working in distinctly Yoruba traditions.

The classic ethnographic work on madness and its treatment in the region is by Prince, and it remains valuable.[14] The interviews I conducted with Samuel Osunwole, conducted about 30 years later, revealed much similar data. Yoruba healers recognize organic and physical problems, bewitchment, and the actions of deities as possible causes of insanity.[15] With regard to the last, Yoruba religions recognize a number of *òrişa,* or deities, and breach of a taboo associated with a deity or other offense may lead the *òrişa* to inflict madness. Gbadegesin also notes that Yoruba psychiatric healers recognize both organic and extra-organic etiologies. Healers treat psychiatric ailments through a combination of ritual, consultations with the family members, and herbal medicines, especially the plant Rauwolfia, which is administered in a liquid and has a powerful sedative effect. Rauwolfia is chemically related to the antipsychotic drugs called the phenoziathines.

People will be said to be *wère* when they have disordered speech, suffer from hallucinations, or are vagrant and inattentive to dress. Healers refer to a number of more specific diagnostic categories, such as *wère àgba,* or psychosis associated with old age, and *wère ilé,* or "madness of the house," which refers to inherited insanity.[16] The association of madness with nakedness in Yoruba culture is so strong that there is a diagnostic category, *wère alálço,* which means "madman who wears clothes" and refers to someone capable of concealing their madness. Madness is also associated with other ailments, most especially smallpox, which is governed by the *òrişa* (deity) Soponna.[17]

Buckley has argued that Yoruba medicine for physical illnesses contain a germ theory of disease and suggests that it is indigenous, not a result of Western influence.[18] Similar arguments can be posed in the area of mental illness; Yoruba medicine has for some time enunciated some tenets now esteemed by cosmopolitan psychiatry. For example, many psychiatrists now agree that a combination of medication and interactive psychotherapy is most effective for a number of mental disorders. While not identical to Yoruba practices, this can be seen as analogous to the combination of herbal remedies and interactive ritual practiced by Yoruba healers. Similarly, contemporary psychiatry has put great emphasis on genetic factors in etiology, as Yoruba have emphasized heredity.

Yoruba concepts of destiny are also important in explanatory models for insanity. Morakinyo has shown the significance of the *àyanmọ́* narratives, derived from the *ifá* corpus, for conceptions of mental health.[19] *Àyanmọ́* translates literally as "that which has been selected as part of oneself," and refers to an *ifá* verse which describes how one chooses one's *orí*, or head, before birth. Morakinyo writes: "Before coming to this world (*aye*) from heaven (*orun*), everybody was obliged to go and choose an '*ori*' from a large number stored in Ajala's house. Ajala is described as the individual appointed by Oludumare (God) to build *orí*. And it was very difficult to determine the quality of an '*ori*' by its physical appearance . . . alone."[20] Those who are kind to Ajala receive assistance in the form of a well-made head; others simply make their own choice. The head determines qualities like aptitude and personality, in ways of which the individual would be unconscious, though it should not be thought of as a fixed destiny, but rather a manipulable one. It can also determine a number of life outcomes, such as occupation, and including the possibility of madness.

A large literature has claimed that less industrialized countries have relatively favorable prognoses for mental illnesses, particularly schizophrenia.[21] This argument has been made for Nigeria and a number of other African countries. Theories to explain the favorable course have included claims for the efficacy of traditional healing and greater social acceptance of mental illness.[22] This discussion is far from resolved conclusively, but if the claims for prognosis are sustained, it would mean that prevalence rates would be lower than industrialized countries, even if the proportion of new cases each year were the same, since people would be returning to the well population at faster rates.

Yoruba conceptions of madness include not only the diagnostic and therapeutic systems of healers but also lay conceptions. These include the common images of the mad as unclothed or half-naked, which are powerfully expressed in the idea that a madman who is dressed is one capable of concealing madness.[23] Kemi Morgan suggests that associations of madness and wildness outside the pale of civilized society have some antiquity. In her adaptation of Akinyele's history of Ibadan, she notes that Ibadan was built on a site first known as the forest of Ipara, and adds that "because no permanent settlement was built there, the forest became a no-man's land where fugitives, outlaws, rascals and criminals from the towns around sought refuge. . . . They became so notorious that people living in the towns and villages around them used to say that only a lunatic would dare go to the forest of Ipara."[24] Lunatics in Nigeria are known to frequent forests, markets, and (in more recent decades) highways and taxi parks, where they are often unrestrained. To a large extent Yoruba society is fairly tolerant of *were,* and men and women with its recognizable characteristics are often not confined. Attempts to restrict the movement of *violent* lunatics are not new to the twentieth century; the leg irons and chains frequently used by the region's traditional healers have been in use for some time.[25]

While it is hard to establish the antiquity of any of these conceptions of madness with precision, there is also no evidence for their novelty. The question arises, in fact, only as an artifact of Western ambivalence toward modernity. Modern Western psychiatry and folklore have dreamed of simpler, "primitive" societies free from the problems of insanity. These dreams have two main features. One is the belief that madness is a distinctive feature of the fragmentation of urban, industrial, and capitalist society. Societies which have not experienced these changes would be relatively immune to mental illness.[26] The other is the notion that earlier societies had dramatically different canons of normality, so that what is considered madness in the modern West might be tolerated or even valued in other societies.[27] The theory holds, for example, that people regarded as schizophrenic in Western society might be seen as seers or shamans in another.

The importance for psychiatric thought of these theories and images of non-Western societies has been immense. They were a part of the cultural background of many British observers in colonial Nigeria and later formed a cornerstone of anti-psychiatric theories that maintained that mental illness was a "myth" or a social construction, as opposed to a *bona fide* disease. These theories have faced significant challenges but remain a part of Western folk knowledge.[28] But there is a further irony to the Yoruba case; although nineteenth-century Yoruba society was not industrialized, the region was urban and hierarchical and had an economy characterized by long-distance trade and production for the market. Far from being a rural society, it developed what Peel has called "that anthropological celebrity, the Yoruba town."[29] Nineteenth-century Yoruba society was also far from free of the "stress" often alleged to cause mental illness, as intermittent warfare afflicted the region.[30] Colonialism did cause major economic, social, and cultural changes, but these changes are obscured more than they are illumined by dyadic oppositions of "traditional versus modern." Rather than referring to generalizations about traditional societies and their conceptions of madness, we should look at what we can learn about the representations of madness in the region before asylums were in use.

There is little mention of madness in classic travelers' accounts. There is one mention by Hugh Clapperton, who called the Fulani leader Uthman Dan Fodio "religiously mad."[31] That this evidence concerns an eminent person may provide a clue as to why so little other evidence appears—lunatics were simply not something that especially interested the travelers. They were more interested in understanding what was *typical* in societies that were for them very strange.

European observers were, evidently, prepared to find the worst in the treatment of madness in the area—in 1849, a British army doctor explicitly noted that the insane were not killed in the cultures on the coastal belt of Nigeria. He also noted that the prevalence of insanity appeared to be low.[32] At least at this early stage of colonial encroachment, large numbers of lunatics were not apparent to a foreign eye.

Madness and the Missionary Enterprise

Missionary records provide more evidence about the representation of insanity during the nineteenth century and also allow some inferences about the dynamics of religious conflict. Medical style was an important theater of battle in the struggle between African and missionary cultures, as different idioms vied for human bodies and minds.[33] Throughout the history of European expansion, medicine was an integral part of the missionary enterprise because it was seen as being "of a piece" with the benefits of Christianity; the curative power of Western medicine would reveal the general power of the Western world view, which for many missionaries was indistinct from Christianity.[34] The self-confidence of the missionaries was such that they believed conversion would be therapeutic for lunatics—although available evidence suggests that healing through conversion was exceptional, not typical.

One early reference to mental disorder in mission records from Nigeria is from May 1855, when the missionary Thomas King wrote of a visit to see an afflicted convert named Rachel:

> She has been suffering from insanity for more than two years, forsaken by the husband, who, instead of paying all the attention to her, thinks this season of her affliction the fairest opportunity to get rid of her, and of making an exchange of her for a better. . . . But as the people have or know no alternative way of treating patients under such distemper, when medical means proved ineffectual, but confinement, specially as she attempted too often to run into dangers in the night.[35]

King was vague about Rachel's "symptoms" so we are unable to judge the nature of her problem. The passage represents an early example of a charge Europeans were to make more frequently when asylums were built—that Africans with insane family members often wished to "dump" the afflicted into someone else's care. While this was sometimes the case, it appears *not* to have been characteristic. There is also some irony to King's implication that "the people"—meaning Nigerians—were, relative to Europeans, bewildered about how to treat cases such as Rachel's, since when "medical means" failed, confinement was the preferred option in Britain at this time as much as in West Africa. King, though, was eager to show that "our religion loves a person not only in health and prosperity, but it sympathizes and loves still in affliction and distress." Doubling the irony, though, Rachel was eventually sent to someone whom King called a "country doctor," probably meaning a traditional healer.

Samuel Johnson, the famous Nigerian historian, had some direct experience with madness. He related the following, which occurred in June 1881: "Arrived home safely, but my joy was tempered with sorrow, having met several members of my family prostrated with fever, and the young married wife of a former inmate of my house in a state of derangement, about 40 days after she became a mother."[36] Edward Buko, a Nigerian clergyman, also experienced madness in a direct and personal way. In an account of his life, he related that "in 1872 my wife fell into a sad sickness (insanity) which obliged me to take her into the colonial hospital at Lagos. . . . In 1875 my wife seemed better at the hospital. I was ordered to take her home. But no sooner she came home than there was a relapse."[37] Buko then shifted medical cultures, without better results: "I obtained the help of a native doctor, but all was in vain. She died January 1876."[38]

Missions actually administered very little therapy to the insane. One missionary recorded speaking to the distressed about their dreams in a manner we might speculate was proto-Freudian,[39] but in general, the sources reveal little psychotherapeutic care. One case missionaries regarded as a success was recorded near the close of the nineteenth century, but while it is detailed on other matters, it is silent on the matter of therapy.

An unusually detailed account was recorded of this case, which was cited as evidence of the healing properties of Christian devotion. The case involved a man who was nicknamed "'Mayunababa' by the Ondos in reference to the demon that was supposed to possess him," and who was re-christened "Jonah" by the mission, a name suggesting deliverance from a creature which had ingested him.[40]

Upon the occasion of Jonah's baptism in 1893, the clergyman E. M. Lijadu narrated Jonah's pilgrimage to grace. Lijadu was from an early Abeokuta convert family, and had taken formal instruction from a *babaláwo*.[41] Jonah had been, Lijadu recounted, "insane up to the time of his hearing the gospel—the only son of a mother who had spent all her living toward his recovery. But on him, fetishes and Mohammedan charms failed alike . . . wherever he went, he stoned people out of his way and was stoned in return." Work and Christian kindness, according to Lijadu, redeemed him:

One day he entered the mission yard and received kind treatments—from Rev. C. Phillips. Repeating his visits, Mr. Phillips managed to allure him to exercise and manual labour. On Sundays he attended the services, and by and by, the week-day classes. Gradually he retained his senses, and now moves among his own countrymen as a living witness of what Christianity can do. This morning, with a peculiar smile on his face, he received the sacred rite of baptism, taking the name *Jonah*—being the name given him in anticipation by Mr. Ogunbiyi some years ago, in accordance also, no doubt, with his natural name "Ikuajunammu" (Death leaves me).

Lijadu elaborated on Jonah's importance as a "living witness":

Although Jonah is still weak intellectually, yet we have many evidences in him of real conversion, and of a spiritual growth. During the influenza attack of last year, he well-nigh reached the grave, but strenuously resisted the temptation to fetish making on his account. Sometime ago, hearing of the dangerous illness of one of the Christians, Jonah visited him and left the sick man 10 cowries, adding the regret that he had not much to give. The sick brother expressed his wonder and satisfaction at this show of brotherly affection, but failed to persuade Jonah to take back his money. The next day he brought a big firewood to the sick man, saying that if it was unbecoming to accept cowries from him, it could not be to accept the wood. His attachment to us is very strong. I cannot easily forget his daring deed of Feb. 6, 1891, when running into the yard, Jonah met Mr. Ogunbiyi carried on sick-bed out of the burning house; he immediately rushed through the flames into the study, saved about a dozen books into the rooms, then ran back with the Mr. Ogunbiyi's bible in his hand. He has always identified himself with our joys & sorrows, and is now the means in God's hand of winning over his mother & two other relatives to Christianity. We pray that not this man only, but all who have received baptism this day may have truly passed from death to life.[42]

As Lijadu indicated, Jonah's story was a double boon to the mission, because his mother followed. In 1891, Phillips recorded that:

an old woman brought her son's *ifá* bag & gave it up to me. The woman was led to become an enquirer by the remarkable cure of her son's insanity, which she attributed to his coming to the church. She had spent nearly all she was worth in past years in sacrifices to different fetishes to procure her son's healing. Since last year the young man who is about 25 years old began to attend the church whenever he heard the sound of the bell. At first we feared to receive him, but finding that he was not violent, we befriended him . . . and set him to work for which he was paid. Whether it was the constant physical exercise or the kindness he received . . . we cannot tell. But he has become more sane since he was coming to us. He has been regularly attending the Sunday services, and class meetings *clothed* & in his right mind . . .[43]

Notice how Jonah was described as "weak intellectually" with a "peculiar smile"; while the mission overtly emphasized Jonah's *cure,* the account shows more definite evidence of *conversion.* In Ijaye, in January 1859, the new year brought a more noisome disorder into the household of Reverend Adolphus Christian Mann. Mann wrote:

Since the 1st our houseboy a young trustworthy convert had a deranged appearance: and turned out to be mad: for a second time he had passed the night in the streets, was beaten, robbed of cloth, etc. In Sunday school, he began to preach etc. The night of the 2nd to third he had 3 attacks to our great fright. At the last about 2 o'clock A.M. he laid hold of an ax and wished to strike another boy—upon the noise I run out—but when he saw, me, he cast the ax away and ran into our bedroom . . . The fright proved very fatal to the health of my dear wife. . . . The boy was bound and secured. . . . He cried . . . "*Jesu gba mi*"—Jesus save me etc. I got irons but when put on they proved too large so he shook them off and said— The Lord Jesus has made them fall away: But they were fastened again . . . He had nightly attacks in which he made great noise, but he improved soon under proper treatment and is now restored.[44]

Mann's houseboy appears not to have been so "trustworthy" as Mann believed; his behavior was related to lingering involvement in traditional religion: "He laboured under the fear of getting poison or threat uttered by the Priest who had made *Ifá* for him."[45] Studies of missionary incursions have frequently shown how incompletely they were able to mold the minds of converts. Converts often judge for themselves what is inalienable in their new faiths more than missionaries like, leading to syncretisms, and appropriation of missionary idioms for different aims. Eventually, although he was "restored," as Mann put it, the houseboy fled the town, "fearing for his life."[46]

Several general points emerge from these anecdotes gathered from the CMS archives. Perhaps most interesting is the *lack* of significant discussion of difference in the manifestation of madness. Far from regarding madness as a radically relative phenomenon, European missionaries perceived it as something they could recognize. Nor did African missionaries emphasize any major differences between European and African conceptions of madness. My point here is not to establish that madness is either a human universal, or relative to different cultures—it is both. What I stress is how in different historical circumstances and with different interests in mind, different historical actors can emphasize the degree of relativity differently. In the colonial period, the emphasis would be on difference.

The CMS records also show that madness was not considered either a startling rarity in the region or particularly common for that matter. Prior to the 1890s, there are no signs of an apparent increase in incidence or prevalence, or indications that madness was regarded as an especially pressing social or medical problem. When an African press emerged in southern Nigeria during the late nineteenth century, it began to comment on a perceived growing problem of lunatics on the city streets.

"Harmless Idiots" or "Raving Maniacs"?
Lunacy, the Press, and Policy

On October 31, 1891, the Lagos *Weekly Record* reported:

> A man named Braima living at Faj has become demented and is roaming about the streets at night armed with a sword and matchet. On the night of the 22nd, a friend who attempted to take him was seriously wounded by him and is lying in a dangerous condition at the Hospital. The insane man is still at large and has been seen at night in the neighborhood of Victoria Road and Breadfruit Street.[47]

The *Weekly Record* began a modest campaign for some governmental action with respect to the lunatics roaming the streets. One editorial in 1895 said, "The spectacle of them roaming about the streets in the pitiable condition which they present is a reflection both upon our *Christianity and our Civilization*."[48] They also seemed to present a threat to public order and safety. In a passage which, with some slight changes in diction, one could easily imagine appearing in a description of a late twentieth-century American city, the *Weekly Record* lamented:

> The demented unfortunates who may be seen wandering about our streets are certainly objects of commiseration. Though most of these poor creatures are harmless of disposition and appear to indulge in their several vagaries without interfering with or molesting other people, yet the squallor [sic] and wretchedness of their condition is such as should excite general sympathy and pity on their behalf. Covered with dirt and filth from head to foot, and carrying a heterogeneous pile of pots, pans and rubbish, the poor creatures wander listlessly about the town without much concern about the matter: their livelihood, such as it is, being derived from odd scraps and pickings from the streets. It is undoubtedly a matter of public concern that this class of people should be cared and provided for. . . . Besides, there is no telling when any of these now harmless idiots may develop into a raving and dangerous maniac. . . . The erection of a lunatic asylum similar to that existing at Sierra

Leone . . . is needed here, and as the government is now well provided with building materials, we presume this could be accomplished without involving any great outlay.[49]

Despite the fears such articles expressed, and the stigma implicit in the notion that the lunatics were especially liable to drift toward violence, the editors of the *Weekly Record* also had sympathy for this class. On February 3, 1900, they insisted that policemen must be considered legally liable for attacks on lunatics, unless the policemen were threatened with imminent danger, in which case the policemen would have to show proof of resistance on the part of the lunatic. "Policemen," they stressed, "should be made to understand that they are not above the law."[50]

Later, the paper also blamed the police for violence sometimes perpetrated by Lagosian lunatics. Although the police could not be faulted for the *existence* of vagrant lunatics, it was their charge to insure that these "roamers are not in possession of any instrument that could be used to inflict hurt . . . [as] sometime ago when a lunatic went roaming about the streets flourishing the head of a man he had cut off . . . [or as when] a lunatic was seen coming along the beach road carrying a matchet in a menacing manner on Sunday."[51] The sensational episode of the severed head appeared in more than one *Weekly Record* article over the years and was symbolic of a perceived growing threat to social order. The Lagos *Weekly Times* also reacted with horror to the deeds of a madman; in May 1890 it reported a suicide by disemboweling and looked forward to when the erection of asylums would insulate the public from such episodes.[52] The Nigerian press was not uniformly in favor of asylums as the solution; a long article in the Lagos *Times* in 1883 condemned asylums and extolled the virtues of native cure.[53] There was, though, pressure on the nascent colonial government to do *something*.

The government was in no hurry, however. In April 1905, about ten years after the calls for an asylum began, one article complained:

The murder of a girl by a madwoman on Thursday adds one more tragedy to the number enacted by reason of lunatics being allowed to roam at large in the town. A few years ago a mad man chopped off the head of a man who was sleeping, and paraded the gory head through the town, all the way . . . to Government House. This frightful murder had the effect of startling the government into action and a lunatic asylum was erected at Yaba. For some unintelligible reason the institution has never been utilized for its

purpose . . . it is rather singular that the Police, from the Commissioner down to the latest recruit, are excessively ardent in chasing
and catching unlicensed dogs . . . [but] maintain an attitude of
culpable apathy towards the lunatics infesting the town.[54]

African critics of the government were lodging other complaints as well.
The issue of care and custody for lunatics came to be seen as part of
a larger pattern of double standards in the colonial medical services.
Protests were also registered over the exclusively European composition
of the colonial medical staff.[55]

One consequence of this composition was that the provision of
medical services for Africans tended to come only in response to scandals. One was the infamous "Adeola incident," in which a woman with
an incurable disease was discharged by the acting Colonial Surgeon,
Dr. Digby, and "abandoned in a nearby shrub."[56] Earlier, Digby had
complained that the hospital was being used as a poor house.[57] Adeola
was refused admission on the grounds that she was mentally deranged
and the hospital did not treat psychiatric cases.[58] The incident was in-
vestigated, at the government's request, by the Nigerian Bishop James
Johnson.[59] Johnson recommended that Digby be dismissed. The colonial medical services were also expanded, with more surgeons being appointed—but the opening of the asylums was still delayed.[60]

Asylums were by that time operating in Sierra Leone and the Gold
Coast, and some male Nigerian lunatics were sent to those institutions.[61] Others were kept in a lunatic ward of the Lagos prison, but this
ward quickly became overcrowded because lunatics were not discharged
after set terms were served, as other prisoners could be.[62] The *Weekly
Record* asserted a double standard, noting, "It would certainly be a
boon to the community if the Legislative Council showed itself as ready
and active in providing for the custody and care of native lunatics, as it
has manifested in the case of lunatics who are foreigners."[63]

In the 1880s, the government began reformulating policy for the custody of lunatics. The Prison Department initiated an effort to transfer
responsibility to the Health Department, an effort that would continue
in the first decades of the twentieth century. This effort was ultimately
successful, in the sense that the insane did come to be seen as primarily
the wards of the medical bureaucracy by the time of independence. A
late nineteenth-century report on the colonial hospital noted, though,
that "idiots and lunatics" were not proper inmates of a general hospital, and neither were those with incurable diseases.[64] Some suggested

building a single massive lunatic asylum for all of British West Africa.[65] In 1889, a Commission of Inquiry proposed an asylum on the grounds that "existing arrangements" were "illusory" and that the "benefits derived . . . would more than compensate for the increased expenditure involved by the erection and upkeep" of an asylum.[66] Nevertheless, an asylum was low on the list of the colony's public works priorities.[67] The ranking reflected colonial development policies of the period, which emphasized transport and other items that would lubricate commerce; social control was secondary, and concern for public health very modest.[68]

There is no evidence that there was an increase in the prevalence or incidence of mental illness in the region in the late nineteenth century.[69] The *perception* of increase was probably caused by a growing number of people in the urban centers, particularly Lagos, who were not being serviced or controlled effectively by traditional methods, because of their distance from families. Kristin Mann notes that Lagos in particular was becoming a city of strangers, many of them immigrants or former slaves.[70]

In 1906 the colony passed a lunacy ordinance, judging it "expedient" to have institutions for the custody of the vagrant insane. "Expedient" stands out as a key word in retrospect. It would be decades before the institutions would make even modest attempts at alleviating the suffering of the incarcerated. The asylums were built more for the people outside them than for those within. Rapidly, the number of those confined grew, outstripping the populations in the other asylums of British West Africa,[71] creating overcrowded and squalid conditions. Created in response to the scandal of untreated lunatics on the streets, the asylums themselves became enduring scandals of the colonial period.

CHAPTER 3

Material Conditions
and the Politics of Care

The history of Nigeria's asylums re-enacted developments common in the comparative history of psychiatric institutions but also illustrates themes peculiar to the politics and priorities of colonialism. In the beginning, the institutions were, like many colonial imports, already obsolete by metropolitan standards, replicating virtually all the faults British psychiatry had come to pride itself on overcoming. For most of the early twentieth century, agents of the Nigerian colonial state vented a rhetoric of scandal and reform, but when reform was achieved in the late 1950s and early 1960s, it was contemporary with Nigeria's gradual shift to independence, and the reform was largely accomplished through the initiatives of Nigerians.

Victorian Britain enacted a series of dramatic changes in lunacy policy, including increased institutionalization, the rise of "moral cures" and other optimistic therapies, and finally a growing disillusionment with institutional options by the early twentieth century. With each of the changes, the psychiatric establishment radiated an image of progress. The tone is well captured in this early Victorian description by Forbes Winslow, a prominent nineteenth-century British alienist: "The Insane are no longer treated like wild beasts; the lunatic asylum no longer resembles the Spanish Inquisition, or the hold of a slave ship . . . the inmates . . . are not exposed to the painful infliction of the whip, nor are they chained like felons to the floor of some dreary, pestilential dungeon, and exhibited to the gaze of those anxious to gratify a morbid curiosity."[1] Foucault and others have, of course, argued that the superficially benign reforms of modern psychiatry have spawned a cultural hegemony and thus social control all the more insidious. But for most of the colonial period in Nigeria this view would have little applicability. The colonial lunatic asylums of Nigeria were simply not benign enough to be insidious. Nor would a view of colonial asylums as "panoptic" really be apt. More to the point is how little these institutions saw, or cared to.

Rather, about a century after Winslow wrote, Nigeria's asylums exhibited the conditions he lamented in disturbing detail. The insane *were* treated like wild beasts, chained like felons in dank, pestilential shelter. They were also crammed together in tight quarters which, while not as horrific as the hold of a slave ship, were nevertheless alarmingly bad— even to the British themselves. If the concept of "social control" has been controversial in the general history of asylums, it should not be in these colonial institutions. But if these conditions are not surprising in a colonial context, the advent of the institutions, and the failure to reform them even as the need for reform became apparent, reveal central contradictions of the colonial regime.

Roughly, asylum policy can be periodized as follows. After the asylums were established in the first decade of the century, there followed about two decades when they were used as purely custodial institutions, with colonial officials having no higher aspiration for them. By the late 1920s, there began to be calls for a reformed, curative hospital, calls that were received with scorn from most in the government at first, but with more sympathy starting in the mid-1930s. Once the government determined that a hospital would be desirable, though, inertia carried the day, until near the end of the Second World War. Development of therapeutic facilities quickened in the mid-1950s, as Nigerian psychiatrists began to staff them.

The Beginnings of Nigeria's Asylums

Other European imports, including cloth, alcoholic beverages, and firearms, had been imported to the Bight of Benin for centuries before formal colonialism, and European medicine made its first significant intrusions with the Christian missions in the middle of the nineteenth century. The asylum came only in the first decade of the twentieth century, after the establishment of formal British rule.

Large institutions for impounding the insane have existed in Europe since the Middle Ages.[2] Incarceration on a massive scale occurred in Western Europe especially during and after the seventeenth century, a story made familiar by Foucault.[3] Foucault's data are strongest for the large French cities he researched most thoroughly.[4] One major difference between the French and British cases is that the "great confinement" came later to Britain. In Britain, asylum use grew especially rapidly during the nineteenth century; Porter reports a hundredfold increase in inmates between 1800 and 1900.[5]

The British diffused these institutions with the growth of their global empire. There were, for example, asylums in operation in India by the mid-eighteenth century.[6] These housed the European insane, for fear they would become vagrant or otherwise compromise British prestige. The asylums in British Africa, by contrast, mostly confined Africans. Asylums were used in southern Africa by the early nineteenth century; these included ones at Robben Island, a predecessor of the notorious prison in which Nelson Mandela was confined.[7] West African asylums in Kissy (Sierra Leone) and Accra (the Gold Coast) were in use by the late nineteenth century. Although built first, these asylums never confined on as large a scale as Nigeria's did.

By the time Nigeria's lunatic asylums were established in the first decade of the twentieth century, the heyday of institutionalization had passed in the United Kingdom. While many early Victorians were enthusiastic about confining the insane, by the Edwardian period most had grown disillusioned—although due to policy inertia it remained a dominant practice. The growing bias against large institutions was reflected in a late 1920s comment by Dr. Bruce Home, the first alienist commissioned to study the problem of insanity in Nigeria. Home wrote that in England, because of "ignorance, public suspicion is directed against the mental hospitals. . . . I see no reason why Nigeria, where such explicit mistrust is absent, should not become a pioneer in the modern and scientific treatment of insanity."[8] Although Lambo's experiments at Aro in the late colonial and early independence period did make Nigeria a pioneer in mental health treatment, it was certainly not because public distrust was absent. On the contrary, Lambo's achievements in dispelling public suspicion were among the features that made the hospital famous.

The Southern Provinces of Nigeria launched an asylum policy in the first decade of the twentieth century, with the enactment of laws for confining lunatics. The Lunacy Ordinance of 1906 empowered the governor to establish a lunatic asylum when necessary and defined a "lunatic" as any person of "unsound mind," including "idiots."[9] Any medical officer could detain an individual as a suspected lunatic for up to a month. Local magistrates could also hold hearings regarding a person's sanity. The district commissioners would have ultimate authority for designating lunatics, and were to hold hearings, call witnesses, and appoint medical supervisors to that end. The medical supervisor was required to certify the individual as a lunatic and "proper subject for confinement," and to specify what warranted the certificate. The first buildings designated exclusively as asylums were the Yaba Asylum in Lagos and the Calabar Asylum in southeastern Nigeria.

Nigeria's colonial prisons and asylums were functionally equivalent. They confined deviant or troublesome individuals and refrained from cure, rehabilitation, or otherwise normalizing their inmates for return to the outside.[10] Yet administrators distinguished carefully between the two. Asylums lay in the middle of a spectrum between prisons and hospitals, reflecting an ambiguity in colonial rhetoric as to whether lunatics were essentially a health or social control problem.[11] By the end of the nineteenth century, prison officials in Nigeria were asking the Health Department to relieve the prisons of "aggressive, homicidal, dangerous, or merely excited persons."[12] Those officials advocating custody over care could depend on inertia and economy inhibiting the development of treatment. Literal overlaps between the asylums and the prisons existed as well. By 1915, for example, with the Yaba Asylum already overcrowded, several cells in Lagos Prison were converted into a lunatic asylum.[13]

In 1906, the Yaba Asylum was developed in the former headquarters of the Nigerian Railways.[14] Although standing in a central urban area across from one of Nigeria's busiest taxi parks today, the Yaba site was at that time a secluded spot, far from the urban center on Lagos Island.[15] Yaba and Calabar were only two small sites for a large and populous country. Many other areas designated prison cells or annexes as asylums. Northern Native Administrations in Zaria, Kano, Maiduguri, and Bauchi used asylums separate from prisons. Sokoto and Jos had prison asylums, as did several cities further south, such as Lokoja and Port Harcourt. Like Lagos, Calabar had a prison extension in addition to an asylum.

Dr. Crispin Curtis Adeniyi-Jones, a Nigerian physician who served in the Lagos Medical Service, became the first director of the asylum. Adeniyi-Jones wrote two reports about the Yaba Asylum in November and December of 1907, which provide impressions of what it was like at that early date.[16] As of the 31st of October, 14 lunatics, 8 women and 6 men, had been admitted, and an additional female inmate was admitted in November.[17] Adeniyi-Jones noted that "the classification as to forms of insanity has not been decided in every case," and that their physical condition had improved since admission. As in many societies, tearing at clothing and ultimate nakedness are among the commonest outward signs of lunacy in southern Nigeria, and this applied to the early inmates at Yaba: "I wrote some time ago for clothing for the inmates as some of the lunatics are very destructive; I beg respectfully to suggest that the materials used be very strong; sail cloth or some such materials. Wrappers for women will be more preferable to gowns; and head wrappers will also be necessary; caps for the male lunatics will also be required." Several inmates engaged in basket and mattress making. Jones added that their comfort could be increased if "necessaries for smoking and snuffing" could be provided. The asylum already had physical defects, including broken locks, gutters, and fences. Jones concluded with a brief note on an adjacent leper asylum that had 21 inmates, noting that some clothes had been sent for them, which he gave to the lunatics, who were in greater need. He also expressed the need for handcuffs and a padded cell to deal with violent cases.[18]

Adeniyi-Jones wrote a number of letters to superior medical officers during his tenure as head of the asylum; they show him to be diligent but already embattled by the lack of resources the government was willing to devote. For a time, thieves had fairly easy access, and he had trouble acquiring adequate supplies. In addition, he had to contend with a number of incidents of quarrels and insubordination from his staff. He was succeeded in 1909 by a European, Thomas Beale Browne, and the asylum would be directed by Europeans until the transition to independence.[19]

The most glaring evidence for the lack of interest the government had in providing genuine care for the inmates is that no psychiatrists were employed in the asylums for most of the colonial period. Visiting alienists wrote three major reports on conditions in the asylums—Bruce Home in 1928, Robert Cunyngham Brown in 1938, and J. C. Carothers in 1955—but these were based on short tours of the region, not regular clinical experience. The government employed one trained psychiatrist in the early decades, Matthew Cameron Blair. Blair, however, opposed the adoption of an official lunacy policy on financial grounds.[20] Blair retired in 1924, shortly before Home's report urged expanded and improved services. There was not a full-time British psychiatrist again in Nigeria until the arrival of Donald Cameron in 1949.

Asylum space was reserved almost entirely for Africans, but this was not for lack of mentally disturbed Europeans. In 1914, 56 Europeans were admitted to a Hospital for Nervous Diseases in the North, which prompted this note in the Annual Medical and Sanitary Report: "It may not be out of place here to draw the attention of the Executive to the danger of leaving officials of a certain temperament too long by themselves in what is known as a 'one-man-station.' Men so constituted are apt to become morbidly introspective and suffer from insomnia, neurasthenia, etc. with the not infrequent result of over indulgence in drugs or alcohol."[21] Coastal West Africa had been famous for centuries as a place that bred ill health in Europeans.[22] By the twentieth century, this image extended to mental illnesses, or as they were called, "functional[23] nervous diseases." The most famous rendering of this image is Joseph Conrad's Kurtz, whose immersion in the African environment led to his insanity. By the 1930s, some colonial officers lamented the greater vulnerability of more recent arrivals.[24] Proposed causes of insanity in a European official included climate, the "standard of amenities," the age of the sick person, and the number of tours served. One official added, in an incredible phrase that distills the ambivalence male officers felt toward European women in the colonies, "the absence or presence of his wife."[25] The official wondered whether the frantic modern world was a cause of European morbidity in Nigeria, and also suggested that the First World War, a famously rich source of mental distress, might also be a factor.[26] Some suspected that unstable persons were attracted to work in the colonies in the first place. The ideal was to repatriate mentally ill Europeans, but this was not always practiced. Prison visitors complained in 1929 that "the keeping of 27 lunatics within the prison seems an unsatisfactory arrangement, specially in the case of Europeans."[27]

Material Conditions

From the inception of the asylums, critics drew attention to their revolting conditions, referring mainly to dirt and overcrowding. In 1928, in the first major report to the government on lunacy in Nigeria, Bruce Home described dark, congested cells, poor bathing facilities, lack of basic supplies, and the use of chains.[28] He added that the asylums in Calabar and Yaba were little better than the prisons. In Calabar, he said, "the unfortunate patients are exposed to view, and are objects of amusement to the public." The later reports by Cunyngham Brown (1938) and by J. C. Carothers (1956) echoed Home's with regard to material conditions. The disgust repeatedly led to calls for reform, but little action.

Although asylums in other regions did not suffer quite as much overcrowding as in Yaba and Calabar, most of them were not much more attractive. Some officials thought lunatics were better off left in the streets![29] The Port Harcourt prison extension was especially dreadful; an official witnessed "several violent lunatics shivering naked in damp, dark cells, chained like animals to a ring in the floor; others also naked, wandered aimlessly around a barbed wire enclosure."[30] Brown observed that the asylum in Kano resembled "a fortress rather than an asylum."[31] The one exception was in Zaria, where "The reporter found the asylum clean, tidy and, according to native requirements, proper in every way."

In order to deal with overcrowding, the Yaba and Calabar asylums tried to exclude so-called harmless lunatics. This did not mean that all the inmates were criminal. On the contrary, the distinction between "criminal" and "civil" lunatics was a carefully kept marker of an inmate's identity. Criminal lunatics were those who had been arrested, usually for violent crimes, and found unfit to stand trial because of their mental state. Civil lunatics were usually people who were considered public nuisances but who had not committed any crime, or at least no serious crime. Whenever possible, the government preferred to leave these people in the care of relatives.[32]

The treatment of lunatics differed little from that of sane criminals. One contrast was that many lunatics were even more restrained in their movement, having to wear chains and shackles, which sane convicts were spared.[33] The similarities between the asylums and the prisons, however, far outnumbered the differences, at least until the late 1940s. The principal similarity was the repugnant material conditions; a 1944 report on crime and correction in the colony lamented that the prisons were "generally accepted as a bad joke."[34]

The material conditions were made more alarming by the expectation that many more lunatics would need to be confined. In 1928, Home "calculated" that provision would have to be made for 4,000 cases of insanity, one quarter of which would require urgent care.[35] The word "calculated" requires quotation marks because there was no basis for his numbers. He was probably trying to stress that a lot of beds were needed, to draw attention to the problem. Ten years later, Brown thought that the 500 or so inmates confined at the time of his visit was a very *small* number for a country of Nigeria's size, and he expected that the country would shortly need space for three to four times that number.

Brown advocated what he called a "village system," a kind of estate where staff could reside and the asylum could exist as a somewhat self-contained unit. This was not quite the same as the village system Lambo developed in Aro, though it was similar in that Brown stressed that "the surrounding conditions should not be too far removed from those to which the patients are accustomed."[36]

By the 1950s, when Aro was starting up in Abeokuta, conditions had still not improved at the other sites. Citing Brown, Carothers wrote in 1955 that "the conditions he observed nineteen years ago . . . exist with little change to-day."[37] One memorandum in 1956 regarding Yaba noted that the building was hazardous and had a leaking roof.[38]

Therapy was obviously not a priority in these conditions. It is possible that the physical health of some inmates may have improved, as the Annual Medical Report for 1927 claimed.[39] This was plausible, given that many of the inmates were impoverished, undernourished vagrants who received regular meals upon admission. Also, medical examinations were given every three months.[40] Still, a number of factors may have worsened the health of inmates. Exposure to rain and unsanitary conditions, for example, may have undermined some of the benefits. The Director of Medical Services reported in 1940 that "the soakaway pits in the male civil and female sections of the lunatic asylum are not good; they were found breeding fly and mosquito larvae in large numbers."[41] The inmates may then have been at high risk for malaria.

Regardless of attempts to maintain the physical health of the inmates, there were barely any attempts to cure any psychiatric problems they faced for most of the colonial period. Very modest occupational therapy was all Yaba offered until independence.[42] Some agricultural work was encouraged for those capable of doing it. In the 1950s the asylum began selling the inmates' handiwork, with dual goals of raising money and reducing the stigma attached to the mentally ill.[43] Sedatives were administered to some inmates, probably more to keep them under control than for therapy.[44]

From Home's 1928 report onward, medical officials urged that asylums offer more therapeutic services. Their reports, even when praised in word, were mostly neglected in practice. This neglect reflected deeper ambiguities regarding the aims of colonialism in the region. If there was lack of clarity as to the uses of asylums, this was partly because of the lack of clarity about the aims of colonialism.

The Contradictions of Indirect Rule

Indirect Rule contained several goals—economic bene-
fits for the metropolitan country, the alleged benefits of civilization for
the colonized people, the preservation of "tribal" customs—that were
incompatible. Asylums—even dreadful as they were—were associated
with the benefits of civilization. The expense of a truly modern asylum,
though, was incompatible with the economic goals of colonialism. At
the same time, financial restraint was justified by the goal of preserving
the African way of life.

The directive to preserve tradition was followed more rigorously
in the north of Nigeria; as a result the Northern Provinces relied on
small Native Administration asylums throughout the colonial period. In
1928, the acting secretary of the Northern Provinces attached a scathing review to Home's call for expanded therapeutic services. He invoked Blair's authority as an alienist to support his disdain for Home's
plan, quoting at length from a world-weary 1926 letter written by Blair.
Blair wrote with cynical acumen; his comments merit extended quotation, to provide a sense of the tone with which asylum reform was
derided:

> I hear a dreadful rumour to the effect that the question of adopt-
> ing a systematic lunacy policy has cropped up again and is being se-
> riously entertained but trust this not be true; for if it be, the results
> are likely to be disastrous. Here, I know what I am writing about;
> for I was an alienist myself for over nine years. If such a policy be
> adopted, this is the sort of thing that will happen—To begin with,
> the Director of Medical and Sanitary Services will have to devote,
> at least, a paragraph of his annual report to Lunacy. In due course
> his report will as usual, be passed on by the Secretary of State to
> the Medical and Sanitary Advisory Committee. When that body
> arrives at the Lunacy section of the report, the Chairman will call a
> halt and deliver himself after this fashion: "Gentlemen, I trust some
> of you know something about Lunacy; for I am sure I don't". The
> long odds are that the other members will declare themselves in the
> same boat. Then the Chairman will say: "Well, gentlemen, I pro-
> pose we have this section extracted and pass to our colleagues, the
> Commissioners of Lunacy . . . for the favour of their comments".
> This motion will be carried unanimously: and then the fact [*sic*]
> will be on the fire with a vengeance. The commissioners will sput-

ter over it, looking at the question from home standards; their comments will establish a state of panic; the Secretary of State will share in it; and the panic will find relief in imposing extravagant expenditure on unfortunate Nigeria. In a very few years we shall have some twenty-five thousand certified lunatics under public control, at a minimum charge of ten shillings a week per head. . . . You can imagine what this means with Nigeria's revenue; and the only people who will profit will be the native lawyers and the food contractors who will charge extravagant prices for the supply of food-stuffs, in not a few cases for the feeding of their own insane relations whom they can well afford to feed at their own cost.[45]

As the appendix continues, it becomes clearer that this debate was not merely over the need or resources for accommodations but cut to the heart of what colonialism was about. The Secretary added that the "loyal cooperations of the local authorities"

might be construed as a polite euphemism for dragooning natives of the Northern Provinces into alien ways and ignoring what is serviceable in their own,— or in other words, pursuing the gospel of Direct Rule. . . .

The assumption that there is no middle course between Native Administration jails and the expenditure of some 500,000 [pounds] a year on providing European comforts and architecture is wholly illogical and wrong.[46]

These responses to Home's recommendations embodied the contradictions of Indirect Rule. They justified parsimony in the name of cultural preservation and assailed reform as an imposition on the native way of life. Underlying this stance was the crucial self-deception that one could, somehow, have colonialism *without* making any impositions.

The government—more by deferring decision than through articulated policy—followed a middle course, avoiding both a significant investment in treatment, as well as a strict "hands-off" policy. Nigeria therefore ended up with institutions that had none of the potential advantages Home called for and all the disadvantages his opponents predicted.

Brown's 1936 report, though similar to Home's, had a different reception. There is no record of his recommendations receiving the derision Home's did. Instead, the tenor of his report was echoed in virtually all subsequent memoranda and reports.[47] In just 10 years, the recognition of the need for expanded accommodation, and the desirability of a curative institution, became conventional wisdom. This change reflected shifts in both colonial and psychiatric thinking. The Colonial Development Act of 1929 signaled the beginning of a move to greater planning and centralization from the colonial state. At the same time institutional psychiatry in Britain itself was becoming more proactive, increasingly admitting voluntary patients from the 1930s.[48] But these changes in thinking were not reflected in significant institutional reform in Nigeria's asylums. As Falola notes, the 1929 act achieved little in its 11-year history because the depression and the Second World War inhibited capital investment, and so the intense emphasis on promoting exports continued.[49] But the arguments against expanded and improved psychiatric facilities no longer ridiculed such reforms as incompatible with the very nature of colonialism itself, but rather more defensively, they cited budgetary restraints.[50]

Responses to Brown's report underscore the ambiguity concerning the purpose of the asylums. Should they be more like prisons or hospitals? Different departments of the government hoped to exploit this ambiguity in order to foist the lunacy problem on others. Prison director Victor Mabb claimed to have no comment on Brown's report, but he did remark tersely that, after all, "the care and treatment of lunatics is a function of the Medical Department."[51] R. Briercliffe, the Director of Medical Services, was not so sure; he argued, "If detention is accepted as the main function of asylums it is not illogical that the Prisons Department should take the chief share in the custody of lunatics."[52] Lunatics, already outcasts, were welcomed by neither the prison nor the medical bureaucracy.

There were several financial obstacles to a mental hospital. The salaries needed for a trained staff and the large amount of water supplies required were seen as prohibitive expenses. Besides the inherent expense, there were competing considerations when the first calls for a curative program were made in the late 1920s—on the eve of the worldwide depression. In the 1940s, of course, the British government was preoccupied with the Second World War and its aftermath. A mental hospital was also more expensive than other public health projects. In 1930, the Nigerian government requested a public health budget from the Colonial Office in which the cost of a mental hospital (33,700 pounds) was almost a third of the total (107,000 pounds).[53] The other items for which funds were requested were training centers for midwives and sanitary inspectors, ambulances, grants to native dispensaries, the leper colony in Benin, general sanitary improvements, and research. None of these items alone approached the cost of the mental hospital.

Ideological Restraints on Reform

Financial expediency was the main reason a curative institution was delayed, but it dovetailed with ideological inhibitions. One inhibition was the belief that a mental hospital was inappropriate for Africans. As Anne Phillips has remarked, "British colonial practice seemed to pride itself on retarding rather than hastening change."[54] This pride was of course misplaced, since there was no way the economic goals of colonialism could be met without hastening change. The theory of Indirect Rule acknowledged that economic, political, kinship, and religious systems were interrelated parts of African life. One goal, therefore, was not only to support those they acknowledged as traditional rulers but also to preserve systems of land tenure.[55] But the encouragement of cash crop cultivation to serve the economic goals of colonialism, along with missionary activity and Western education, were causing significant disruptions.[56] The ideology of Indirect Rule — what Freund has called the "cult of tradition"[57] — nevertheless had significant effects; one result of the contradiction between ideology and practice was half-measures like asylums — measures which dimly recognized the social changes colonialism incurred but also denied responsibility for them.

At the same time, the "hands-off" policy involved some grudging respect for traditional healers. CMS missionaries respected the talents of *babaláwos*, and some government officials continued this attitude.[58] Although officials usually saw little ambiguity in the identification of African lunatics, the *cure* of these persons was seen as beyond colonial competence.

The medical treatment of African lunatics was complicated in part because lunacy was seen to belong to the realm of "witchcraft." Witchcraft was one of the master categories of colonial discourse, but like most key words, it contained ambiguities. This was noted during the colonial period itself; B. G. St. J. Orde Browne wrote of witchcraft legislation that "certain features will be conspicuous. Perhaps the most noticeable is the lack of accurate definitions. Terms such as 'witchdoctor, charm, ordeal' are freely used, though the exact meaning of them is disputable."[59] Witchcraft was really a blanket term for African practices and beliefs perceived as inconsistent with European rationality.[60] Differences among African practices were acknowledged, but they were not important in comparison with the difference they were *all* supposed to have with European science.

So "witchcraft" was part of a world in which many in the government disavowed interference. In the 1930s, K. Dewar, Assistant District
Officer in Benue, wrote a report entitled "Notes on Witchcraft and Its
Relation to Administrative Problems." As Dewar put it, interference
"might altogether destroy the religion into the fabric of which they
[Africans] are so closely woven."[61] Citing ethnologists such as Evans-
Pritchard and R. S. Rattray, Dewar represented indigenous beliefs as
a closely knit textile, dangerous for white men to pull at, constantly at
risk of unraveling. This logic became a staple of colonial psychiatric
thought, where African psychopathology was thought to be caused by
the dislodging of the subject from the sphere of tradition, the basis for
all stability in society and the person.[62]

But preternatural influences were a major cause of insanity according
to most Africans, and criminal acts by the bewitched therefore raised
confusing issues of responsibility. E. E. Evans-Pritchard considered this
in his classic *Witchcraft, Oracles and Magic Among the Azande,* which
was recommended reading for officials in Nigeria:

> As in our own society a scientific theory of causation, if not
> excluded, is deemed irrelevant in questions of moral and legal re-
> sponsibility, so in Zande society the doctrine of witchcraft, if not
> excluded, is deemed irrelevant in the same situations. We accept
> scientific explanations of the causes of disease, and *even of the causes
> of insanity,* but we deny them in crime and sin because here they
> militate against law and morals which are axiomatic. The Zande
> accepts a mystical explanation of the causes of misfortune, sickness,
> and death, but he does not allow this explanation if it conflicts with
> social exigencies expressed in law and morals.[63]

This question had direct relevance to the colonial treatment of insanity. One official wrote:

> There are certain cases bordering on the line of witchcraft and
> hallucination which should be dealt with similarly. Two such cases
> have come to my notice. In the first a man who had killed a bush
> cow had omitted to carry out the necessary rites. Some months
> later he killed at point blank range his fellow hunter under the hal-
> lucination that he was a bush cow. In the second case a man killed
> his wife under the hallucination that she was a banana tree. Both
> cases were quite genuine and both accused pleaded that they had
> been bewitched. In neither case was the death penalty exacted,

though detention . . . was imposed. This to the African mind is unjust. Where the victim is not the cause of the "bewitchment," compensation would be payable. The African must, however, learn to accept modern ideas upon cases of this description.[64]

In such cases, he concluded that the accused should be "treated as insane at the time of the commission of the deed." He also argued for medical intervention: "The closer study of the condition mental and physical of a person bewitched by those properly qualified."

Who, though, was "properly qualified" to examine the bewitched? Were the bewitched manifesting a universal medical condition, which was colored by local idioms but was in the end best studied by enlightened physicians from Edinburgh? Or was bewitchment essentially a cultural condition, to be referred to cultural experts, the stewards of local knowledge? This remains to this day the central fault line of debate in cross-cultural psychiatry. The ambiguity itself bewitched the colonial mind. In the 1950s, Lambo would devise a dazzling resolution in the Aro village scheme: cosmopolitan and local experts would, in concert, accommodate a "both-and" rather than an "either-or" approach.

In a review of Jock McCulloch's book on colonial psychiatry, Anthony Appiah has warned, "Anyone who wants to add the colonial mental hospital to the long bill of indictment against colonialism . . . would do well to ask how these people would have been treated by their own societies; and should ponder, too, the fate of the mentally-ill in postcolonial Africa."[65] Without denying that many of the mad who were not in asylums during the colonial period may have suffered from stigma or abuse, I think the indictment must stand. In the care of traditional healers, supportive therapy would often have been available to patients, in a context that was familiar to them. In colonial Nigeria's asylums, they were not patients at all but inmates solely, depersonalized in deep ways and living in conditions that alarmed the very people responsible for them. Real changes did come concurrently with the transition to independence.

Decolonizing Psychiatry

By the 1950s, just as it was clear that the colonial state was moribund, there was official recognition that the custodial model of care that had characterized colonial policy needed to be abandoned. In 1951, shortly after arriving in Nigeria and becoming its first full-time psychiatrist, Donald Cameron divided the mentally ill into the following groups:

1. uncertifiable Cases
2. certifiable Cases
    a. in early stages with recovery possible
    b. chronic [66]

What is significant about this taxonomy was that Cameron said that group 2b ought to be excluded from both the mental hospital *and* the asylum, indicating the hope that the institutions would cure, whereas for decades the buildings had been seen as the last resort for hopeless cases. In Lagos, Yaba Lunatic Asylum became Yaba Mental Hospital in the early 1960s. A German psychiatrist, Alexander Boroffka, came to oversee the transformation and Yaba began employing a battery of therapies, including drugs and electro-convulsive therapy derived from Western psychiatry. But it was the Aro Mental Hospital which paved the way in the 1950s and which deserves close examination because of its innovative treatment plan.

Funds were first committed, and planning begun, for the development of Aro in the 1930s.[67] Brown noted then that "the Alake [King] of Abeokuta is actively interested in the welfare of the insane of Abeokuta";[68] the Alake had, in fact offered a lease of land, at nominal rent, for the hospital as early as 1929.[69] But some officials continued to believe that a mental hospital for Africans was an extravagance, some arguing for public health initiatives directed more toward infectious diseases.[70] Lambo relates that during the 1930s he remembers passing a sign indicating the future site of Aro Mental Hospital while he was walking to school and not knowing then what a mental hospital was.

The Second World War provided the essential catalyst for the Aro project, because of the repatriation of soldiers who had served with Allied forces.[71] West African soldiers received free medical care for disabilities resulting from service, as well as employment assistance, upon their repatriation.[72] Rehabilitation centers were set up in Lagos, Freetown, and Accra, which dispensed artificial limbs manufactured by Italian prisoners of war. Upon repatriation, five mentally ill Nigerian soldiers were transferred to Abeokuta from Yaba, where they could not be accommodated due to overcrowding.[73] Carothers noted the "frequent need for repatriating on medical grounds West African soldiers of psychopathic personality."[74] Their presence did not generate a distinctive terminology analogous to "shell shock," or "post-traumatic stress disorder," but a disproportionate number of soldiers seem to have returned from combat with psychiatric problems.[75]

The responsibility the government assumed for insane soldiers highlights the element of bad faith in the prior claim that Europeans could not treat mental illness in Africans. The returning soldiers were too many to stay in Yaba, which was badly overcrowded. And it would have been an impressive feat of ideological rationalization to deny them treatment altogether. After their experiences fighting for the Allies in Asia, preservation of their "African way of life" could hardly be seen as a pressing aim.

The soldiers were lodged in a building formerly used as the Abeokuta convict prison—at that time also an overcrowded institution—the name of which was changed to Lantoro Lunatic Asylum.[76] Lantoro, which became the nucleus for Aro, was a curative institution and excluded all cases "associated with crime or violence."[77] Asuni has referred to the "unfortunate circumstances of Lantoro's origin," which, he said, resulted in a stigma being attached to the patients there.[78] Lantoro was, however, kept as a relatively "closed" extension of Aro, for what Asuni described as the most "disturbed and uncooperative" patients.[79] Despite these disadvantages, Lantoro claimed a good remission rate, and consequent discharges.[80]

Dr. Donald Cameron was an important voice stressing the need for a mental hospital. Cameron was, as Boroffka has put it, "a character": "It is reported he was transferred to Nigeria for disciplinary reasons from Jamaica after he opened all doors of the Kingston Mental Hospital to spite the then Colonial Government for not complying with his requests for the patients."[81] Over the first half of the twentieth century, the Nigerian government enacted a stasis, a failure to reform when reform was deemed essential, which had been common in the history of European and American psychiatry. It is therefore apt that Cameron's gesture, in the manner of Philippe Pinel, re-enacted an archetypal scene of reform in the history of psychiatry, a scene mythologized in Tony Robert-Fleury's "Pinel Freeing the Insane," a painting which has been reproduced and scrutinized in more than one history of psychiatry.[82]

Civilian patients were admitted to the Lantoro site beginning in 1946.[83] Construction of Aro began in the early 1950s about seven miles from the Lantoro site. The initial staff of Aro consisted of 13 attendants transferred from Yaba.[84] Although there were still no psychiatrists in attendance, medical officers from the Abeokuta General Hospital supervised. The professional staffs of both Aro and Yaba at this time were still dominated by Europeans. In 1951, Abraham Ordia, the first Nigerian trained as a psychiatric nurse, began working at Yaba. Ordia, who had spent 32 years in mental health nursing in Holland, England, Sweden, and Switzerland, helped oversee the beginning of the transition of Yaba from asylum to hospital.[85]

During the 1940s, while a colonial government was planning mental hospitals for Nigeria, the Nigerian doctors who would be the future architects of psychiatric care in Nigeria—Asuni, Lambo, and A. A. Marinho—were in the United Kingdom working on their medical degrees. None of them, in fact, planned to take up psychiatric specialties at first. Lambo studied medicine at the University of Birmingham and later specialized in psychiatry at the University of London. Asuni and Marinho were both native Lagosians who studied medicine in Dublin; Marinho is Catholic and chose Dublin in part for that reason, and partly because it seemed relatively safe from the bombing taking place in England during the 1940s.[86] Asuni had originally been interested in engineering but made his decision to take up medicine in large part because it was one of the few professions in which one could work on one's own and avoid employment by the colonial state.[87]

Although Asuni, while in medical school in Dublin, had no plan to become a psychiatric specialist, he did belong to a psychoanalytic circle there. This circle was mainly composed of lay people, artists and writers, interested in exploring psychoanalytic perspectives on culture. According to Asuni, it was the only social circle he found in Dublin which accepted him as an equal, overlooking differences of class, race, and religion (Asuni is Muslim)—a profound commentary on the exclusion Africans studying in the West have experienced.[88] Asuni underwent psychoanalysis himself at this time. It was, however, only when he returned to Nigeria and saw that the creation of the Aro Hospital meant a demand for psychiatrists that Asuni chose this specialty. When he did, he employed little psychoanalysis. Asuni did not reject psychoanalysis, or even question its cross-cultural utility. Asuni simply did not think that it would be helpful in dealing with psychiatry's greatest challenge in Nigeria: the large number of vagrant psychotics in the urban centers.[89]

Lambo and Asuni were also cultural nationalists of a kind.[90] Neither was a revolutionary theorist the way Frantz Fanon was, but their work and careers were critical of colonialism in both explicit and implicit ways. Lambo quite self-consciously regarded the use of traditional healers at Aro as a retort to the arrogance of Western medical science and its assumption that it alone provides the keys to health. While promoting benefits of scientific medicine in Third World countries, Lambo has also been a champion of traditional healing in Geneva, the world capital of public health. Asuni has been more critical of traditional healers but saw his very career choice as a way of achieving autonomy from the colonial regime. This was a common strategy; J. F. A. Ajayi notes that starting in the early twentieth century, law and medicine, which offered the possibility of private practice and success independently of the colonial government, became the favored careers of educated Nigerians.[91]

Even during this period, work on Aro Mental Hospital proceeded slowly, and it was not completed until 1958. In the early 1950s, reflecting the continued sense of alarm about the number of psychiatric cases, Lambo decided to take up psychiatry as a specialty. He studied psychiatry at Maudsley Hospital in Great Britain and assumed authority over Aro in 1954. He remained at Aro until becoming chair of the Department of Psychiatry at the University of Ibadan in 1963. Aro's physical plant was not yet completed in 1954, but Lambo, whose enthusiasm and commitment were becoming legendary, was not to be stopped. Making necessity virtuous, he and his wife, Diana Lambo, devised the Aro village scheme, an outpatient care system which permitted the beginning of treatment.

Lambo's roots in Abeokuta were crucial. He persuaded a number of families near the Aro site to allow mental patients to live with them in exchange for work, mostly help in farming, and a lodging fee. The patients could go to the hospital for treatment in the morning and work in the farms in the afternoon. In addition to the rents the villagers were able to charge, they received several public health benefits: piped, purified water, pit latrines, and a mosquito control squad.[92] Nurses were available to the patients on a 24-hour basis.[93] Landlords were able to borrow money from the hospital in order to build extensions to their houses so they could accommodate patients.[94]

Lambo was acutely aware of the ways the mental hospital was alien to African cultures. Understanding how cultural familiarity was critical to mental health interventions, and also strongly convinced of the therapeutic efficacy of local medicines, he traveled across Nigeria and handpicked 15 traditional healers from different cultural backgrounds to serve as mediators between the hospital staff and the patients. It was crucial to have diversity among the healers, since patients were coming from throughout the country. The healers had a significant role in treatment.[95] Also, through the healers, the psychiatrists gleaned data on cultural conceptions of mental illness. The hospital's treatment program, though, strongly emphasized interventions which were then state of the art in Western psychiatry: electro-convulsive therapy (ECT), psychotropic drugs such as largactil and insulin, interactive psychotherapy, as well as an expanded occupational therapy program.[96] In the early 1960s, the United Nations made a film about Lambo and the experiments at Aro which stated that at the time of filming fully two fifths of the residents of Aro village were patients.[97] The village system became a model for mental health care in a number of African countries, including Ghana. At a time when the world psychiatric community was searching for alternatives to institutionalization, the Aro plan offered an imaginative compromise—outpatient care which could help the patients reintegrate into society, in close proximity to the medical technology of the hospital. To appreciate the prescience of this system, note that it preceded by about a decade powerful and influential sallies against institutionalization such as Erving Goffman's *Asylums* and Foucault's *Madness and Civilization*.

The Aro village system had a number of advantages. For one, it prevented complications brought on by the hospital setting.[98] Another advantage was that the village system worked to counter the stigmas attached both to mental hospitals and their patients. Bruce Home, recall, hoped that Nigerians would be more trusting of mental hospitals than Britons; by the 1950s, Carothers recognized that quite the contrary was true but praised the Aro scheme, which he said "nullifies the repugnance" rural Nigerians felt.[99]

According to Asuni, another advantage of the village system was that mental patients were exposed to "real-life" situations. Patients were less withdrawn and more integrated with the normal life of the village. The villagers meanwhile derived economic benefit from renting rooms. In general, everyone would benefit from the realization that mental patients could live safely and productively in a community, so the usual stigma attached to mental patients would be reduced.[100] One disadvantage of the village plan was that it excluded some urban patients because doctors thought it was inappropriate to make them work on farms. They were treated as inpatients at the hospital as space allowed.

A tremendous amount of optimism surrounded these reforms. One measure of the enthusiasm Asuni and his colleagues had for their new hospital was that they searched the streets of Abeokuta looking for vagrant psychotics to recruit as patients.[101] Conversely, by 1956, attempts were being made to close down some "native asylums."[102] Finally, there was the repatriation of Nigerian mental patients from abroad; on June 27, 1956, "there was a great deal of excitement in Kano Airport," as a plane carrying deportees and mental patients from "various other countries" landed.[103]

Emplotting Reform

Since the 1970s, two narrative structures relevant to the history related here have come under increasing challenge. Much Africanist historiography of the 1960s was redemptive in the sense that it tended to introduce a conflict (colonialism) but to conclude with a happy ending (nationalism and liberation). This narrative structure is less compelling now, as analysts have recognized that despite political independence, most African nations continue to be impoverished, while many are subject to authoritarian and capricious rulers.[104] Similarly, the story of progress in the history of psychiatry has been muted by the influence of Foucault.

The power of these challenges to naively redemptive renderings of both African independence and psychiatric reform must be recognized. But there are dangers in replacing them with a lachrymose irony that would obscure the real benefits of these changes. As Crawford Young writes, in a work devoted to showing the continuities with colonialism that have plagued postcolonial Africa, "African independence remains a historic accomplishment of epochal dimensions."[105] The Nigerianization of psychiatric institutions provides an example of the creative energy for which independence provided greater scope. At the most basic level, the transformation of the asylums from near-prisons into hospitals, while indeed a change in the form of "social control" of the mentally ill, was a departure from the most crudely coercive and dehumanizing form of control. And this change needs to be understood in the context of Nigeria's independence, not only because it provided more opportunity for Nigerian physicians to use their expertise publicly, but because the welfare initiatives which characterized colonialism in the 1950s represented, as many in the government themselves understood, a collapse of the basic logic of colonialism itself. The Aro village plan merits particular recognition as a significant achievement. The village system was not completely novel; it resembled, for example, Belgium's

Geel Colony, where lunatics traveled in search of cure and lived in the community, and which was a model for some fitful experiments in Britain in the nineteenth century.[106] Outpatient care was a growing trend in European psychiatry when Lambo was studying psychiatry, as antipsychotic medications came into use; in Britain, this trend was represented by the development of Maudsley Hospital, which was a reaction to the large, long-term custody mental hospital.[107] There was also an African precedent in the outpatient care developed by Dr. Tigani El-Mahi at the mental hospital in Khartoum, which Lambo had observed at first hand. The use of traditional healers in active conjunction with biomedical care was also not completely innovative; Alexander Leighton, Lambo's collaborator on *Psychiatric Disorder Among the Yoruba*, promoted a similar plan in the 1940s among the Navaho.[108] But while there were precedents for the Aro plan, Lambo executed it with a practical conscientiousness that made it justly famous.

A measure of this care can be gained by comparing the Aro plan with the deinstitutionalization movement in the United States. Deinstitutionalization was no doubt well-intentioned in some aspects, and in some respects successful. It too frequently, though, failed to think through exactly what "community care" should mean—What was the community? What was in it for the community? Indeed, the combination of a desire for fiscal restraint and an often blithe invocation of the merits of "community care" in the deinstitutionalization movement inadvertently echoed the rhetoric of Nigeria's colonial policies. If this seems a harsh charge against deinstitutionalization, consider how specifically criticism of Home's report anticipates the language of the deinstitutionalization movement. Advocates of deinstitutionalization also saw hospitals as impositions, as a form of cruelty worse than the disorders they were supposed to correct. In the United States, the critique of institutions dovetailed conveniently with the desire to cut government budgets. Many advocates of deinstitutionalization also rejected disease models of mental illness to begin with, just as Home's opponents sought to decouple "mental abnormality" from sickness. And, just as the critic hoped to solve the problem more simply with medication, deinstitutionalization became viable in part because of developments during the 1960s in psychotropic drugs, which offered the hope of less involved, less expensive care away from large hospitals.[109] Indeed, the ease with which psychotropic drugs can return a deviant individual to apparently normal functioning must be counted as one of the reasons for psychopharmacology's attraction for the psychiatric profession. Many critics of deinstitutionalization have noted that while the rhetoric of the policy called for "community care," in only a few instances was a "community" carefully identified, consulted, and articulated with the planning in a meaningful way.[110] This was precisely the merit of the Aro village plan, and a principal reason why the village system there has been maintained and even expanded to the present.[111]

If colonial asylums were not subtle enough in their social control function to merit a Foucaultian approach, it is in the reforms of the late colonial period that one might look to such an approach. But while we remain alert to the exercise of power and control in the context of reform, it is also important to measure the use of power in comparison to the alternatives available at a historical moment, and not against a utopian scenario in which no power relations exist.

Much has been at stake, as the number of confined mental patients increased over the course of colonial rule, reaching close to a thousand by independence. This remained a small proportion of the population, but the rate of increase far exceeded any likely rate of population increase. Moreover, the numbers exclude a great deal. For example, they do not include those lunatics confined in Native Administration asylums or prisons.[112] More significantly, archival sources often refer to the much larger number of lunatics turned away from the asylums due to lack of space. In the 1950s, Carothers estimated a total number of insane people in Nigeria as high as 30,000. This number cannot be considered accurate but is nevertheless a symptom of considerable numbers of people cast in the social role of "lunatic." Similarly, many of the healers Prince interviewed in the early 1960s stated that mental illness was on the increase in that period, as the breakdown of the traditional family led to a loss of respect for authority figures, and thus an increase in the hostilities and jealousies which lead to curse and sorcery. This explanation may be questioned, but it is important that the perception of an increase in madness was not unique to colonial officials.

The social role of "lunatic," itself a kind of institution, increasingly subjected the persons assigned to it to incarceration in institutions of madness. During this process, lunatics were subject to a third kind of "institutionalization," in the form of representations in medical and official documents that, in cursory but revealing ways, described their cases. This documentation, analyzed in the following two chapters, allows us to peek in the windows of the colonial asylums and ask, Who are these people? How did they get here?

CHAPTER 4

"Proper Subjects for Confinement"

I have come to realise that there is an element of sense in every nonsense spoken or written down.

—Mr. O., Patient in Yaba, 1987[1]

To be confined in an asylum, somebody has to claim you are insane. Distinguishing the normal from the pathological, though, is a complex process that involves social value judgments as well as purely medical ones. Indeed, the notion of a purely medical judgment has been questioned in recent years, as scholars have shown that the designation of pathology expresses social values.[2] How then did British-administered institutions determine "lunacy" across the cultural frontiers that separated them from Africans?

"Displacing Everything": Reading Patient Records

For how many minutes per day do you demonstrate your madness

—Anonymous patient in Yaba, 1987[3]

The evidence in this chapter comes from two main sources: the Nigerian National Archives in Ibadan, and case files from the early years of the Aro Mental Hospital, to which the hospital graciously allowed me access. These sources help to reveal the social processes set in motion as lunatics collided with police, magistrates, clinicians, district commissioners, traditional rulers, and neighbors.

These sources are unconventional in some respects, so a statement of methodology is called for. I am particularly concerned with patients' experiences, but also cautious about looking to case records for an "authentic" source. Most of the records were written by administrators and, in the later years, by clinicians. But, as Lorna Rhodes has put it, "all clinical situations are polyphonous,"[4] meaning that case records are not just written by the person who puts pen to paper but are produced asclinicians and patients—themselves representatives of complex social worlds—work with and against each other. This "polyphony" leaves ambiguous, contradictory traces in the records, undermining the quest for a reified "patient experience."[5]

In a fascinating minority of cases, patients wrote the documents either partly or wholly themselves. The special problems, and promise, of such sources can be seen in this account I found in an unnumbered case file at Aro. Ayo, a 28-year-old clerk admitted to Aro in August 1959, described his path to the hospital during the year before Nigeria's independence in this elliptical but captivating account:

> I was well till 26/8/59. Suddenly, I took my notebook & started writing "nonsense" in it like: "I am the new money with 5 heads. All the world shall use it."
> Awolowo + Awolowo = Double Awolowo
> Double Awolowo = Double Victory
> I drew a flag showing where the boundary of the Western Region should be, i.e. the River Niger. Then I wrote, "We are wonderful." Then I packed my clothes, bible, ruler & prayer garment (I am an Aladura), my wristwatch my shorthand fountain pen. I gave them to my brother. I was displacing everything, so I was brought here. When I got to Abeokuta I heard the voice of a spirit which asked me to say "*Irapada*" [redemption], so I shouted "*Irapada*."[6]
> When I got here, I did not take food, in obedience to the spirit which asked me not to take food. It said "Have you not taken food before?" Later I thought that I was in the House of Representatives.
> Since then I have known that we are not in the House of Representatives. We are in the Hospital. . . .
> The day I received my salary, I had another attack.[7]

One thing this example shows is that the accounts can be *hard to read;* they are "displacing everything," often following a highly emotive symbolic logic. One reader of a version of this chapter thought "highly emotive symbolic logic" to be another way of simply saying "incoherent," but this is the view I reject. There is ample precedent in African studies and other fields for attempting to interpret a symbolic logic of utterances under spirit possession, for example. To say that Ayo's language does not merit such analysis because he was sick seems to me only prejudicial.

Ayo himself described some of this writing as nonsense. But as Emily Dickinson wrote, "Much madness is divinest sense"—an attitude implied in Ayo's quotation marks around the word "nonsense." While Ayo was "displacing everything," he also wrote with splintered eloquence about the themes of Nigeria's imminent independence. In this, and in many of the preserved accounts, the language of the confined is saturated with political and religious meanings. The identification with Obafemi Awolowo (the most prominent Yoruba politician of this period, founder of the Action Group political party, and Premier of the Western Region at the time of Ayo's writing) and the concern with the boundary of the Western Region reflect brewing anxieties about ethnic conflicts. The cry of "*Irapada!*" possibly expresses a redemptive elation associated with the end of colonial rule, while the confusion of the hospital with "the House of Representatives" conveys a sense of the hospital as a political institution—perhaps also expressing a sense of the "Westernness" of the institution. Indeed, it is striking that prior to his admission, Ayo was divesting himself of items associated with his Western education—wristwatch, fountain pen, bible—in a purging process anticipating redemption.

None of these interpretations has significance if we regard Ayo's words as *simply* the raving of a madman. That point of view, typical of the most reductive biopsychiatry, holds that what the lunatics *said* is not so important as what they *had*. I propose instead to treat "raving" itself as a valid object of social analysis. As Ann Braden Johnson has put it: "Often, their [insane people's] peculiar mannerisms and behaviors represent their best attempt to communicate something important. . . . No matter how failed the transmission . . . there is always a message buried somewhere in the . . . bizarre behavior of the mentally ill person."[8] The argument that these buried messages are worth excavating is developed in what follows. For this reason, I am critical of biopsychiatry not so much because I regard it as wrong, but because it is incomplete. Proponents of strictly biological psychiatries may concede that the content expressed in madness varies according to context, though the "underlying" pathology remains the same. In the rest of this chapter, I hope to show 1) that attention to this content is crucial, and 2) that the content has both political and cultural significance.

My approach presupposes that the insane do not differ from "normal" people in an absolute sense but instead occupy a position on a spectrum containing the normal and the pathological.[9] The precise borders within that spectrum are subject to ongoing negotiation, as recent debates over the pharmacological treatment of depression and attention deficit disorder illustrate. Even if one accepts that medications should be used for these conditions in some cases, neither disorder provides an unambiguous, observable symptom that allows one to separate sharply those who need medication from those who do not. The potentially treatable population shrinks or expands depending on one's view of what normal is, and the ultimate path to treatment depends on negotiating one's views against those of family members, peers, supervisors, and clinicians.

But as I trace these negotiations in colonial Nigeria, I guard against a possible misunderstanding. This approach is quite different from arguments which deny outright the reality of mental illness, call mental illness a "myth," or treat the insane as merely people with "problems in living" whom one persecutes by calling them ill. Such arguments are useful for framing skeptical attitudes toward medical expertise, but in their strongest form they are a fittingly simplistic mirror image for biopsychiatric reductionism.[10] In other words, while I hold that insanity and sanity form a continuum rather than a dyad, this does not mean that there is no difference between them. In some cases, there is strong evidence of a political content to allegations of "madness," but this cannot be used as an indictment of the entire category of mental illness, a category that virtually all human societies seem to have found necessary. The number and range of documented societies with a category similar to madness surely puts the burden of proof on researchers who would posit otherwise.

Several factors conspire to make the stories of mental patients obscure. Because of legitimate concerns about privacy, incomplete documentation, and the sometimes cryptic language of the mad, the "voices" of patients are always difficult for historians of psychiatry to uncover. In 1936, Robert Cunyngham Brown observed that it was hard to learn particulars about asylum patients, such as their age, marital state, occupation, and life history generally, *even when he could approach them and talk to them face to face.* This was partly because they were disordered in mind and also because their social connections had been severed.[11] For the Aro case files, thorough case records could not be kept because of staff limitations in this period.[12] Finally, a number of records refer, as Ayo did, to the "nonsense" uttered by lunatics, but in many cases the inability of the author of the document to understand the utterances of an inmate may have more to do with the author's linguistic limitations—asylum officials spoke little Yoruba or other African languages until the significant advent of Nigerian clinicians in the 1950s. Yet all of these factors also indicate why these sources are especially valuable; they open windows to hidden chambers of the colonial estate.

The Limits of Epidemiology

The available records have significant limitations for answering epidemiological questions. For example, the reason for the increase in the number of people confined in the asylums cannot be determined precisely. Even if one believed that mental illness were an easily defined, and therefore easily counted, entity (and I do not), there is no reliable way to know how many people were treated in other settings, or not treated at all.

Wage earners and city dwellers also seem overrepresented in the asylums, compared to the population in general.[13] This does not necessarily show that such people were prone to mental illness, although the notion of "detribalization" as a cause of insanity was common in colonial literature. As Margaret Field noted, rural Africans who became mad were not noticed by the officials because they did not show up in asylums.[14] The occupations of the inmates therefore tell us more about the institutions and *which* lunatics they housed than they do about lunatics generally.

One epidemiological question deserves, I think, special attention. Among *institutionalized* mental patients in Nigeria, males have outnumbered females in a ratio of about 3 to 1, a ratio that held constant for most of the colonial period. This ratio is curious, and potentially very significant from a comparative perspective, since the preponderance of women as mental patients is often taken as a commonplace in Western scholarship, especially over the past two centuries.[15] The preponderance of male mental patients may be widespread in West Africa; Leland Bell reports similar ratios to the Nigerian ones in Sierra Leone. The meanings of the Western ratios remain in dispute, though. The notion that women are innately or biologically more susceptible to mental disorder, a notion which influenced some colonial psychiatric thought, has been mostly discarded. In searching for a more social explanation, students have posited that the strictures of male-dominated society have led women to become mad in higher numbers (in other words, that there is a higher true prevalence); that the biases of male psychiatrists have simply led women to be diagnosed more frequently; that women and men have different help-seeking patterns, and that new diagnostic categories have disproportionately been applied to women.[16]

While it is possible that several of these factors interact, the Nigerian data yield similar puzzles and require much more interdisciplinary research before a convincing explanation can be advanced. Before beginning my fieldwork, I conjectured that the Nigerian ratio was an artifact of treatment patterns—that male patients were more closely articulated with the colonial sector and female patients were being served by traditional healers. That interpretation makes sense, since males were predominant in most colonial institutions in Africa—general hospitals, schools, prisons.[17] But at the same time, traditional healers also report a predominance of male patients, dating back to their parents' practices, in very similar ratios. It may be that psychopathology in southern Nigerian women takes forms which do not occasion strong and obvious measures of social control. Alternative treatments that I did not investigate, such as spirit possession cults and healing churches, are probably a factor. Prince argued that the *gèlèdé* cults among the Yoruba were an important treatment site for insanity, and in their work on *gèlèdé* Henry John Drewal and Margaret Drewal stress the ways *gèlèdé* rites honor women.[18] In general, I think it likely that the gender ratio of mental patients in Nigeria is an artifact of treatment patterns more than a reflection of the "true" prevalence of mental illness.

Getting In, Getting Out

The social processes of determining who was a lunatic can be studied by looking at the processes of confinement and discharge. As I have stressed, cases where Africans and Europeans disagreed outright on the madness of a case seem to have been rare. Most of the confined seem to have been people who caused considerable distress and confusion to those around them. For the most part, patients were not brought in voluntarily by themselves or their families but involuntarily by police or other relative strangers. Asylum administrators were usually willing to release patients if someone would care for them, though there were exceptions to this.

Some officials were aware that the labeling of insanity was problematic, especially in a colonial situation. In 1950, an official named J. H. Pottinger provided guidelines for detention. A careful diagnosis must be made, he said, because lunatics should not be lightly deprived of liberty. Pottinger also argued that asylum life would worsen the chance of recovery for a patient: "Life under detention is regular, food and drink appear at stated times without effort on the part of the individual and shelter and clothing are available. The patient therefore tends to lose initiative. . . . He gets out of touch with the life he has previously known, and after a prolonged detention becomes positively unfit for any other kind of life."[19] Pottinger issued these cautions:

> Paranoia is an uncommon condition, is found in persons of more than average intelligence, is not accompanied by hallucinations, and the delusions expressed nearly always sound as if they could be true.
>
> It is a good habit to write a note at least every 3 months on every patient. Carefully avoid the easy entry of "No change."
>
> Refusal to work, noisiness, fighting, etc. are not necessarily evidence of insanity. Many normal people do or would do these things in the same circumstances.
>
> In attributing delusions be very careful that they are delusions. Remember the classical case of a fisherman who was stated to have delusions because he boasted that he had saved the Russian fleet and had been given a Golden casket by the Emperor of Russia. It happened to be substantially true (he helped save the lives of some sailors of a Russian fleet and had been presented with a gold cigarette case bearing the monogram of the Tsar).
>
> Belief that "juju" has been put on him cannot be assessed as delusional if it's common to the majority of other people of the same society.[20]

We shall see that Pottinger was well advised to urge caution with regard to "delusions."

Family members wrote letters to administrators requesting the release or confinement of patients; many of the letters are preserved in the archives.[21] There were very few requests to confine family members; despite occasional colonial complaints about families "dumping" unwanted lunatics into the asylums, this was not typical. There were apparently occasional instances of families or communities who, frustrated with attempts to manage chronic cases, sought the state's help, but this was exceptional. By contrast, 87 of the letters request the release of a patient, and of these, 78 concede the insanity of the confined but urge home care instead. The archival file also contains 84 letters from administrators granting a request for release, and only 20 letters turning down such a request. Of these 20, 17 allege continued and dangerous insanity.[22] So administrators were often willing to release patients when relatives could care for them.[23] Often, the freed patient was deemed a good candidate for effective "native" treatment, or simply harmless.

Another striking aspect of these letters is the rarity of dispute over the madness of the inmate in question. Rather than deny the patient was insane, most letters proposed that a local healer should care for the patient. This may have been a rhetorical gambit; letter writers may have thought their chances of getting someone released were better if they conceded the madness, and this may have even become known as a formula for procuring release. But I think it more likely that the concession to the inmates' madness was sincere. Asylum inmates were likely to be the most unambiguous cases—that is, people whose dramatically anomalous behavior caused widespread apprehension.[24] Ulli Beier relates an example of an inmate at Lantoro who "in his own society . . . was not considered mentally disturbed in our [Western] sense of the word," and it is likely that there were many other cases of whom this could be said. But the case Beier relates is one he concedes would have been treated by a healer, in the absence of the asylum.[25]

One letter claimed that the inmate was bewitched but, rather than viewing bewitchment as the cause of the insanity, treated it as a categorically different condition. Debule A.'s release from Yaba was sought by relatives in this 1939 letter: "He is not insane at all, neither a mad man, but it was the people who hated him and conjured and cast upon him a very powerful divination and that stupefied his brain. We cry only for his release into our care, and we shall try our level best to bring him into a good state . . . by our native different herbs and medicines."[26] The letter *recognizes* a universal category of madness, but exempts its subject from inclusion in it.[27]

While Nigerians did not always question the ability of colonial institutions to recognize madness in Africans, they did frequently question the institutions' ability to care adequately for mad persons, and traditional treatment was sought as an alternative. In many cases, authorities agreed.[28] Official support for local healers was partly a matter of convenience; the more patients who were handled by healers, the fewer who burdened the asylums. There was, though, some concession to the abilities of healers. An intriguing case was Ruth B., whose release was sought by her uncle, a Lagos policeman, in late October of 1947: "From my own experience, though unsupported scientifically, I could seek . . . complete release from her illness, by my conclusions during my regular visits there. . . . If my request is granted, I shall endeavor to give her some other treatments necessary."[29] Ruth's caregiver stated in her medical report that she was

> afraid to stay in her employer's house because of auditory and visual hallucinations. She was rather violent at times and had to be confined in an isolation cell. . . . She was certified . . . as a case of melancholia with delusions. . . . Occasionally she is startled and complains of being chased by mermaids. Recently one of her compatriots living in Lagos visited the Asylum and gave the information that in their country, the people worship mermaids. Her failure to "placate" the mermaids before sailing "over the seas" to Lagos has resulted in the mermaids penalising her with the result that she is now insane. . . . From my experience this is a case that should improve with proper native treatment. . . . She shows no homicidal or suicidal tendencies, I recommend she should be released to the care of her uncle.[30]

One remarkable aspect of this response is that Ruth's release for treatment by a healer was authorized despite some record of violent behavior.

Conversely, when petitions for release were turned down, medical officers sometimes claimed that native cure had been tried and failed, even if this was not the only reason for the denial. Such a case was John O., whose release from Yaba was sought by his mother in 1955. She wrote, "I am taking him to a native doctor who assured me he would cure him of his mental disease." Donald Cameron, however, noted that John "was out on trial for treatment by a native doctor in 1951 and in fact got worse."[31]

Once a person was confined, it could be difficult to get out. Psychiatric labeling can follow a downward spiral through which the belief that someone is insane prompts more evidence to support it, while contradictory evidence is not noticed.[32] As a result, inmates entered not only the physical space of an asylum but a bureaucratic labyrinth with few avenues for exit regardless of their behavior. This can be illustrated even with cases that were eventually discharged. One case where remission was claimed was Aiyebusi O. of Ishan, a criminal lunatic whose mother requested his release in late 1953. Aiyebusi had been charged several years earlier with the accidental assault and killing of his father. The Senior District Officer for Ekiti Division wrote to a medical officer at Yaba, "The lucid letters he writes home encourage his people to believe that he has regained his stability."[33] Another Medical Officer responded that "any letters he may have written to his people were irregularly sent out of this institution. All letters from patients are dealt with in the usual official process." Attached to the medical officer's letter was Aiyebusi's medical report from that year, which said: "He is quite rational now. Behaviour is normal. Keeps himself clean. Washes his clothes. He is a hard working patient. Does not give any trouble whatsoever. I cannot certify that he is permanently sane now and recommend further detention here."[34] The case for Aiyebusi's continued incarceration was obviously not so solid. His mother's cause was adopted by the Onishan[35] of Ishan, whom she probably contacted in search of an alternate authority. The Onishan, unable to see medical grounds for the imprisonment, offered to take responsibility for him.[36] Aiyebusi was finally released, on the order of the Resident for Ondo Province, several months later.

An apparent restoration of health was grounds, then, for a return to liberty, but there were also cases where a return to liberty prompted the announcement of cure. Laiwole B.'s remission was declared, as a *fait accompli*, after his escape from Aro on October 1, 1948, a year after he was admitted with the diagnosis "Dementia Paranoides." Laiwole's original medical certificate said: "Patient talks a lot incoherently . . . walks up and down the wards of the hospital talking a lot of nonsense and creating a lot of fun. Sometimes he takes off all his clothes leaving only a pair of knickers on. . . . Says that he has been a driver to all the kings in Yorubaland."[37] His medical record after his escape, though, states that Laiwole was "well-behaved and a good worker," and that "at the time of his escape he had improved considerably . . . [and could be] discharged." A similar case was that of Sule, a criminal lunatic who escaped from Aro in 1948. Sule served a year and a half hard labor for theft but was detained in Aro because he could not "give a reasonable account of himself and his whereabouts." The file also notes that "he ate up his bed ticket and his temperature chart." Following his escape, his record recommended that he be officially discharged.[38]

Officials based the release of patients more on their harmlessness than on their health. If someone assumed the care of the patient, and the patient was not considered a public danger, release was granted even when the symptomatic behavior was still present. Henrietta A., a 41-year-old petty trader, was originally brought in by her mother. A police magistrate called Henrietta "paranoid," and medical officer J. Femi-Pearse maintained that "she may be a little mentally defective, but the main trouble seems to be a sex mania. She apparently is a prostitute. [She is] continually laughing . . . states that she stays wherever the spirit dictates to her, no definite place of abode . . . she is excitable and become confused." [39] In November 1941, her mother wrote to the commissioner of the colony to ask for permission to look after Henrietta herself.

Pearse was sympathetic, indicating that Henrietta could be discharged despite her behavior: "[She] is still weak mentally and shows very little sign of improvement. . . . She is physically strong. She eats and sleeps well. She might be handed over to the care of her immediate relative." [40]

The boundaries of incarcerable behavior were wider, though, for people far from kin and community, even if these people were not violent. One official noted in 1950 that the Western Province resented spending money on non-Yoruba lunatics, but also argued: "Generally lunatics while fairly harmless are looked after by their families, but they have a nomadic tendency and when far from their homes constitute a nuisance and are locked up. Any asylum in this country has a large percentage of lunatics from remote localities." [41] The medical certificate for Momo Y., who was confined in the late 1930s, lists these signs of insanity: "He behaves in a childish manner, giggling & acting in a shy manner when addressed . . . breaks out into prayer . . . he is constantly praying & does not answer rationally . . . it would appear that he is behaving like a mental defective with a religious mania as a prominent feature." [42] Laughter, prayer, and shyness would seem to be innocuous conduct, especially considering the scarcity of asylum space. The certificate also notes, though, that "no person is found who can give information as to his previous movements or life." Momo had migrated to Ijebu-Ode from Kano; to the extent that he was truly shy, it should be taken in the context of his status as stranger. His "irrational" answers may have reflected discomfort in southern languages; his "religiosity" might seem pious rather than manic in a more familiar setting. [43]

Many inmates were "criminal cases," people charged with violent crimes and declared unfit to stand trial, or people attempting a guilty but insane plea. In 1941 Omo B. was an "unconvicted prisoner becoming insane." Omo was charged with stealing; while he was awaiting trial, his medical certificate indicated that he "talks a lot of nonsense—giving wrong answers to questions—confused and stupid looking."[44] By contrast, there was a 1930 criminal case in which Nigerians—including the accused—claimed insanity, whereas the asylum found the suspect sane. Neighbors had for several years regarded the suspect, Idabie, as a "violent and dangerous lunatic."[45] He was arrested for murder and brought to the Yaba asylum but was certified sane and released. Idabie, probably attempting a guilty but insane plea, admitted his crime and said he realized that his mind was "unhinged," remarking that several traditional healers had failed to achieve a lasting cure. Idabie said he knew he was mad at the time of the crime and could not control himself.

Eccentric behavior could help implicate an individual in a crime. This is not unique to colonial Nigeria; it is a widespread stigma attached to the insane that they are prone to criminal activity. A possible case of scapegoating concerned a man named Falade, who came before a magistrate in 1935 with a wound on his head inflicted by a farmer. At the hospital, people claiming to be his parents said he had been insane for some time.[46] Falade denied they were his parents. The magistrate concluded, "There is no doubt from the man's behavior and appearance that he is hopelessly insane."

The farmer was later found murdered. No motive for the killing was known, and on the basis of this highly circumstantial evidence, a magistrate concluded that Falade was the killer.[47] Falade was confined in Yaba, his madness having made him a convenient and defenseless suspect. The farmer's death provided an occasion for incarcerating Falade, who, according to his professed parents, had been "behaving foolishly . . . the past four years." A certificate written after his confinement provides an unhappy coda: "Since his admission to the hospital . . . he has been shouting and raving practically continually. . . . He continually repeats the same phrase which I am informed is meaningless."[48]

Criminals were probably only a modest majority of asylum inmates. Many of the so-called civil lunatics were also detained by police or other authorities for being nuisances, if not exactly criminals. Often these were people who walked naked in public, urinated or defecated in the open, or threatened people for no apparent reason. While the behavior could be simply odd, such as giving away money at random, it was usually bothersome to other people. Sometimes, entire communities petitioned to confine a threatening person.[49]

When physical threat was absent, financial drain or the failure of traditional treatment were common complaints.[50] These requests often show exasperation. A 1952 letter from Ladipo O. requested asylum space

for his mother: "The woman had been out of mental order for over ten
years ago on whom all efforts for mental restoration had proved abor-
tive . . . this lunatic talks as from 10 P.M. till day break in which in addition some respectable neighbour landlords with their wives and children had been subjected to day light attack with injuries and damages
done to their properties. . . . I am really fed up of her."[51] The opening
of Aro—"Lambo's hospital," in some popular usage—aroused hope for
many. It meant that families with chronic cases could unburden themselves and place kin in a benign environment. For example, a 1947 editorial about Aro prompted a letter from a Kaduna man who sought help
for his wife who had lost her reasoning power due to "poison . . . everything seem to her as if she is in some deep dream or under some spiritual spell."[52] The man had spent a lot of money on "native and English
doctors" trying to cure his wife, but "believe me since 1945 that my wife
fell ill, life became a drag not worth living and nothing interests me again
till I read the cited editorial in your worthy paper." And while they remain to this day a small category, self-referrals emerged as a new category of institutional mental patients in the 1950s.

   With an idea of how incarceration and discharge worked, we can look
more closely at the conflicts—social and internal—embodied in the inmates' stories. I discuss these conflicts under two major (and partially
overlapping) rubrics: the problem of "somatization" and medicaliza-
tion, and what I call the political construction of delusion. What connects these themes is the illustration that madness is not simply "socially
constructed"—a phrase which conjures a kind of architectural stasis to
my ear—but politically fraught, and ambiguous in ways the mad and
those around them actively puzzle through. Madness raises questions
about no less than the nature of reality—physical, cosmological, and
political.

SOMATIZATION, MEDICALIZATION

   The opening of Aro in the 1950s widened the scope of
potential inmates, so public nuisances were not the only candidates.
People whose problems were mainly nuisances to themselves became
patients. Many of them were people who suffered from physical problems which clinicians labeled psychosomatic. Lambo published an article in 1955 arguing that in Africans, psychological disturbances were often "masked" by their transformation into physical complaints.[53] This
"somatization" of psychological problems in Africans has continued to

be the subject of clinical literature.[54] Morakinyo has argued that phobic states are often missed by clinicians working in Africa because of their transformation into somatic problems.[55] Prince has suggested that "members of many African cultures must employ physical complaints to be permitted to enter the sick role. Psychological complaints would not be considered sufficient grounds."[56] Prince further argues that physical complaints are likely to take locally prominent forms, the most prevalent diseases in the area involving, for example, rising temperature, as with malaria and smallpox.

There are grounds for questioning just how uniquely African "somatization" is, given the numbers of complaints which clinicians in Western countries believe are psychosomatic.[57] At the same time, Prince is probably right to indicate that the sick role in Western countries encompasses a wider range of psychological complaints. Rather than try to resolve this question, however, I consider two examples of how the ambiguities themselves influence clinical situations.

The first example concerns a patient named Julius who, in 1955, went to the new medical school in Ibadan with physical complaints. A doctor there thought his problems were psychosomatic and referred him to Lambo at Aro, where he was treated with a combination of sedatives and stimulants: adrenaline, electro-convulsive therapy, and largactil.[58] After his treatment, Julius wrote what he called his own "sick history":

> In the first place, I am sincerely thankful to the doctor for my improvement and am still wish to complain of these more serious cases about the sickness.
>
> Sometimes my brain stirs and confuses making me to feel like being unconscious with the result that I scarcely concentrate upon one thing up to two minutes time.
>
> Suffer a continual acute and crushing headache. At times blood gushes out of my nostrils and as an effect of this torture the right ear is now deaf.
>
> Exceptionally very weak and tired at the depressed heart, while the entire body shakes and quivers me especially along my hands.
>
> Occasional paralysis throughout the whole body and a very painful aching waiste. As if, of course I know not the bones, of course I know not are broken.[59]

Despite the thanks offered for his improvement, one is struck by the fact that he remained in excruciating pain. Note as well how intensely *bodily* his complaints were. His upper body especially appears to have been in agony. How closely his own description of his symptoms resembles the Yoruba diagnosis of *orí ọdẹ*, or "hunter's head," also strikes me. Describing *orí ọdẹ*, Prince names "sensations of burning, crawling, or thumping in his head. . . . Insomnia, dizziness, and trembling may occur."[60] I make this connection not to suggest that this was the "real" diagnosis but to suggest how Julius's own understanding may have differed from his clinicians'. Julius was essentially told he had mental problems with a physical manifestation, where such a separation may not have been meaningful for him. He did, after all, seek general medical help, not psychiatric. Available records do not show the grounds by which clinicians determined his problems were psychosomatic, but the bodiliness of his description draws attention sharply to a central feature of such a diagnostic description—it questions the patient's self-understanding, ascribing a kind of "false consciousness." But we need not question the sincerity of Julius's thankfulness or the probity of the clinicians. What I do want to explore further is the friction the concept of psychosomatic illness can bring to clinical situations.

This friction is evident in the case of Philip, a 43-year-old postal clerk who came to Aro complaining of weakness, pain in the ribs, blurred vision, "heaviness in the chest," "tiredness in the head," shallow breathing, sleeplessness, and constipation.[61] The record of his case suggests some haggling between him and a clinician over the nature of his problem. After describing Philip as a formerly "brilliant student," and his home life "excellent," the clinician continued: "Mental state—no abnormal mental manifestation. Does not appear, however, to have been very cooperative in his answer, because he believes his trouble is general weakness, & he suspected I was asking him irrelevant questions because he is 'mentally unbalanced.' He is very eager about letting one understand the point."[62]

The clinician, though, added "hypochondria," to the list of complaints, a diagnostic label that seems inevitably to involve a pejorative judgment. Despite Philip's eagerness to press his side of the case, the diagnosis of hypochondria undermined Philip's physical complaints. By calling Philip hypochondriacal, the clinician invoked a model of illness derived from Western biomedicine, which sees psychosomatic ailments as less than "real" diseases and barely distinguishable from downright malingering.

But the case does not only provide an instance of a patient resisting the diagnostic process. There is also an unsettling ambiguity in the view of the clinician, since along with the diagnosis of "hypochondria"—a psychiatric diagnosis of sorts—he indicated that there was "no abnormal mental manifestation." The contradiction shows just how confusing "hypochondria" is as a category. Kleinman has observed that hypochondriasis is revealing of a gap between lay and clinical experiences of illness; invoking the heuristic distinction between "disease" as objective biological phenomenon and "illness" as culturally mediated experience, Kleinman writes: "Hypochondriasis creates a reversal of the archetypal medical relationship in which the patient complains of illness and the physician diagnoses disease. Rather, in hypochondriasis the patient complains of disease . . . and the doctor can only confirm illness."[63]

There are still further inherent ambiguities in the question of somatization. Csordas has pointed out, for example, that the word itself has at least four potential meanings: 1) the presentation of physical symptoms in the absence of organic pathology, 2) amplification of organic symptoms beyond physiological expectations, 3) presentation of personal or social problems as somatic symptoms, and 4) a mechanism where emotions give rise to somatic signs and symptoms.[64] In addition, the exact grounds for terming patients' problems primarily "mental" but "masked" by physical symptoms is not always easy to determine. Asuni has noted, for example, that "'stomach pain' may be indicative of physical illness like helminthiasis; psychosomatic illness like peptic ulcer; or neurotic illness or even somatization of depressive illness. Other symptoms which are difficult to classify are weakness, headache, and dizziness."[65] The diagnosis of somatic problems can therefore reveal not only friction over the validity of the patient's self-report but also more general negotiations over the relationship between mind and body.

However much the psychiatry an institution practices may be based on organic conceptions of disease, the mind, and the person, mental hospitals must, by their nature, attempt distinctions between what is "mental" and what is "physical." Aro was a mental hospital new to a region where such a firm division was problematic, if not absent. Idowu argues that the Yoruba èmí is close to the English word "spirit" and is something that can inhabit a physical body, but is nonetheless distinct. Morakinyo and Akiwowo, by contrast, argue that èmí is better rendered as "life-force," and connotes no separation of the physical and mental.[66] These ambiguities are fairly resistant to resolution, though most scholars take a view closer to that of Morakinyo and Akiwowo. Philip's case illustrates how the ambiguity itself can generate tension in a hybrid clinical setting. As a species of madness, somatization might oxymoronically be called "physical mental illness," and a case of it is thus an interrogation of the very terms "physical" and "mental."

The cases of Philip and Julius both illustrate how Aro began generating new idioms for understanding distress, and Philip's case seems to indicate the limits of the acceptance of those idioms. Those limitations also apply to spiritual conflicts. In a study of Nigerian syncretic churches in the 1970s, Asuni reported of their preachers and prophets that "practically all of them had some psychiatric problem prior to being converted and later taking up their jobs."[67] Given the pliable nature of psychiatric diagnoses, and the hairline fracture that often separates madness and divine inspiration, one might like to know more about the evidence for psychopathology. But there is no question that the records of Nigeria's mental patients are highly charged with religious content. In the nineteenth century, the madness of religious converts was interpreted in spiritual terms; some inmates of Aro, by contrast, found their spiritual conflicts interpreted in medical terms.

In 1959, Lambo received a letter from a physician at the Baptist Theological Seminary in Ogbomosho concerning a lunatic named Richard. Richard was a student at the Seminary and was admitted to the hospital and given largactil after displaying "antisocial behavior" at his dormitory.

> He stated on admission that he was afraid to go to sleep because he might die. Further questioning brought out the following history. He is the son of a drummer for the shrine of his local religion. During his earlier life he worked as a clerk for the United Africa Company. During that period he enjoyed himself with drinking and, as he says now, taking bribes. On becoming a Christian he completely changed his life. He stopped drinking immediately. Sometime later he vowed to preach (the implication being that if he did not preach the Lord could just kill him). He stayed with Mr. Agbowu of Warri during the period immediately after his conversion and played in a religious orchestra supported by that man. He subsequently went to a Bible School in Benin City where he continued to be riding on a cloud of religious euphoria. At the bible school, he preached often, and participated in daily religious services of some sort. Since admission to the seminary he has done fairly good work, but as . . . [he] himself puts it he has felt like dead wood. He has not been able to preach as often as before because of the language difficulties. He has been pressed in his studies until now he tends to lay some of the cause of his trouble to excessive reading. He and his closest friends have talked of leaving the seminary to go back to the experiences that meant so much to them earlier.

His present illness was precipitated on Sunday two weeks ago when he was invited to preach at a small nearby church. On going to the church he says that he was unable to preach or teach a Sunday School class. He was able to talk about other things, but unable to make his voice preach. He left the church in emotional distress, and since then he has a felt heavy guilt of condemnation.

He has vacillated concerning his willingness to come to Abeokuta for treatment, however he states that he is willing now to do whatever is necessary to expedite his cure.[68]

Richard developed a "symptom"—his inability to preach—that led his fellow Baptists to send him for psychiatric treatment. His case also raises the possibility that spiritual experiences were being increasingly medicalized. What seems to be a crisis of faith is referred to medical authority. And there is evidence that Richard himself may not have regarded his problem as medical. In a note left in his medical file he wrote: "I, Richard . . . hereby state that I am leaving Aro hospital of my own free will and that I have been advised not to do so."

THE POLITICAL CONSTRUCTION OF DELUSION

Conversion in any historical setting seems apt to provoke these kinds of conflicts, but surely one reason for any spiritual ambivalence evident in the stories of lunatic converts was the close identification of Christianity with the colonial state.[69] A vivid illustration of this identification appears in a remarkable set of letters written by a patient named Josiah A. to the District Officer for Ijebu-Ode in the spring of 1943. Josiah left Lagos in 1920 to study in Sierra Leone. He was "advised to leave school owing to his mental condition . . . [and] booked for England . . . to study for medicine."[70] In England, he became a law student, but landed in an English asylum in 1921. His father actually sent a traditional healer to England to cure him.[71] His certificate called him an Anglican Christian who was "unable to work." On his return to Nigeria, he was treated by five healers and was "reported to be irresponsible in his behaviour and dirty in his habits," and he was placed in Yaba.[72] Josiah wrote a series of letters. They merit substantial excerpts, which read as a troubled prose poem on the partition of Africa:

The British government is now called the government of God. God, who is called Jehovah, great I am, is the author of the Ten Commandments and all the sacred Laws of the Holy England. The

English are fighting for the government of god, whereas the Germans are fighting for a Nazi government, an invention made by Satan, the Devil.

Hitlerism must be destroyed. The man Herr Hitler, that German Devil, must pass away a mad man.

I am Josiah A., a poor gentleman whom your worship sent to Lagos, Yaba Asylum for medical treatment. I am quite well and returned to Ijebu-Ode a discharged lunatic on Friday, April 19th 1943.

All places inhabited by the black African race, in former times (before the First Great War) were governed by different powers from Europe, such as the English, the French, and the Germans. But now, by the justice of God, all these places are governed by the English. . . . All these places under the British government are collectively known as "The Nigeria of God."

God appeared to me, Solomon, King of Israel, in a dream by night, and said, "Ask what I shall give thee."

And I Solomon said, "Thou hast made me king instead of my father David, and I am but a child. I know not how to conduct myself before thy chosen people. Give me an understanding heart, that I may distinguish between good and bad, judge thy people righteously."

And God said to me, "Because thou hast asked this, and not long life, or riches, or the life of thine enemies, I have given thee an understanding heart. And I have also given thee that which thou hast not asked, both riches and honour. . . . "

And I Solomon awoke; and behold it was a dream. Soon the time came when I had to put to the test the good gift of wisdom which I had received.

One day there came to Solomon two women, England and Germany, who lived in the same house, Europe. Each of them was the mother of a baby-boy, Nigeria; and the one infant, England's Nigeria (This is called the Nigeria of God) was only three days older than the other, Germany's Nigeria (the German Cameroons, etc.). But the one mother, Germany, had lain on her child by mistake in the night, and killed it. When she awoke and found that it was dead, she took it and laid it beside the other woman, England, while she slept, and carried off her living child. The other, England, soon found out the trick that had been played upon her. So a dispute arose between the two women, England and Germany. Each of them claimed the living Nigeria, and they came together to me Solomon to settle the matter.

> I Solomon, having heard what each had to say, called for a
> sword, and bade one of my guards divide the living Nigeria in two,
> and give half to England, and half to Germany. Germany thought
> this was a good plan, but England exclaimed against it, saying, "Oh
> my Lord, give Germany the living Nigeria, and on no account di-
> vide it."[73]

In this way, by Josiah's account, the true parentage was discovered, and
the living Nigeria was given to England. The letter seems to caricature
the "paternalism" of colonialism, which was reflected in an imagery of
parenthood that pervades colonial discourse.[74]

In May 1943, Josiah added a letter addressed to King George III at
Buckingham Palace:

> I am wisdom, the Conqueror of every foe of England. I am a Law
> Student, the "Palace of Arts," of the University of London, and the
> Founder of all British Universities and Schools.
>   I am that I am,
>   Josiah A.

The letters end, then, with the ultimate gesture of grandiosity, and a
glorification of England. Indeed, they interweave English and biblical
history; Nicolson refers to Lugard's "immodest adoption of Solomon's
Seal as the badge of the new country."[75] Some speculation about the
letters' preservation in official records is also warranted. It may have
touched a nerve because the glorification of England is so extreme as to
seem grotesque, as if lampooning the project of colonial hegemony.
There may also be a subtle anticolonial message buried in Josiah's letters.[76] The last letter was directed to George III, Britain's monarch
when the American colonies decided to rebel, launching a crucial sally
in the gradual dissolution of Britain's global empire. (George III was
also famous to history as the mad king, "easily the most closely observed mad person in English History.")[77] But Josiah's writings are
more striking for the way they differ from the majority of records with
political content, in which resentment toward the state is more or less
overtly evident.

J. C. Carothers, while working in a Kenyan mental hospital, separated
Kenyan schizophrenics into those with persecutory delusions and those
without and maintained that Africans were especially prone to persecutory ones.[78] How should we understand such an extraordinary focus on
this particular symptom? "Persecutory delusions" are a common symptom in mental patients anywhere.[79] But in many of the Nigerian cases,

judgments about psychopathology are inextricable from the political culture of colonialism. The commonly noted symptom of "persecutory delusions" was overdetermined by the persecutory nature of colonialism itself.

A number of cases do not point in obvious ways to the colonial context. L. S. was repatriated from Britain, where he had been studying carpentry and developed "a strong persecutory mania" in the mid-1950s, which led to disorientation and auditory hallucinations. He was treated with deep insulin and electro-convulsive therapy, which "relieved" his most obvious symptoms, but his return to Britain was blocked because of his "dependent" personality.[80] Another example was Rufus A., who, in 1951, was a 42-year-old petty trader in Oye. Rufus, according to witnesses, killed a neighbor's sheep. The Oloye added, "He used to spoil people's properties . . . he threatens people."[81] A petition for his entry into a hospital stated that he had been insane for three years, but the call for medical intervention did not come until his neighbors perceived a physical threat.[82] Rufus was found insane and confined; his certificate said he was delusional in believing that relatives and others in the town were conspiring against him.[83] The file of a soldier named Momoh, who had fought in Southeast Asia, indicates that he was "depressed—continually mumbling incoherently" and showed "no interest in his environment." He was diagnosed as schizophrenic, with "delusions of persecution," and tried to kill himself by cutting his throat.[84]

Appiah has reminded us that there are dangers in overestimating the reach and cultural significance of the colonial state, and many of these cases do not seem to convey political content.[85] At the same time, the sheer frequency of this alleged symptom compels us to consider the broad political context.[86] More concretely, we may well wonder about the "delusions" of a soldier fighting in the name of the free world in the service of a colonial government. The delusion may well echo the disillusionment the war occasioned for many soldiers who were not thought insane. If this comparison seems a stretch, consider the example of Bassey, a "lunatic soldier" who was diagnosed as a "psychopathic personality," with a "history of erratic and violent behavior," and was repatriated from Southeast Asia. His file contains a daily log of his rationality and aggressiveness, which shows a general tendency toward increasing irrationality. Soon after his admission to Aro, he was said to have developed a "persecutory complex against the British and became increasingly difficult to handle."[87]

Millenarian and other religious movements that articulated anticolo nial nationalist statements are a well-studied theme in the historiography of colonial Africa. The alleged irrationality of these movements was a preoccupation of colonists, and the leaders of them sometimes characterized by colonists as insane.[88] Conversely, asylum inmates sometimes delivered oratory with millenarian and nationalist imagery. This is an example of the continuity (but not identity) which can exist between the normal and the pathological; in the absence of an objective dividing line between "insane" and "inspired," perspectival factors—in these cases related especially to political position—come into play. In Nigeria there was at least one case of an incarcerated religious leader whose politics above all landed him in the asylum. This was Oke A., the founder of an "Ethiopian" Church based in Ife, who was taken for medical observation in 1936 after having been tried in the Lagos Supreme Court for the "offence of breaking and entering into the Nigerian Treasury Store with intent."[89] There was initial reluctance to confine Oke in Yaba, because he was an educated man, and the living conditions were thus considered inappropriate. Nevertheless, Brown described his condition as "delusional insanity of paranoid form" with grandiose and persecutory ideas, and he was placed in Yaba.[90] In 1953, his followers claimed he was sane and sought his discharge. The medical officer in Yaba responded: "He has systematized delusions of persecution and grandeur and occasionally refuses food because it is provided by the British government in Nigeria who persecute him. He is an Apostle sent by God to deliver the world. He is very stubborn and uncooperative. There has been no change in his mental condition since 1936 and therefore not fit for discharge. His diagnosis is paranoia."[91] Examples like this recall the overstated aphorism that "when a man speaks to God, we call him pious, but when God speaks back, we call the man schizophrenic"—as well as the old joke about paranoid people knowing what's really going on. In fact, the exact grounds for calling Oke a madman, rather than a religious rebel, are unclear from the existing documents; they surely seem to be related to his critical stance toward the colonial regime.

Regardless of the "reality" of mental pathology in these cases, we need to read them with the recognition that resentment and aggression are predictable in a colonial society. In Bassey's case, for example, a man trained to fight for colonial superiors in a remote place and then confined against his will should be *expected* to show rancor against the dominating power. His brother supported this view and wrote that "Bassey while at home, was very rascally and I believe that he might be well and due to his rascality he might be detained on the grounds that he is not well."[92]

Diagnosis was thus problematic not only because of "cross-cultural" differences but also because of perceptions of appropriate social relations rooted in colonialism. These differences in a sense produced the diagnoses. Ambiguities in the diagnostic process are not unique to colonialism; cultural and political differences are always factors in the process. But particular social contexts foster particular inflections. "Delusions of persecution" arose as an important category because colonialism is by its nature persecutory. The term "persecution" is not commonly used in the historical vocabulary on colonial Africa; "domination" and "hegemony" are more recognizable in recent writing. Yet I think the term is an apt description of a process whereby a foreign power intrudes, demands taxes, sets up often unpopular local rulers, coerces labor, and rationalizes all this with a delusion of its own, namely, the delusion of racial superiority.[93]

Africans and Europeans in colonial contexts had different cognitive realities not only because they had different cultural backgrounds—important as those were—but also because their view of the colonial situation itself differed. Many have remarked that close to the end of the colonial period, officials believed it would be a century or more before Africans would be ready for self-government. The appropriateness of British rule seemed to them natural and self-evident, more a practical necessity than a persecution. This can be illustrated by the very existence of asylums that were functionally equivalent to prisons; it was important to the colonial self-image to separate patients from criminals, even when they were unwilling to make the investment to treat them differently. Actions and utterances that questioned colonial ideology were bound to catch attention and seem bizarre, especially if they were accompanied by other strange behavior. Labeling these behaviors "deluded" reinforced the ideology that British presence was appropriate. Labeling the deviant reaffirmed a colonial vision of normality.

Resentment among inmates was operative on several levels. The very fact of being in an asylum could produce persecutory feeling. Brown wrote: "Experience in all countries has shown that proper provision for exercise, grouping, occupation and the substitution of other methods for the employment of coercion and mechanical restraint, and in general *the removal, so far as is compatible with safety, of the pricks against which the insane 'persecuted' kick, is followed by a notable improvement in their conduct.*"[94] Asylum inmates *were* subject to processes of exclusion and confinement—by their communities, in the asylum, by the structures of domination in colonialism. These levels of explanation are not exclusive but complementary.

Another way of looking at the problem of persecutory delusions is to posit that to the extent these inmates were mad, their disorder allowed sentiments to flourish that might have otherwise been concealed. A similar notion can be found in some psychoanalytic theory that regards neurotic behavior as expressing unconscious wishes or conflicts repressed under "normal" circumstances.[95] It may be naive to believe that the mad are more properly regarded as seers or prophets.[96] But it is a belief with origins in the observation that the mad can have an unsettling degree of insight. The mad may seem endowed with special powers of sight because their madness frees expression—a principle analogous to that of *in vino veritas*.[97]

The insane also sometimes identify with holders of power and prestige in uncomfortable ways, voicing common fantasies. A famous example in literature is the narrator of Nikolai Gogol's *Diary of a Madman*, who progresses toward his coronation as King of Spain, which for the reader is his forlorn admission to an asylum.[98] Glass has proposed that this kind of identification forms a counterpart, or flip side, to paranoid delusion; by identifying with the powerful, one defends against the annihilation threatened by the persecution.[99] Consider the example of M. A. of Ijebu-Ode, who portrayed himself as a rival to one of the most famous black men in the world in the early 1950s—Ralph Bunche, whose efforts in the settlement in Palestine earned him a Nobel Prize. M. A., who was a convert from Islam to Christianity, reproduced his claim in triplicate:

> I forward herewith one copy of an extract from my statement of policy, summary of actions since my stay in this land, an explanation of the issues involved in Korean War . . . one chart indicating my activities towards maintenance or attainment of peace in Korean field, and one baptismal certificate. . . .
>
> It would be seen that I possess an exclusive claim both to last year's award wrongly made to Ralph Bunche and this year's award yet to be made. A close scrutiny of my chart and religious qualifications will certainly justify the claims. Under the circumstances, kindly take step to make Bunche vomit what he has shrewdly swallowed. I am the owner.
>
> In both cases, kindly remit me a sum of 16,000 [pounds], representing the 8,000 [pounds] last year, & 8,000 [pounds] for this year.

> [With regard to the Korean War] the conflict has been that
> of Democracy versus communism . . . Xtianity stands for Democ-
> racy, Mohammedanism for communism. In Holy Koran, the regu-
> lation savours of communism, the rule being four wives to a man.
> In Xtianity, the order is one. . . . Christ's policy has been that of
> peace while Mohammed maintained a belligerent one.[100]

In the mid-1960s, an American psychoanalyst, Helen Tartakoff, posited "a new nosological entity, the Nobel Prize complex."[101] Tartakoff
held that in postwar America, there was a strong discrepancy between a
culture that idealized achievement and the institutional means it provided to attain it. This discrepancy caused pervasive distress for analy-
sands of the time, with the Nobel Prize presenting a widely shared com-
pensatory fantasy. As a discrete "nosological entity," the Nobel Prize
complex has not gained wide currency. Yet Tartakoff may well have
touched on an idea with wide significance. As Tartakoff noted, "modern Western culture . . . is not more conducive to the development of
fantasies of omnipotence than other cultures, either past or present."[102]
If contradiction between ambition and means of achievement was a key
factor in the "Nobel Prize complex" in America at this time, in Nigeria
such a contradiction was at least as likely, as the number of educated
people was growing faster than the number of jobs commensurate with
the skill level they had attained.[103]

Lunatics sometimes draw their references more closely from "everyday life," as, for example, in the adoption of a policeman's comportment. The police were visible daily reminders of the colonial state in Nigeria, and they figure prominently in the visions and "delusions" of the
insane—not least in the minds of "criminal lunatics," such as Awudu
B., "a violent lunatic believing that 'the Judges and Police Magistrates
of Lagos have given him permission to carry out wholesale murders
about town.'"[104]

Sometimes fantastic claims can be oddly modest, as with Laiwole B.,
who said he had been a driver to all the kings in Yorubaland. In Nigeria
though, as elsewhere, the claims could be outlandish. A patient named
Baba, identified in his file as a Muslim Yoruba and a beggar, was admitted to Aro in 1947, aged 60. His certificate calls him "very deluded."

> He states that he is the owner of all land extending from here . . .
> to Lagos. All the government officials are responsible to him and
> hence must be able to give an account of them. . . .

> The patient talks a lot of nonsense, making unnecessary and un-related jokes that generally make people around him laugh.[105]

This terse clinical description raises some interesting questions. What, for example, constitutes a "necessary" joke? How do jokes need to be related? Cases like this above all raise the question of why social control, in the form of hospitalization, becomes necessary. Baba and Laiwole shared two traits—they liked to tell jokes, and they assumed roles considered grandiose. I venture that in many cases the behavior of the "harmless" lunatic was not just anomalous or deviant but odd in ways (such as grandiosity) that were threatening to those around them, because they drew attention to structures of power in ways which denaturalized those structures.

The Making of the Mad

> *I consider inner life an object of inquiry that has its own unique dignity and peculiar lawfulness. A prominent characteristic of such a perspective is the belief that everything that goes on—thought, feeling, attitude, action—has many layers of meaning. . . . The psychoanalyst is the ambassador of a neglected reality—our inner life.*[106]
>
> —Leon Wurmser

Jean Comaroff and John Comaroff, in their influential book *Of Revelation and Revolution,* suggestively claim, "Between the conscious and the unconscious lies the most critical domain of all for historical anthropology and especially for the analysis of colonialism and resistance."[107] I propose that the study of asylums, asylum inmates, and their incarceration provides an inviting gateway to this poorly mapped domain of partial recognition. For madness, considered here as a social phenomenon, directs social analysis away from conscious intent and its furious attempts to make sense. And here I refer not only to the lunatics, who mocked the various regimes of colonial society, but also to those who responded to them, who "constructed" them as mad.

If the "inner life" is a remote domain, requiring diplomatic emissaries and translators to negotiate its demands, the insane are its tourists, refugees, émigrés—and in more threatening cases, its terrorists. If asylum inmates shared one feature, it is that they acted out impulses or fantasies others would, literally, only dream about. The action could be as dangerous as murder or as innocuous as "inappropriate" laughter, but even the most harmless behaviors were transgressions. These transgressions met with a series of acts: apprehension (in the double sense of acknowledgment and arrest), labeling, classification, trial, and confinement.

That madness is a disputed border region between the inner and social worlds is a universal, but like most universals, it contains a tautology that reduces its interest. For a historian, the particular nature and shape of the dispute is more absorbing. It would be misleading to ask if these people were mad by "Yoruba" or "Western" standards. Such a line of inquiry, which is only recently waning in cross-cultural psychology, assumes boundedness and homogeneity in cultures themselves. It is reminiscent of the discredited "dual economy" thesis which depicted southern Africa as divided into separate economies, without recognizing the ways that these apparently separate realms were interwoven, with profound consequences for relations of production in each.[108] Asylums were sites of a kind of "creolization" of pathology, where what Vaughan has called the "idioms of madness" were not so much African, European, or universal, but specific to colonial Nigeria.

To develop this case, I raise a comparison discussed by Gananath Obeyesekere.[109] The category of depression, Obeyesekere argues, poses a question for a Buddhist culture such as Sri Lanka's, in which the notion that unhappiness is pathological is absent.[110] A fundamental tenet of Buddhism is that living existence is suffering. The "symptoms" which a Western clinician includes in a diagnosis of depression exist in Sri Lanka, but they are not "fused into a conception" as an illness. Depression, therefore, should not exist. An especially effective rhetorical tactic Obeyesekere uses is to show that many in the West suffer from the symptoms of an East Asian syndrome called "semen loss," but that if he were to suggest that they had this illness, he would be "laughed out of court."[111] In Sri Lanka, different cultural work is thus done on these putative "symptoms." What I want to address in particular is Obeyesekere's discussion of those in the Sri Lankan mental hospitals diagnosed with—and suffering from—depression. If depression does not exist in the culture, why are those people in the hospital? Obeyesekere answers that Western medicine is a culture of its own, with enormous prestige, power, and influence in parts of Sri Lanka. This power actually *creates* depression. One is reminded of Karl Kraus's quip: "Psychoanalysis is the disease of which it pretends to be the cure." The point is given a finer irony by adding that neurasthenia, which was a major diagnosis in Western psychiatry in the late nineteenth and early twentieth centuries, is now used in Southeast Asian countries where it was imported, although it has dropped out of Western nosology.[112] Following Obeyesekere, we could say that the Nigerian asylum inmates were suffering syndromes "fused into conceptions" in Britain and the West, and then imported to Nigeria. But I would like to take Obeyesekere's argument a bit further.

Nigerian asylum inmates were not simply mad according to Yoruba standards, or those of Western medicine. Rather, these cultures—immensely complex and contested in themselves—were in a process of interaction; the insane in colonial Nigeria were insane according to the polysemic standards of a colonial society with many cultural values in interplay. An example is M. A., who complained that he had been deprived of the Nobel Prize. M. A. was clearly mad—in the social sense that his belief aroused the call for treatment from those around him. It would be misleading to consider his deviance uniquely "African" or "Yoruba"; there was mention in the 1960s of an American "Nobel Prize complex." At the same time, there is a particularly Nigerian inflection to his letter, which combines an appropriation of Ralph Bunche's fame and honor with a discourse on conflict between Islam and Christianity. This does not mean that the "symptom repertoire" of lunatics was entirely new; the association of madness and nakedness, for example, has some antiquity among the Yoruba and continued into the colonial period.[113]

Obeyesekere's also rightly draws attention to the power of Western medicine, which results in the ironic effect of creating illnesses. But while brief vignettes illustrate his points about the cultural work that Buddhism prescribes, no examples are given of people in the hospitals. The specific content of their depression and the context of their diagnoses are omitted.[114] Proponents of a universal psychiatric nosology concede that "content" of a disorder varies culturally. But this content *demands attention;* without it the patient is decontextualized, and the social dimension of affliction is obscured.

Even the briefest records I have treated refer to the context of domination in which they were produced. I alluded earlier to glimpses of affinity between the language in these documents and that used by millenarian leaders. This raises the question of resistance, a much discussed theme in Africanist historiography. It was common in the historiography of the 1960s to view millenarian and other religious movements as proto-nationalist. While this approach can be criticized for its teleology, and consequent neglect of what these movements were in themselves, an important insight may be salvaged. Many millenarian movements *were* nationalist, sometimes self-consciously so. To recognize this does not necessarily mean denying that they were other things as well, nor need it entail a stages scheme. Protest and other forms of political expression can take place in many forms and idioms at the same time.

A similar analysis applies to certain expressions of madness. I am, of course, not trying to install the lunatic as a model of anticolonial liberation. Apter has called for a restrictive definition of resistance, explicitly contrasting "effective" and collective political action as a worthy object of study, and as opposed to "utopian lunatics."[115] Such a restriction has appeal, and the expansion of the term "resistance" in African studies has threatened to dilute the term of meaning. But I am arguing that a form of political expression need not be organized, collective, or even "resistance" by any standard to have significance as a gauge and representation of social pressures and contradictions. The "symptoms" of Nigeria's lunatics and the psychiatric labels that were affixed can be understood as inchoate articulations of the stresses of colonial society.

In a sense, it should not be terribly surprising that the mad would draw their references from the political world surrounding them. But the point is worth stressing in light of the highly universalizing tendencies of psychiatry. And these are tendencies that have been growing with the ascent of *exclusively* biological models in psychiatry.[116] Attention to social environment and even to life history are receding in contemporary Western psychiatry, as the search for genetic markers gains attention in explanations of etiology and medication eclipses the "talking cure" as a preferred treatment modality. It would be tempting to dismiss this perspective as "positivistic," or to point out that it is itself "socially constructed knowledge" whose dominance we do not have to cede. Such a critique would be not so much untrue as truistic. It would retain a materialist-versus-all-others dichotomy that is also deeply Western in its assumptions. Even if mental illness is a reality, even if those confined in the asylums were genuinely mentally ill, even if the symptoms of madness are partly caused by genetic or other organic factors, and even if these symptoms could be dispelled by medication, the specific content of the symptoms retains significance.[117]

In *The Wretched of the Earth,* the psychiatrist and anticolonial theorist Frantz Fanon wrote: "In the period of colonization when it is not contested by armed resistance, when the sum total of harmful nervous stimuli over-step a certain threshold, the defensive attitudes of the natives give way and they find themselves crowding the mental hospitals. There is thus during this calm period of successful colonization a regular and important mental pathology which is a direct product of oppression."[118] Fanon proposed that the overcrowding of colonial lunatic asylums was the result of internalized anger. This explanation of the epidemiology of confinement rests on the questionable assumption that the overcrowding was a reflection of true prevalence. But Fanon's works remain trenchant studies of the psychopathology of everyday life under colonialism. His theory remains a discerning foray into the psychology of the inmates. There is, frequently, a relationship between madness and resistance to social order, even if madness does not actually constitute resistance. We will see this clearly in the story of Isaac O., whose relatively detailed story in fact indicates struggle with a *number* of social orders.

CHAPTER 5

The Confinements of Isaac O.

A Case of "Acute Mania"

Commitments

By his own admission, Isaac O. began acting a little strange in June of 1932. Thomas Cullen, a "duly qualified medical practitioner," wrote that he was

> very excited, shouting and yelling. He threatened people round about him with violence. He spat at one within reach. Said that he had bought a motor car which he saw on the road for a million pounds. Called Europeans who came within his line of vision Eskimos. . . . On being brought before a European missionary his hands were tied. On his hands being released, he immediately whipped out a knife and attacked him. Before being overpowered he wounded two boys with a knife.[1]

So ran the order which mandated Isaac's confinement in Yaba Asylum.

Isaac did not substantially dissent from this account. He did, though, dispute that he was insane and requiring confinement. He also convinced others of his mental balance, at least temporarily. In this instance, the order of committal was revoked. After standing trial for his disorderly behavior, Isaac was judged sane and not dangerous. He was freed, with supervision mandated to watch for relapse. But by the time Nigeria's freedom from colonial rule was achieved in 1960, Isaac had been confined in, and freed from, Yaba Lunatic Asylum at least four times.[2]

Isaac was born in a rural village, was educated in a Wesleyan mission in the sprawling metropolis of Ibadan, worked in another rural area as an agent of the Wesleyans, was brought to trial in a colonial court, and was faced with confinement in a colonial lunatic asylum in Lagos—all before his twentieth birthday. He navigated, then, several sites of continuity and change in the region. His story touches a variety of themes: religious change and conflict, the ideology of scientific medicine, problems of cross-cultural translation, struggles between metropolitan and local powers.

Origins

Isaac was 19 in 1932, the year he was first certified insane. Nigeria's first lunatic asylums, in Lagos and Calabar, were thus created 7 years before his birth. Yaba—the large, dank, dirty, noisy, and overcrowded building with leaking roofs and breeding mosquitoes—was Isaac's home for a good deal of his adult life.

Isaac's story illustrates how Nigerians and Britons could agree on the lunacy of a patient and at the same time enact complex drama of miscommunication and interpretive improvisation. And Europeans also agreed Isaac was not a fit subject for native treatment.

A product of Wesleyan missionary education, Isaac was an exemplary student. Before June 1932, he appeared as lucid and promising as Dr. Henry Jekyll. Moses Akunda Awosanya, a teacher at the Wesleyan mission in Ifaki, who testified at Isaac's trial in 1932, knew him to be perfectly well since they were students together in Ibadan in 1925.[3] By 1929, Isaac was a respected catechist in the Wesleyan establishment. As Edward John Jones, the superintendent of the Ifaki mission testified, "I know Isaac. . . . He is a catechist of our mission. . . . He entered Wesley College in Ibadan in 1929, according to our records. . . . Each student has to be medically examined before he enters Wesley College. . . . He must have been perfectly fit to be accepted. . . . He passed out of college with a clean medical sheet, and an excellent reputation for general diligence."[4] The mission, Jones made clear, could not be faulted for failing to anticipate Isaac's outbursts.

Some foreshadowing of the disorder to come was, however, recognized later. Jones did recall that Isaac was perhaps slightly troubled, but this did not hamper a proper Wesleyan commitment to industry: "He seems to be possessed of a highly strung temperament & inclined to worry. But there was no fault to find with his work. His church records were better than any other records kept by my catechists. His manners always, however, inclined to be bad and boorish."[5] Jones did not

reveal what exactly "bad and boorish" manners were, though the episodes which brought Isaac to trial suggest hostilities and conflicts which
had been simmering for some time.

Awosanya recalled a pivotal episode: "One day he did tell me that
there was trouble at Ifisin about a juju tree which the Christians had
been ordered to cut. He said that there was a big religious quarrel: that
one Alosanye, a native doctor, and the *Bale* [chief, or governor] of Ifisin
were making bad juju against him."[6]

Jones had sent Isaac to Ifisin in March 1932. As an emissary of the Wesleyans, he was a natural target of anti-Christian sentiment in the event
of religious conflict in the area. Isaac was forthcoming about this early
on. Jones indicated that

> Early in March . . . [Isaac] reported to me that he was having some
> trouble. The *Bale* of Ifisin had ordered the Christians to cut down
> a juju grove. . . . [Isaac] and his Christians had objected to doing
> this particular work. . . . Isaac reported to me that bad jujus were
> being used against him & the Christians as a result of this objec-
> tion. . . . However, I heard nothing further of this trouble, until
> June 12th when he mentioned it in his ravings.[7]

Note again Jones's implied bewilderment about Isaac's double nature.
Despite a worried temperament, and the troubles at Ifisin, the Isaac that
emerged in mid-June was a shock to those who knew him. A fellow
student, Gabriel Laleye, had known Isaac in Ibadan the previous year,
when, according to Laleye, he was "quite sane and well." The next time
Laleye saw Isaac, it was in Ara. Isaac was "obviously out of his mind."[8]

The abrupt, unprecedented onset of Isaac's lunacy would be equaled
by his brisk adoption of calm comportment at his trial.

The Road

At the time of his arrest, Isaac was acting out a stereo-
typical role. He was found on a highway, tearing at his clothes. In the
latter decades of colonial rule, the sight of lunatics on the highways developed as a cultural stereotype of the madman. This stereotype, which
may reflect the greater risk strangers and travelers faced of being labeled
mad, complemented nakedness in forming a stereotype of the mad. Recall that the association of madness and nakedness is so strong that there
is a Yoruba diagnostic term, *wèrè aláṣọ*, which literally translates as "mad-

man wearing clothes," but which is an idiomatic expression for someone capable of concealing their madness.[9]

Michael Tayo was a messenger of the Alara of Ara. Upon learning of a disturbance on the road leading to Ara, the Alara sent Tayo to apprehend the troublemaker. Tayo testified to the court that the lunatic "had taken all his clothes off and was standing naked in the road."[10] Isaac, he said, promptly slapped Tayo in the face. Isaac, who verified most of the accusations against him, interrupted Tayo's testimony to protest that Tayo had in fact struck the first blow.

Tayo finally subdued Isaac and brought him to the Alara's palace. The prisoner was not happy. He sent a message to Jones, which included a request for money. Jones sent Laleye and Awosanya ahead with the money. In the meantime, Isaac was an unruly prisoner. Tayo said that he "was very violent, and held the Alara's gown and tried to tear it. He flogged me with his belt. . . . He tore his clothes & said the townspeople would have to pay for them."[11] When Laleye arrived, he found Isaac

handcuffed and chained. He was obviously out of his mind. When he saw me, he said he had many cases to bring to the D.O. [District Officer]. He said he was sent to Ijebu Ode about a Boy's Brigade, that he had been sent to arrest the chief the Alara of Ara and a man called Babamu Jamu. . . .

On Sunday morning, after morning service, June 12th, he suddenly became enraged, & most destructive. He started to tear down the pictures on the walls. He broke a number of plates and tore his clothes and the clothes of Mr. Awosanya who tried to check him. *There was no apparent reason for his being so angry. He was just crazy—a lunatic.*

He told me just before this violence that something was wrong in his head because the people of Ifisin poisoned him.[12]

Because of this erratic behavior, Isaac had to be under constant restraint and surveillance. Thus when Jones finally arrived, he also found Isaac tied up:

I ordered his hands to be released & gave him some aspirin. Almost immediately he pulled a knife out of his pocket. His feet were still tied. He struck with the knife at a teacher, Mr. Abraham Adeluse. Mr. Adeluse just did get out of range, & then four of us jumped at him and with some difficulty disarmed him. We tied his hands again.

[Isaac] remained very violent. He raved and shouted and threatened to kill anyone who came near him. He said he would kill all the people he had met in Ara; he would kill me and all other Europeans in Nigeria. And through these ravings he kept on repeating that he had been poisoned by the Bale of Ifisin.

There were no signs, as far as I could see, of any physical disorder; nor did . . . [Isaac] complain of pains.

He was at Ifaki from Saturday 11th June until Tuesday June 14th, when I brought him to Ado Ekiti in my car. . . . All the time . . . [Isaac] was violent and unreasonable. He seemed quieter in the mornings, but in the afternoons was very wild. I do not think he slept at all and was very noisy in his nocturnal ravings.[13]

At Ado-Ekiti, Isaac was put in prison. The prison clerk reported behavior which was by now familiar—struggling to escape, raving all night, tearing his clothes. Isaac also "tried to bite the wardens who fed him" and refused food for several days. The clerk, Emmanuel Adeshiyan Koku, also reported that "he complained about the presence of snakes in his cell, but there were no snakes. He said that all the Europeans in Nigeria were to be killed this Thursday morning. . . . On Tuesday evening June 21st . . . [Isaac] began to show signs of a return to a more normal mentality . . . he has shown no signs of violence and has talked properly and coherently. He is still not normal, but is improving."[14] The foregoing quotations are from the testimony given by the various witnesses at the first day of Isaac's trial. A clerk recorded the trial in longhand, producing an unusually detailed document[15] It is obscuring in some respects—it does not, for example, tell who was present at the trial besides the witnesses (if anybody), and it does not even give the name or title of whoever presided. Still, it is a remarkable document because it provides copious information on the events leading to Isaac's arrest. Most of this information appears in Isaac's own words, which is even more remarkable, since the insane are rarely given a chance to speak for themselves in any society. Perhaps because of his apparent return to normalcy, the court was eager to hear the prisoner's side of the story.

Confession

The hearing was reopened on June 24, and the court allowed "the alleged lunatic" a chance to "show why he should not be dealt with . . . [under the lunacy ordinance] and ordered to be confined." I will quote Isaac's testimony extensively, omitting only some repetitions.

He began almost as if he were responding to a psychiatric diagnostic interview—perhaps indicating that he was already beginning to be "psychiatrized," familiar with the role of the mental patient. He established orientation of place and time, and past history. He also provided family history, recognizing the role that heredity plays in the genesis of madness, according to Yoruba belief. Starting by stating his hometown, he continued: "I shall be twenty years of age on July 16th 1932, as I was born in 1912 on July 16th. I have a baptism certificate giving these particulars. . . . At the present I am a teacher, catechist of the Wesleyan Mission, employed at Ifisin in the Ifaki circuit. I have never had epileptic fits in my life. I have not been sick and none of my relatives have been sick like this before." His family not only lacked a history of insanity, but also had a royal pedigree. His misadventure began with his attempt to reunite with his younger brother:

> On Tuesday June 7 I went to the superintendent. I told Mr. Awosanya that I am sending my younger brother to him. The next morning I left for Ifisin and ordered my younger brother, Moses Adeyinka, to catch motor to Ilesha and from there to home. On the same day I sent two of the scholars at Ifisin to Ifaki, and on their return I was told that my younger brother went on foot. Then, after school, I went again, to the superintendent at Ifaki, and asked for permission to go in search of my younger brother. Then I returned to Ifisin the same night. The next morning I started with five boys from Ifisin, and I took the path from Ifisin to Ijero. I got there 6 P.M. I went to the C.M.S.[16] mission, and the headmaster whose name I don't know told me that my younger brother slept there the day before. . . . Then . . . I left for Ara. We got to Ara by 10:15 that night. I am ordered by the headmaster of Ijebu C.M.S. school to sleep at the C.M.S. mission at Ara, but immediately I entered the town I heard somebody singing one of the Christian songs. Then I went to his house. I asked permission to sleep there. He gave me the chance to sleep in his house. I slept, but I was always thinking of my younger brother on my bed that night.

If he began the night troubled in mind, it would get worse. He related a growing restlessness that would culminate in his "nocturnal ravings" while imprisoned:

> [I] saw something in the night as being troubled witches. Then I woke up. I prayed and then woke up the owner of the house. Afterwards we looked at the time and it was about 12:45 A.M. I told him

that I would be going; that I shall get to Effon before day-dawn. Then he pressed me that I should not go by that hour. He put out the light & we went to sleep again; and I could not sleep before dawn again.

Though we cannot assess the quality of his memory, we can see that Isaac strenuously attempted to recover as many details as possible. He was trying, perhaps, to demonstrate the soundness of his mental state while speaking, in contrast to that displayed during the events depicted. He also may have been groping to understand an episode that was as puzzling to him as to the court.

"Day-dawn," sunrise, has a history as an optimistic metaphor for missionary endeavor inland of the Bight of Benin. The next day, though, began inauspiciously for Isaac, as it marked his first encounter with the law enforcement system. He started making threats.

When the day dawned I left Ara with three boys; two of the five had returned at Ijero yesterday. Before I got to the main road . . . I saw a policeman. . . . He rode a bicycle & I asked him why he took the right hand & not ring his bell. By which he told me that it was because he was climbing a hill. Then I said he should bring his bicycle and let me climb the hill; and then ring and let him hear. He refused; and I told him that I would report him officially to the D.O. [District Officer] at Ado. After that I saw a man going to farm. I asked him whether I can get carriers at the next village. . . . He said I could not. Then I said I would come back and then called for him. He went away saying I could not take him as a carrier to Effon. I asked for his name and his town. He said his name to be Samuel Oni, and said he was a C.M.S. member at Ara. . . . I had not taken food then since 12 noon the day before at Usi: I asked two of the boys to go and buy food . . . and then call carriers. They came back with neither food nor carriers. Then I said that I should take them by force.

He then began disrobing:

I gave my brigade belt to the two boys: that they should take it to the Bale of Erio [a small village] and give them two men who would take my loads to Effon as carriers. They came back telling me that the people of the town refused to show them the Bale's house and even ran away.

I saw two boys coming from Ara with cutlasses on each other's hand. I asked them to come and take my loads to Effon. Then they ran away. I ran to catch them. The one in front escaped and I pursued the second one. I was then with a tennis shoe. I kicked him with the shoe. He fell down. When he stood up he left his cutlass and ran again. Then I took the cutlass and ran after him. When I caught him I beat him with the cutlass for about eight times.

After the last stroke he had a mark on his neck. Then he pretend to be as one who has fainted. I took the cutlass and left him there.

Isaac was also oddly candid about his indignant attempts to take advantage of people. These mainly involved finding someone to help him with the carrying of his loads. In order to elicit it, he posed as a representative of colonial authority:

Before he got up I saw a woman coming from Ara. I saw that she should help to take my loads to Effon. When I knew I could not catch them by saying I want carriers, then I show them my brigade uniform & told them that I am one of the messengers of Government officials. I told her that she ought to take the load by force. She then told me that she had been sick by smallpox & just recovered by which she would not be able to take the load.

I said if she will not take the load she ought to give me her name. She being afraid gave me 3 shillings & said that I should give that to any carrier I see. I asked her if that would be carriers fare to Effon. I said, if that was so, she should take the road [sic][17] & would give her 3 shillings carriers fare from my purse. She knelt down and begged that she cannot take the load, but that I would receive the only 3 shillings she has got. I had pity on her and took the three shillings & let her go. Immediately I saw another woman coming from Erio with a basket on her head as I was in that uniform looking like a Nigerian policeman I said she would either take the road [sic] or give me her name. She, being afraid to give me her name & would not take the load, ran back to Erio. I ran after her & took from her her shawl-*Iborun*,[18] thinking that she would on account of that come back to me. But she left the Iborun & her basket and went away. . . .

Many others I called and they ran away. About five minutes later I saw men and women from Erio marching along. About not less than fifty without children. Then they began to curse me saying I am taking their people by false [force?]. I stood up to meet them. Then they ran to their village: but at last I saw a man who was bold enough to come near me. He was in a gown with sword under his arm. The name of the man called yesterday Babamujemu. His name I was told by the Alara of Ara to be Adepile, a native of Erio. He cursed me as much as possible, then beat me, slapped me. Then the boy (who said his name to be Oni, yesterday) came back to me. Babamujemu held my hands and twisted & I was then powerless. Then the man I have first seen who called himself to be Samuel Oni came and opened my felt hat, and in that I had two currency notes . . . paid to me by Reverend Jones. He threw the felt into the bush & slapped me as much as possible. I was then held by Baba-mujemu and could do nothing. Another man altogether asked Babamujemu to leave me. He said he would take me to Ara, & I said he could not take me to Ara by force. Then they began to scat-ter my properties. I tore the gown of Adepile when I was having much pain. He leave me when I tear his gown and slapped me again.

Someone with beads on his neck was coming from Erio whom I supposed to be their Bale. He asked of the case. I told him all about the past events. He told me he was not the Bale & that he was go-ing to Ara court. Then I was vexed, asking if he was not going to deal with the matter why did he detain me here to tell him all that had happened.

He left for Ara & said he would tell Alara about the whole. Not less than ten minutes & not more than fifteen minutes later I saw about 8 farmers, one of whom is the father of the boy I hurt with his cutlass. They said they would take me to Ara by force. I saw they could not, telling me that they were sent by the Alara. Then I proved it to them that the chief who had left ten minutes ago could not have gone to Ara, which is 2½ miles to Erio, to report. Though the eight are natives of Ara they are from their farms. The father of the boy I hurt said I must not go: they must take me by force because I have done what is bad.

Then they took me by force and beat me as much as possible. But they could not take me more than a quarter of a mile before, after beating me as much as possible, they were tired of me. Imme-diately there was a motor lorry from Ara. The driver I know to be Dosu. Another person was the houseboy of Rev. Jones whose name is Ajimoko. The motor had three N.A. [Native Administration] Po-lice; telling me that they were sent to Ilesha: and the Alara's mes-senger who stated his case here yesterday [Michael Tayo].

One of the Olopa [policemen] came out of the motor, whose

number is E.K. 14. The Alara messenger came down too. In the presence of the driver Dosu & the houseboy of Rev. Jones, Aji-moko, the Alara messenger slapped my face & asked the Olopa EK 14, "there is the man! Where are the handcuffs you are given?"

I was then tired & hungry. Even I nearby fell down and they slapped me. It was about 11 A.M. & I haven't taken my breakfast. When I hear the word "handcuff" I told the Olopa that he could not take me by force.

Then he said he would not take me away by force because I am a gentleman & he didn't put the handcuffs on my hand. He said I was wanted by the Alara of Ara. And I asked him what of the rest who had beaten me & done what-nots to me. Then I pointed to them, not less than 8 from Ara & three from Erio. . . .

Then I said I would take my bath when we got to a river. The Olopa said "all right," but when we got there he refused. I entered the Ara town in that poor condition. When he told me to go to the court I told him I must go right away to report to the D.O. at Ado & before that to . . . the superintendent at Ifaki.

Then the Native Court Clerk, the Alara of Ara & the Olupas in the court began to insult me: & blamed the Olupa EK 14 for not putting handcuff in my hand. And I said to the Alara it is only that I respect him. I say "had it not been so I would not have entered the court because they cannot take me by force." Then the Cor-poral Olupa who was coming to put handcuff on me also stopped, when he had heard how I had drubbed the Native Court Clerk & the Alara of Ara.

So concluded the accused's narrative account. The court demanded more of an explanation.

"Not Myself": The Catechist Questioned

The record continues:

By Court: What have you to say about your conduct at Ifaki and Ado?

Answer: All that I have done whilst I was not myself. I was out of sense. Now I am getting better I can say I have been poisoned by juju at Ifisin where I am working. The only thing is that I cannot prove it but I am sure, because there have been quarrels. One of the members at Ifisin can bear me out. I do not think they put poison in my chop [food] they made juju.

By Court: But you are a Christian catechist—surely juju cannot affect you?

Answer: When I see witches in the night I just pray. Had I taken medicines all this might not have happened. My prayer might not have been answered, being that I am a sinner.

Isaac did not deny the charges against him. But he did not feel that a simple insanity defense would, in the literal sense, do him justice, since he was not insane at the time of trial. His mission training did not seem, however, to provide an explanation for his erratic behavior. When the court pressed him on the contradiction between his explanation and his profession, his speech became more disordered, if the clerk's rendering is accurate:

By Court: But surely you don't believe juju can hurt you?

Answer: I don't believe now, but because of this I believe when I see snakes that others don't see, when I see many insects that others don't see; when I saw that you when I first saw you were Mr. Hodges whom I know well. I should not call you that now I am getting better.

Three days later, the hearing reopened, and Thomas Cullen, Medical Officer for Ondo Province, judged that Isaac had been suffering from "Acute Mania" and had been dangerous but was at that time "quite sane and rational." He discharged the prisoner but recommended "a complete mental rest for about three months." The court released him, and Isaac was spared confinement at Yaba. Isaac's father was "bound over to report to the District Officer Ijebu-Ode any relapse . . . within three months of this date."

That was in the summer of 1932. As far as I have been able to determine, Isaac drops out of the archival record for the following 14 years. He reappears in 1945, aged 33, a patient at Yaba. The medical officer at the asylum noted, in a letter to the commissioner of the colony, that he "appears quite normal, and has been like this for five months. But this is his third time in the asylum." [19]

If Europeans and Africans both believed individuals should be kept out of the asylum whenever possible, in practice Isaac was a confusing case. An August 1946 memorandum from E. C. Erokwu, a medical officer at Yaba, stated, "He has behaved normally since the past five months and I have no objection to his being released." [20] It is not clear whether or not Isaac *was* released after this endorsement, but if so, he was back in Yaba by the following year. One medical officer at Yaba petitioned for his release in February of 1947. In response, a colleague wrote that Isaac was

> recently released from isolation cell when he became violent and excited. Now appears normal and quiet. He puts his recent state of violence to thinking of the bonus he had squandered during his state of "mental sickness". Now quite coherent and accurate in his speech . . . although looking like someone who had passed through an ordeal . . . it is quite clear that I cannot guarantee the improbability of another attack.
> I consider him still potentially dangerous to himself and others.[21]

The officer petitioned again in November 1947 and was again informed that Isaac was too dangerous for discharge. At this point, there is another lacuna in the archival record, until January 1955, when Isaac's brother secured his release. Isaac was then given six months' trial leave. It is not clear whether he was readmitted over the course of the following 10 years when, contemporaneous with the transition to Nigeria's independence, Yaba was transformed into a mental hospital and began dispensing psychotropic medications and electro-convulsive therapy.

The Problem of Resistance

The word "resistance" has complex resonances in both the study of madness and the study of colonial Africa. As discussed in the previous chapter, "resistance" has been one of the key words in Africanist scholarship in recent decades, particularly in studies of colonialism. In the study of madness, "resistance" has had two distinct meanings, which are perhaps mirror images of one another. One meaning comes from psychoanalysis, where "resistance" refers to the analysand's vigorous denials of the analyst's interpretations. These denials reflect the patient's inability to confront painful truths; the patient's liberation is won when the resistance is overcome. Resistance, in this view, is a symptom. Some anti-psychiatric scholarship, and particularly some feminist approaches, by contrast, view symptoms as resistance in a more political sense. The mad are seen as challenges to established social order. The psychiatrist, in this view, is a representative of the order, whose "cure" mainly serves to silence an inchoate critic.

Isaac's periodic eruptions *were* challenges to the social orders he traversed. Yet their distinctive form needs to be precisely distinguished from clearly articulated political protest.

Cullen reported that Isaac referred to Europeans he encountered as "Eskimos." This may be taken as the ravings of a disordered mind but also as a symbolic expression of the "northernness" of the colonists, the strangeness of their presence, let alone rule, in a tropical country. His grand claim that he would kill all the Europeans in Nigeria recalls the oratory of the leaders of the anticolonial millenarian movements and is reminiscent of the explicitly anticolonial Oke A. we encountered in the previous chapter. Isaac's move from threat to prediction, as reported by the prison clerk—"He said that all the Europeans in Nigeria were to be killed this Thursday morning"—has a particularly millenarian tone.

Isaac's imagery provides further evidence that "delusions" must be contextualized politically. For delusions are not formed at random. Isaac's claim that he purchased a motor car for a million pounds is a case in point. With it, he appropriated two prominent symbols of British power and encroachment (money and cars) at one stroke. In this fantasy, Isaac inverted his frustrating experience of standing in the road by Ara in the hot sun with his heavy loads, vainly struggling to find a driver for the three-shilling journey to Effon. The close association of the roads and highways with madmen is also significant. If it was agreed that disturbed Africans were better cared for in their "communities," the distances people were forced or encouraged to travel for work and education were also undermining this agreement.

Isaac's decision to disrobe in public seems to have been an been an "overdetermined" symptom.[22] It was midday, the sun was hot, and he had not taken his bath. In any event, disrobing is not a behavior unique to Nigerian lunatics but seems to occur in a variety of contexts. Since the insane are people who have already begun transgressing social rules, retaining their clothing may come to seem absurd.[23] But it also worth considering what clothes he was wearing. He related that in his dress he looked like a policeman; in fact, his arrest and encounter with Nigeria's judicial system was ironically preceded by his "acting out" the role of policeman. According to Elizabeth Isichei, "The impostor was one of the more curious afflictions of the early colonial period. Official records in both northern and southern Nigeria make constant reference to those, such as ex-soldiers and ex-carriers, who made use of a modicum of acquaintance with the white man's ways to pass themselves off as government officials and demand money, food, and so on from vulnerable villagers."[24] Despite Isaac's attempt to deploy the costume to his advantage, his concern about the Bale's curse, and his surfacing anti-European rancor, may have made his clothes that much more uncomfortable.

We can imagine that Isaac's utterances about Europeans were striking to Cullen and Jones. *We* must be attentive, though, to Isaac's explanation, which stressed that the conflict with the Bale of Ifisin, and the consequent curse, provoked his disturbance.[25] This emphasis may have been produced merely for the benefit of the court, but Jones had testified to its prior importance in Isaac's preoccupations.

The precise meaning of what Awosanya called a "juju tree" is elusive, but we can infer why the Bale of Ifisin ordered Isaac to cut it—and why such an order so vexed Isaac. Jones referred to it as a "juju *grove*," and the grove may have been a floral delimitation of an *òrìṣà* shrine. In any event, it does seem that the Bale was being willfully provocative. He seems to have been testing the faith, and loyalties, of the Christians. Ayandele notes that "wherever missionary propaganda became successful . . . the chiefs noticed and regretted that they had lost considerable influence and power."[26] He also says that for Nigerian converts, "their notion of Christianity was that it conferred many positive advantages . . . absolving them from the legitimate tribal functions such as clearing of roads . . . they looked to their pastors to protect them against the consequences of the breaking of their own tribal laws."[27] By asking Isaac and his co-religionists to perform a task that was not "legitimate," but probably taboo in the local context, the Bale effected a daring play on Christian defiance. He was asking the converts to prove the extent of the cultural distance they proudly claimed to have ranged, to prove the depth of their faith in the powers of their protecting pastors.

Although he did summon Jones when subdued by the Alara's people, Isaac may have had doubts about this protection. Ayandele has emphasized the extent to which Nigerians who allied themselves with missions did so for educational opportunities and social advancement. If this motivation led any to feel spiritually divided, the feeling may have been doubled for Isaac. As the son of a local ruler himself, he may have been sensitive to the Bale's claims to power, political and spiritual. Challenged in his allegiance to a metropolitan ideology, Isaac was firm in deed. But he was troubled in mind, deeply concerned by the Bale's threat.

It was central to Isaac's situation that he felt unable to make common cause with anyone. His anger may have been internalized in part because he was unsure where to direct it. He ended up aiming it at everyone, almost at random. Most people understand what is at stake in, say, a tax revolt, but no one seemed to know what to make of this flailing mayhem. There are, of course, many instances where colonial social science "pathologized" collective resistance.[28] These instances alleged *group* psychoses and acknowledged, however derisively, that the action followed some kind of warped inner logic. Isaac's behavior was seen to lack any kind of logic, of the group or the individual. Where he might have been someone to mediate between the colonial edifice and local structures, Isaac instead laid mines on the road of mediation. This is why the people of Ara, the Alara, Jones, and Cullen could agree that he had to be controlled.

Diagnosis and Control

Isaac was diagnosed with "acute mania," a term which has lost status in Western nosology.[29] In the 1930s, the term was already considered to have historical interest in an American psychological dictionary.[30] A contemporary British psychiatric textbook considered it a subspecies of manic-depression, explaining that the patient, who is overactive and impulsive, "has an air of utter superiority, he orders every one about, and his conversation and conduct are so disordered that *residence in a mental hospital is imperative* . . . violent assaults are made on the officials and nurses, the furniture and the bed-clothing are broken and torn . . . but just as suddenly there may be a return to a state of good humour, and apology may even be expressed for the previous conduct."[31] "Acute mania" seems to have been used in Nigeria as a rough catchall for people who acted wild—who were the people most likely to be considered for the asylum. Home wrote that mania "in its various forms, accounts for the largest number of cases. Noisy and irrational conduct is a common symptom in Mania, and so the sufferer is liable to be sent to the hospital or to fall into the hands of the police."[32] According to Brown, acute mania was, though "not of frequent occurrence, compared with other forms of mental disease, it is, paradoxically perhaps, one which offers very favourable prospects of recovery."[33] Joop T. V. M. De Jong has proposed that the first task of any medical system must be to serve an explanation, to give meaning to the sufferer's pain.[34] The term "acute mania" did not hold much force for Isaac, whether explanatory or therapeutic. However earnestly he may have sought to absorb the viewpoint of the mission or the court, the only paradigm that made sense of his troubles was the one promoted by his nemesis, the Bale of Ifisin.

If the term "acute mania" failed to have explanatory or therapeutic value, the crux of the matter may be that *it was not intended to*. It was, rather, meant to authorize Isaac's confinement. Situations like this surely warrant some concept of social control. Horwitz urges a conceptual shift from seeing mental illness as a "disease" toward an emphasis on its manifestation as unsanctioned behavior.[35] Horwitz, of course, is not the first to advocate such a shift. His approach differs, though, from some other loosely anti-psychiatric approaches that see mental illness as a "myth" (Szasz), a predictable product of sick societies (Laing), or a function of societal reaction (Scheff).[36] For Horwitz, it is not crucial to debunk a medical perspective on etiology. He is more interested in understanding reactions to mental illness. He also develops a nuanced concept of social control, regarding psychiatry as only one aspect of a broad network of control, although one which makes a critical and authoritative intervention.

Horwitz recognizes the culturally relative quality of particular deviant behaviors. But he contends that the criteria which lead behavior to be marked in English by the words "mental illness" are found in a broad array of cultural settings and that therefore mental illness can be regarded as a universal. The first criterion is that the "symptoms" (behavior) must deviate from what is acceptable to a particular cultural setting. This criterion is not sufficient, though, because it would include criminal behavior, tactlessness, and other forms of behavior which are censured but which do not necessarily require psychiatric intervention. The deviance must also meet the second criterion of *incomprehensibility*. Criminal behavior may be seen as wrong, but rational.[37] The Yoruba word *were* can be translated into English as "mental illness," not because they refer to the same behavior but because the behavior meets these two criteria within their cultural contexts.

The designation of what constitutes mental illness need not be unanimous; canons of deviance and normality may be shifting and contested. It is because of these contests that medical authority (an alienist, psychiatrist, healer) is invoked to settle the matter. In Isaac's case, Cullen had the final word.[38] And yet *all* witnesses to Isaac's behavior seem to have agreed that it was dangerous and incomprehensible.

Horwitz further claims that two types of psychiatric social control are meted to the mentally ill. Supportive therapeutic treatment is likely when the patient shares the cultural background and social status of the controllers. When the patient is culturally distant, or lacks status and resources, coercive means of control are employed and the patients are placed in large custodial institutions.

In some ways this does describe Isaac's path to Yaba. He was a stranger to both Ifisin and Ara, where he lacked kin—recall his eagerness to find his brother. His cultural distance from Jones and Cullen was perhaps even greater; they were "Eskimos." Yet Isaac's case was also ambiguous. He was not—as many of those confined in the asylums probably were—without allies. Jones and his colleagues were, presumably, not eager to lose a valued intermediary in their efforts to impose European cultural forms in Africa. And if Isaac sought his brother during his drift into deviancy, his brother sought him after his confinement. For those who wished, Isaac's periods of normalcy provided opportunities to release him.

Isaac's trial established that he was guilty of deviant and dangerous behavior and also that no one could comprehend it. His explanation, also, seemed to underscore the cultural difference between him and the locus of authority. In a foray to measure this difference, the court sought to test his Christian credentials, to scrutinize the depth of his acculturation to a colonial norm. "But you are a Christian catechist—surely juju cannot affect you?" As I argued earlier, his Christian catechism did not provide an explanation that made his behavior comprehensible to *him,* any more than the throwaway label "acute mania." "Juju" *did* provide such an explanation.

The use of the term "juju" in the court also merits attention. It represents the use of a highly generalized *European* word for African behavior. It refers to no specific practice or belief but gestures to a general world beyond European interest or ken. Like "acute mania," it is a word which obscures, a label which seeks to reduce and control the incomprehensible.

Some vital work in recent African studies has analyzed the cultural and ideological construction of the term "African" itself.[39] Much of this work, though, focuses on the rarefied level of academic texts. Isaac's trial may provide an opportunity to look closely at the quotidian aspect of this process, as it was in part a dialogue about identity. First, Cullen and Isaac traded labels: If Cullen were to be called an Eskimo, this bizarre accusation would have to be explained by the label "acute mania." But this was an explanation that held little meaning for Isaac. It might as well have been in Inuit. So Isaac provided an alternative account. Debates over the applicability of Western categories to African cultures form some of the deepest and most unstable fault lines in academic African studies; they have origins in the day-to-day operations of colonial rule. Isaac's dialogue with the court itself approached becoming such a debate.

When the court pressed Isaac on the betrayal of his European education, he explained that the weakness of Christianity, or at least his Christianity, accounted for its inability to protect him: "My prayer might not have been answered, being that I am a sinner." And Jones's magical cure-all—aspirin—failed its clinical trial in Isaac's case.

The dialogue that concluded the trial was a record of failure in the creation of colonial hegemony. Isaac failed the court: the phrase "But surely you don't believe juju can affect you" rhetorically vented the colonial cliché that Africans never change. Isaac too had reason to be disappointed; in a time of crisis, European religion and medicine failed equally to protect, explain, or cure. Yet despite these failures Isaac was given his provisional freedom because he was able and willing to moderate his deviancy—at least for the time being.

The Confinements of Diagnostic Categories

Isaac became an asylum inmate only after having been thought a nuisance by a wide range of people and places. In his hometown, or during his education in Ibadan, he may have been high-strung or "boorish," but no one was ready to commit him. Away from the supports these environments offered, he became a nuisance to the Bale of Ifisin, initiating a friction that propelled him into a series of further conflicts, starting with the various strangers he accosted on the road near Ara. Subdued by the Alara's forces, he called out to his mission supervisor for help, only to attack the latter—who had assigned Isaac to Ifisin and was, in a sense, responsible for his difficulties—on first sight. He moved through several lower tiers of authority before being called before the court. In the end, he traveled from the local conflict over the "juju grove" in Ifisin to the asylum in Lagos—a powerful symbol of metropolitan domination. It was a prisonhouse from which he could escape only in fits and starts.

This cyclical nature of Isaac's difficulty was for contemporaries one of its most puzzling aspects. His cycles bring to mind the description of "bi-polar disorder" in the *Diagnostic and Statistical Manual of Mental Disorders* (*DSM-IV*). In the years since Nigeria's independence, personnel in the mental hospitals have been unimpressed by assertions of a radical difference between the experience of madness in Africa and that in the West. Consider the following excerpts from *DSM-IV*, which enjoys the same status in Nigeria's hospitals as in the United States, with regard to bi-polar disorder:

> a distinct period during which there is an abnormally and persistently elevated, expansive, or irritable mood . . . inflated self-esteem or grandiosity, decreased need for sleep . . . flight of ideas . . . the person may spontaneously start extensive conversations with strangers in public places. . . . Lability of mood (e.g. the alternation between euphoria and irritability) is frequently seen. . . . Individuals . . . may travel impulsively to other cities. . . . They may change their dress, makeup, or personal appearance. . . . When no longer in the Manic Episode, most individuals are regretful for behaviors engaged in during the Manic Episode.[40]

This is an apt description of Isaac—the fit is too close to ignore. The evidence, moreover, for a genetic role in the etiology of bi-polar disorder is stronger than for virtually any other mental disorder.[41] Many also believe that the use of lithium in treating bi-polar disorder has marked one of the more impressive success stories of psychopharmacology.[42]

But even if valid, this retrospective labeling would explain Isaac's story only in very truncated ways. I contend, rather, that the foregoing analysis retains such validity as it has regardless of what mental disorder Isaac had, regardless of whether or not he had a mental disorder, regardless of whether mental disorder is a "disease" or a "myth." Again, the content of madness *demands attention;* it should not be treated as a distraction from the essence.

Isaac was labeled with the abstraction "acute mania"; such an abstraction was necessary because the goal was not comprehension or therapy but control. Biochemically directed psychiatry risks a similar lack of attention. A psychiatric label can itself become a place of confinement, where patients are corralled, given the correct synthesized substance, and released with their symptoms dispelled—at least at the grossest level. What would be lost is a vast archive containing densely textured and symbolically charged transcripts of their political situations, cultural predicaments, and daily trials.

CHAPTER 6

Psychiatry and
Colonial Ideology

Objectivity can sometimes become an obstacle in the search for truth.[1]
                                                          —T. A. Lambo, 1955

For the native, objectivity is always directed against him.[2]
                                           —Frantz Fanon, 1963

       If critiques of the objectivity of scientific and medical research are fairly common now, it is striking to see them developed by two major (perhaps *the* major) psychiatrists of the late colonial era in Africa, over a generation ago. For both Lambo and Fanon, the context of such a critique was the experience of working in psychiatric institutions originally developed by colonial powers. This chapter explores the colonial psychiatric discourse generated in Nigeria, seeking to show how objectivity could be thought an obstacle to truth, how objectivity could be directed against the "native."

       The confining of hundreds of alleged lunatics occasioned a psychiatric literature that sought to explain the apparent rise in prevalence. The social meanings of madness were discussed in generalizations about African character that equated difference from the West with incommensurability. One could as easily have used patients' symptomatology to show identity between European and African psychopathology. Indeed, generic (European) nosology was used avidly, showing that for individuals, similarities in presentation were recognized.

       Colonial psychiatric theory, more than the social history of madness in Africa, has a relatively well-developed historiography. Elaborating a major theme in the comparative study of colonial medicine, a central accomplishment in this area has been to show the irony of how colonial medical theory located the source of pathology in the "innate character" of Africans, at the same time that colonial policies were generating the social changes which were altering epidemiological patterns.[3] This irony of colonial medical theory followed from the ways in which clinicians viewed Africans as representatives of a race, rather than as individual patients.

This literature has tended to treat colonial psychiatry as a single discourse. This approach has provided important contributions; McCulloch, for example, has shown how even writers who worked in isolation from each other reproduced similar ideological features in their work. He concluded that the social context—colonialism—determined the contours of the theory.[4] If so, Nigeria, which differed substantially from Kenya, South Africa, and other African colonies whose psychiatric practices have received more attention from historians because it was not a settler colony, might provide a useful comparison. The Nigerian literature, I will argue, was both similar and different in revealing ways; its colonial psychiatric theory was relatively "liberal," less reliant on the most overt and virulent forms of racism. But it was nevertheless limited by its colonial origins in its ability to abandon rigid conceptions of cultural difference, even as those conceptions were recognized to be inadequate.

Specifically, I examine the writings of Bruce Home, Robert Cunyngham Brown, and John Colin Carothers, the three most important colonial psychiatrists with Nigerian experience. With the partial exception of Brown, these experts most venerated by the colonial state were among the least relevant actors in the day-to-day process of labeling the mad. None of them did very much treating of patients in Nigeria; they were brought in to to do a report and make policy suggestions. All three were reformers in the sense that they urged the government to provide more beds and curative services. But in this chapter I want to focus less on their direct social impact than on what they can reveal about the production of knowledge in a colonial context. I also concentrate less on the accuracy of the observations in these writings than on their status as ideological artifacts.[5] My primary concern is with how the link between evidence and theory is socially formed, how social position shapes the range of plausible theory[6] and, in particular, the generation of stereotypes.[7] Some recent research in the history of medicine has shown how social location and stereotyping can cause resistance to evidence;[8] the value of internal textual analysis lies in showing resistance to evidence *contained in an author's own text.* When we know for certain that an author had access to a given datum or point of view, we can see clearly that extra-evidential factors are at work when the data are overlooked.

Bruce Home: The First Foray

> *It is difficult to distinguish temperamental and racial peculiarities from eccentricity and psychoneurosis, and fortunately such cases do not as a rule require mental hospital treatment.*[9]
>
> —Bruce Home

In the early colonial era, colonial officials formed proto-psychiatric ideas of a distinct African mind and personality. These were mainly pejorative ideas—J. F. A. Ajayi notes that key features included mendacity, drunkenness, hypocrisy, and immorality.[10] As the colonial era proceeded, these stereotypes were increasingly rationalized by the impress of science; in keeping with a growing organic bias in psychology, the "African mind" came to be a reflection of the African body—in particular the brain. Colonial psychiatry therefore had a distinctive role in colonial ideology, but not a discrete one. It drew upon other forms of writing which were themselves forged out of the longer history of the West's discovery of other cultures, and of itself. Analyses of this longer history exist elsewhere,[11] but it is worth noting that colonial officials were provided with ethnographic reading lists which show that, by the beginning of the twentieth century, imperialists were forming ideas of a distinct African mind and personality.[12]

There was, then, a "proto-psychiatric" discourse in place when Home's 1928 report, *Insanity in Nigeria,* was produced. *Insanity in Nigeria,* though, was important for setting the tone of much subsequent psychiatric writing on Nigeria and Africa. It contains, in compressed forms, many of the debates that were to follow over questions such as the prospects for cross-cultural diagnosis, the role of "civilization," sex ratios of mental illness, and the prevalence of depression.

Home was commissioned by the Colonial Office in 1927 to study forms of mental illness in Nigeria and to recommend steps for care and treatment.[13] He visited 25 regions and sent a questionnaire to Residents and Medical Officers. He also met personally with insane people who were in hospitals, asylums, and prisons. His conclusion called for increased services and curative institutions, modeled on European hospitals.

The main problem Home addressed was the prevalence of insanity. He discussed two extreme positions, neither of which persuaded him. One was the expectation that a "primitive" society would not have mental illness. Home countered that "insanity occurs throughout Nigeria, and no race, tribe or class is exempt from attack." [14]

The other extreme position was that Nigeria was experiencing an epidemic of mental disease, a ravage wrought by civilization. Africa, of course, is not the only context where "civilization" has been thought to cause insanity, but the theory took on special significance in colonial writing because of the long historical distance Africa was thought to be traveling in a short time. On this point, Home was contradictory. On the one hand, he noted that the number of reported cases was not necessarily equal to the "true" prevalence. This principle is often used to show that prevalence is greater than it seems, but in this case, Home used it to suggest that it was less. He argued that "a-social conduct" was noticed and resented more in civilized communities, leading to an illusion of increasing incidence of insanity, as more communities became civilized.

Home did not maintain this thesis consistently, though. He also argued that the greater stress of "civilized" life would be likely to cause a rapid increase in the incidence of insanity in the Southern Provinces of Nigeria. An axiom of the colonial mind held that aspects of modernization were thus seen as causes of madness in Africans and could be expected to increase incidence; the power of this axiom is underscored by the fact that it was adopted even by Home, who elsewhere denied that there *was* increased incidence.

In fact, the view that "civilization" could be a cause of mental illness became more pronounced in *Insanity in Nigeria* once Home's early denial of it was abandoned. It led to an odd sequence of propositions in which statistical estimates, admitted to be flimsy and ambiguous, were used to show confidently that the proportion of lunatics to the rest of the population in Nigeria was considerably lower than in England and Wales: "In replies to the questionnaire on Insanity 652 lunatics are reported, apart from those in asylums or prisons, but the replies from twenty-two districts stated that no figures were available, or that the number was impossible to ascertain, (one reply was 'plenty'). It is not possible therefore to estimate the proportion of insane from the figures submitted." [15] Despite this apparent caution, Home confidently esti-mated the insane in Nigeria to be 20 per 100,000 of the population, compared with 365 per 100,000 in England and Wales—in keeping with the assumption that less "developed" societies were compensated with less insanity.

We can get another view of the contours of Home's mental landscape by investigating his mention of sex ratios of mental disorders. His com-ment on the subject was terse: "The nervous system is less stable in the female than in the male, and in most countries insanity occurs more fre-quently among women. Of reported cases in Nigeria the male are to the female in a ratio of 3 to 1. This ratio is the basis on which hospital ac-commodation must be calculated." [16] The view that the female nervous system is less "stable" than that of the male was widely held among Western psychiatrists at the time. Conflicting Nigerian data did not lead Home to question this premise, or even to wonder why the nervous sys-tems of Nigerians deviated from a known pattern. The data presented a clear conflict between the key formations of difference by gender and by race.

Home's reasoning could have taken decisive turns at this point. He might, for example, have questioned the assumption that the predomi-nance of female patients in Western treatment settings was due to an immutable biological factor and not a social artifact. His inability or un-willingness to make this move can be compared to the account Freud gave of Viennese psychiatry's response to Jean-Martin Charcot's theory that hysteria occurred in males. The notion was absurd, they protested, since the etymology of the term referred to a part of female anatomy. It could have been argued as logically that the term itself was flawed and should be jettisoned. We can only speculate about whether for Home, the additional variable of racial difference seemed to obviate the need to question his assumptions about European women—that is, the women writ large into phrases like "the female nervous system." The sort of turn I have suggested was not possible in his mental map. Confronted with an inassimilable fact, Home restricted his gloss to the practical im-plication: More beds would be needed in the male wards of the mental hospitals.

Home was, of course, commissioned by a colonial government seek-ing practical suggestions. As I noted earlier, nonmedical officials de-nounced Home's advocacy of increased accommodation and his com-mitment to treatment as inconsistent with the aims of Indirect Rule in the colony. But the growing number of vagrant lunatics was nevertheless causing a sense of crisis, leading to Robert Cunyngham Brown's larger report in 1938.

Robert Cunyngham Brown: Psychiatric Liberalism

Be it said there is here no question of good and bad, or of superior and inferior, but only one of difference.
—Robert Cunyngham Brown

Difference is that which threatens order and control.[17]
—Sander Gilman

Robert Cunyngham Brown was born in Shetland in 1867 and educated at the universities of Glasgow, Durham, and Frankfurt. He had worked in a neuropathological laboratory in Frankfurt, a hospital for epileptics and the paralyzed in London, an asylum in Chester, and the British prison service. In 1911 he became Deputy Commissioner of Lunacy for Scotland and later served as a medical officer for the army in the First World War. By the time he wrote his reports on West Africa in 1938, he was in the last decade of his life and toward the end of a successful career.

With the assistance of the local residents and other officers, as well as the traditional rulers and emirs, Brown covered every major population center in Nigeria over three and a half months. He inspected asylums, prisons, hospitals, dispensaries, and other sites where the insane were found, including their homes and the practices of "native doctors." He studied incidence and prevalence rates for mental disorders, their forms and relative proportions, and the conditions of housing and treatment. Unlike Home, he saw many patients face to face. In a phrase hinting at apprehensions, he described them as "the opposite of hostile in demeanour."[18]

Brown's report was more developed and rigorous than Home's, but he shared some of his predecessor's inconsistencies. For example, Brown's report overtly claimed to put relatively little emphasis on categorical differences between Africans and their cultures on the one hand, and Europeans and theirs on the other. Instead, he stressed diversity *within* Nigeria, especially the difference between the coastal peoples and those of the north. He nevertheless added that these differences were weak in comparison to the gulf separating the "intellectual, emotional, and ethical qualities" which "distinguish the West African from the European." [19] He declined to guess whether the difference was based on anatomy and biology or on cultural and "mental" factors.

Brown believed that cultural differences represented developmental stages. He described Nigeria as recapitulating the stages of (European) human incubation, prior to the birth of the generation of Brown himself. The different social organizations in Nigeria included "well-developed" Muslim states, as well as "primitive pagan communities": "In consequence it may truly be said that Nigeria today furnishes examples of almost every chapter in the long and doleful history of the insane of all countries, from its first recorded beginnings in the days of antiquity up to modern times, with the exception as yet of late nineteenth and twentieth century developments." [20] To Brown, then, Nigeria in 1938 seemed on the verge of entering that very nervous time, the *fin-de-siècle*. But Brown was more forceful than Home in denying that insanity was increasingly prevalent and stood apart from many of his European contemporaries in explicitly repudiating a "clash of culture" thesis. [21]

The "clash of culture" thesis held that the "impact" of the West would be likely to increase mental disorder among "uncivilized" peoples, who now had to cope with the alleged strains of reading, regular work rhythms, and the like. Brown countered that this was an illusion produced by the fact that lunatics who were most exposed to the centers of colonial administration were more apt to be noticed by colonial observers. [22] Yet Brown did consider "uncivilized" societies relatively inoculated from mental illness. He counted in the year of his visit 290 persons certified and confined, or 8 per 1 million of the total estimated population—as compared with a ratio of 8 per 10,000 in England and Wales. [23] As Nigeria became more modern, its true prevalence would rise *and* the detected cases would also increase in proportion to those hidden. Like Home, he therefore recommended more beds and a therapeutic program to confront the growing problem.

These discussions of increasing prevalence reflected colonial anxieties. The doctrine of Indirect Rule was always tied to uneasiness about the consequences of intervention in indigenous society, and the perceived prevalence of African lunatics provided a mirror for colonial projections of their own apprehensions. This kind of projection, apparent in all the debates over the effects of modernization, can be seen most clearly in the emerging debates over the effect of literacy. [24]

To the historian of psychiatry, theories which see literacy, reading, and education as "risk factors" for insanity reappear over the centuries with a certain monotony. They have often referred to dominated groups whose status is in flux.[25] Brown, however, criticized the theory that the "town" African was more prone to mental illness.[26] He argued that those who became insane in rural settings were simply not noticed by the colonial regime.

Brown's report was greeted more warmly by officials than Home's had been; although he also called for expanding services, he drew none of the contempt Home had, indicating that it had become hard to deny that the colony had a problem with insanity. At the level of concrete policy, however, inertia carried the day, so that when Carothers visited in the mid-1950s, conditions were in many respects identical to those Brown described two decades earlier. By the 1950s, efforts to create a curative hospital were well under way, but this was largely due to the initiatives of Lambo and Asuni.

I term Brown's report "liberal" in the colonial context because it resisted theories of racial difference and on the policy level called for the reform of expanded services. Yet I have also stressed that there were also important ways in which Brown's report was shaped by colonial ideology, ways in which his dissent from colonial assumptions was tempered. We see in much of Carothers's work, on the other hand, instances of explicit apology for those assumptions.

J. C. Carothers: The African Mind as Pattern and Threat

Many attempts have been made to describe African mentality but, in recent years at least, have usually been made apologetically—saying, for example "This is the classical conception," "This is the popular stereotype," or "It has been said." Such apologies are not so necessary; these "classical conceptions" are largely true today. Their meaning is another story.

—J. C. Carothers[27]

J. C. Carothers was born in South Africa and went to medical school in England. He served for nine years as a Medical Officer in Kenya, and subsequently for twelve years as Director of Mathari Mental Hospital and of H. M. Prison in Nairobi. He also acted as Psychiatric Consultant to the East African Command throughout the Second World War. On retirement from colonial service, he worked for 18 months as a psychiatrist at St. James' Hospital, Portsmouth. Late in his career, he produced a report on conditions in Nigeria[28] and was commissioned by the World Health Organization to write *The African Mind in Health and Disease*.

Carothers was the first colonial psychiatrist in Nigeria with previous African experience. Because he worked in and wrote about several very different colonies, his work provides an interesting comparative case. Gilman has proposed that familiarity with "the other" works to moderate stereotyping, since experience or empirical observation tempers the construction of the images. Gilman writes: "The actual amalgamation of the stereotypes of blackness and madness could not take place in Greek medicine; such a telescoping could not occur for the reason that blacks were present in the daily experience of the Greeks."[29] This logic is too general to be taken as anything more than a possibility to be considered in different research contexts. Carothers's experience in Kenya, in any event, produced the most virulently stereotyping colonial psychiatry. His writing on Kenya, where he lived and worked, relied on a much more rigid category of the "African mind" than his writing on Nigeria.

The demand for Carothers's expertise during the twilight of colonial rule and the awakening of African nationalism in itself reflects apprehension among supporters of empire about the changing situation. Some social theory proposes that the labeling of behavior as mental illness indicates that, to the labeler, the behavior is incomprehensible.[30] This notion took on a particular political significance under colonialism, since imperialists and Africans inhabited different cognitive worlds, having different views of the appropriateness of colonialism itself. In Carothers's work, the pathologization of resistance and the resistance buried in pathology become especially clear. His writing is constantly in tacit dialogue with liberal opinion, anticipating its objections, conceding its force, and resenting its presence.

These themes are presented most boldly in his *The Psychology of Mau Mau*.[31] In the Mau Mau rebellions, a European psychiatric researcher would be faced with Africans who were emphatically not, as Brown's phrase put it, "the opposite of hostile in demeanour."[32] A number of writers have shown that it was politically useful for British colonialism to depict the Mau Mau rebellions as irrational, the result of disordered minds. For example, A. S. Cleary writes that Britain tried to contain damage to its public image by popularizing the view that Mau Mau was "a small, unpopular, easily controllable, savage tribal uprising, *perhaps the symptom of some form of mass psychosis,* the result of the Kikuyu tribe's inability to cope with the modern world" (emphasis added).[33] But to see this depiction as simply a cynical manipulation would be to underestimate the complexity, and ultimately the power, of ideology. Carothers did see Mau Mau as a psychological disturbance, but this reading was naturalized by the colonial situation, not just functionally expedient for it.

The Psychology of Mau Mau, like all of Carothers's writings, opens by denying any "fundamental" difference between Europeans and Africans —the word "fundamental" meaning "physiological." This disavowal, though, serves as a warrant to search for *cultural* incommensurability. Similarly, he stressed early on the diversity of African cultures, only to expound later on their essential character. For example, despite the diversity of African cultures, he generalized that, for the African, "reflection, foresight and responsibility are rather components of his culture than of himself; misfortunes are never wholly his own fault."[34] This aspect of the African character had direct relevance for an uprising like Mau Mau:

> Without the tribal group or in one's dealings with outsiders who have been seen as evil, the traditional rules not only have no application but are positively incorrect.
>
> Where there are no specific rules, behaviour can be governed wholly by the emotions of the moment.[35]

It was common in colonial writing to describe Africans as so deeply determined by culture that slight historical change could leave them utterly without mooring, a theme Carothers echoed: "When European influence impinges on the African, his whole cultural machinery is apt to collapse quite quickly."[36] In Nigeria, as in Kenya, the government was apprehensive about such a collapse and commissioned Carothers to write a report on psychiatric services for them in 1955, a year after his treatise on Mau Mau.

Although *The African Mind in Health and Disease* also began with a statement of Africa's diversity, Carothers defended his right to paint "African mentality" in broad strokes. In a key passage, he wrote:

> This monograph is not concerned with the Christian, the Mohammedan, the urban, or the "educated" African as such, nor even with those groups (such as the Yoruba) who have developed cultures that diverge from the usual patterns insofar as they diverge. *Yet although many, if not most, Africans today diverge in some degree from the model as defined, the ancient cultural modes are a far more vital*

force than these remarks imply. Few Africans are wholly free from tribal custom. (emphasis added)[37]

Note the shift that occurs in this passage. It begins by exempting certain Africans from the scope of the study on the grounds that they are no longer really African, but then re-expands the scope on the grounds that Africans do not really change. In theory his book was not relevant to the Yoruba, who were urban and exceptional. The passage repeats a recurring turn of mind in Carothers's writing, a turn which is probably central to all stereotype formation—exceptions to the formula of the African mind are taken to make the exceptions somehow less African, rather than to indicate any weakness in the stereotype.[38]

In *The African Mind,* Carothers again denied physiological difference—but with a tone of melancholy regret. He eagerly cited research into anatomical differences between Africans and Europeans (particularly brain differences), some of which was frankly eugenicist. A forlorn reference to a 1943 South African study of intelligence scores reveals how Carothers regretted the disrepute of this research. After conceding that a culture-free intelligence test was a "contradiction in terms," Carothers added: "Since the publication of Biesheuvel's masterly monograph of 1943, no one in Africa has had the temerity to plunge into seas which are so inviting, yet have such treacherous undercurrents; and 'the rest is silence.'"[39] Of course, a lot had changed between 1943 and 1953; from Carothers's point of view, such "masterly" inquiries had become, regrettably, politically unacceptable. In any event, his concept of African culture was so coterminous with race—he omitted North Africans from his study, while including American blacks—that the distinction between race and culture became meaningless.

If cosmetically avoiding a physiological explanation for African difference—a move that anticipated liberal objections and also staked out a ground for specifically psychiatric study—Carothers did require some explanation. Taking a psychoanalytic turn (a turn avoided in Home and wholly absent in Brown), he relied on weaning. Citing John Bowlby's work on the formation of bonds in infancy, which was just beginning to become influential in psychoanalytic thought, he represented the African child's relationship with the mother as "warm, intimate, and continuous," just as Bowlby advocated.[40] "In these respects, therefore, the African infant's experience seems to be ideal."[41] But Carothers saw this as ultimately damaging because it failed to prepare the child for the "demands of reality," and "no firm foundation is laid for clear distinction of the subject and object."[42]

Having a developed idea of African difference did lead Carothers to wonder whether there were limitations to European nosology, but he decided to use it anyway, assuming that "the principles described in psychiatric textbooks apply in Africa as well as Europe."[43] He questioned, for example, the utility of the distinction between affective disorders and anxiety neuroses for the African context but retained it, "with a view to following standard procedure as far as this is possible."[44] Schizophrenia was described as "par excellence the chronic form of insanity in Africans as in Europeans."[45] Depression, on the other hand, he thought rare: "There seems to be no good reason to doubt that the recorded rarity of depression in standard forms in Africans corresponds to a reality. If the hypochondriac cases previously mentioned are fundamentally 'depressive,' then confusion takes the latter's place and one can say only that circumstances have so altered the expression of this illness in the African that it is not the same disease."[46]

This observation signals the unraveling of the nosology by granting that cultural differences in presentation make it hard to verify that the disorders are identical. It might have followed that "depression" was not a useful category in this context. But Carothers was nevertheless concerned to account for its rarity, which he claimed was due to a lack of personal integration and responsibility.

Carothers elaborated the colonial cliché of the irresponsible African at length in the *Journal of Mental Science*,[47] where he developed it in rich, racist, anecdotal detail. It is not necessary here to reproduce these anecdotes; as German puts it, "Responsibility was defined in terms of European priorities, while the responsible pursuit of African values was usually regarded as a sign of backwardness."[48] At times Carothers admitted that colonial rule lacked legitimacy for Africans, but this recognition was subdued compared to the glowing confidence with which he rendered African resentment as pathological.

In his conclusion to the article, which inspired a powerful rebuttal from Lambo,[49] Carothers compared the normal African to the lobotomized European. In Europeans, he asserted, the main effect of a lobotomy is a failure to see an event as an element in a total situation: "It would have been possible to write the analysis of the leucotomized European's mentality in words that echoed the analysis of the [normal] African's; but it would have made wearisome reading."[50] Here again, Carothers tried to disavow physiological reductionism; the African's frontal lobe was not missing but undeveloped, due to "African culture."

Carothers's writing represented the apotheosis of several contradictions in colonial psychiatry. Despite the diversity of African cultures and the disavowal of a biological theory of difference, an incommensurate African mind was rationalized as an object of inquiry. Yet the universal applicability of Western nosology was subject to only modest reservations. What was at stake was not so much a definitive statement of whether African cultures were similar or varied but the policing of the cultural boundary which was held to separate all of them from European culture. This became crucial the more that boundary was threatened.

Yet given this theoretical background, what is most striking about Carothers's report on Nigeria is how relatively liberal it is. This 68-page report contains not a single line alleging special common mental characteristics of Africans. There are occasional swipes at traditional healers and some mention of the problems causes by urbanization—though these were not held to reflect any peculiarities of the "African mind." Indeed, that collective singular form, which was the key phrase in Carothers's major monograph and was echoed ironically in the title of Jock McCulloch's book, is absent from the Nigeria report. Where *The Psychology of Mau Mau* and *The African Mind in Health and Disease* are filled with caustic generalizations about Africans and their deficiencies, Carothers's report devoted to Nigeria is a tame echo of the calls for expanded services made by Home and Brown.

This is not to suggest that a short trip to Nigeria changed Carothers in any important way.[51] It does indicate that lack of experience is not what encourages the formation or reinforcement of stereotypes. On the contrary, the essence of stereotyping is that, since a complex of political and emotional factors drives it, it is a mode of thought that can be immune to evidence. Colonial ideology was dependent on certain racial assumptions, and these influenced all the psychiatric writing, in all the colonies. The ideological elements in colonial psychiatry were, though, related above all to the degree of perceived threat. A context like Kenya, where colonial rulers sought to suppress a violent uprising, occasioned a psychiatric literature that was noticeably more reactionary.

Lambo's broadside against "objectivity" appeared in a critique of Carothers, which Lambo published in 1955.[52] His article acknowledged that presentation of symptoms could vary culturally, and that Africans could therefore differ from Europeans, but he stressed that this was a sign of cultural difference and was therefore not innate. He wrote, "There is no such thing as 'African culture' and therefore no 'African mentality' . . . diversity of human cultures in Africa has been emphasized by many competent anthropologists,"[53] and therefore any comparisons based on an African mind were inherently hazardous. Colonial psychiatric writing presented itself as objective science, but to Lambo it was clear that the knowledge it produced was positionally determined— that is, it was a distinctively *colonial* science. There was thus a profound political dimension to Lambo's writings during this period, even if it did not take the form of direct social criticism.

While many lament "reflexive turns" in contemporary scholarship, one could only have wanted more critical self-awareness from colonial psychiatrists. The concept of the "African mind" was more a barrier than a useful theoretical tool for understanding the psychopathology in Africans. Yet it provides a point of entry for examining colonial psychology.[54] To a degree they could not acknowledge, colonial psychiatrists represented *colonial* anxieties and preoccupations, while ostensibly probing the psychopathology of Africans—of whom they conceded they had little close knowledge.

It would be surprising if colonial psychiatry did not contain racist elements. Imperialism is a discredited political doctrine, scientific racism is a discredited scholarly pursuit; these considerations could lead us to consign these writings to a discredited past. But to understand this period, it is important to stress that Home, Brown, and Carothers were read with equal seriousness and considered safely within the realm of acceptable psychiatric inquiry. In any event, the permanence of the scientific racism's disrepute is far from secure.[55]

I do not, though, wish to minimize the challenges which Home, Brown, and Carothers faced. While the search for genetic sources of psychiatric disorder and the spread of psychopharmacology have prompted triumphant soundings from the more biomedically inclined, cultural difference continues to vex psychiatric research.[56] And strenuous efforts to forge a globally reliable nosology have not prevented subjective factors related to status and power differences from significantly influencing the diagnostic process.

The strength of these factors in the colonial context is above all reflected in the features shared by relatively liberal writers such as Home and Brown and a more reactionary figure like Carothers. What most strikingly connects their work is not simply the assertion of a uniform African mind but rather the presence in their writing of evidence and logic working, vainly, against that assertion.

CHAPTER 7

Conclusion

One of the major achievements of African historical scholarship in the postcolonial period has been to show that "the meanings of such units as the 'Yao,' 'Kikuyu,' 'Bakedi,' and 'Hausa' were socially constructed in time and could only be defined 'in motion.'"[1] Over the same period a considerable scholarly and scientific literature has also developed about mental illness in southwest Nigeria, and by the postcolonial period, the "Yoruba case" had become a staple of ethnopsychiatry. But just as Yoruba identity must be defined in time and in motion, groups and categories as "the mad" and "schizophrenia" are not primordial or unchanging entities. Much of the anti-psychiatric literature which flourished in the 1960s erred in concluding that these categories were thus "only" myths, or therefore not "real" illnesses. To show that these categories are "in motion" is not to deny their reality or force, any more than to emphasize the historically formed character of the category "Yoruba" implies that it is unreal or inauthentic.

There is now an understandable fatigue with the concept, and certainly the phrase, "social construction" in recent scholarship. Charles Rosenberg has worried that the phrase has unduly stressed an arbitrary nature to medical categories.[2] Rosenberg notes that constructivist approaches have focused on diseases that either lack definitively known biological pathogens (which includes many mental illnesses) or that have a great deal of cultural resonance (one could cite AIDS, for example). I would take this observation in a different direction from Rosenberg, though, and stress that it may be precisely for those diseases whose biological reality makes their "constructedness" less obvious that constructivist approaches may be most fruitful.[3] Michael Taussig has pointed out that for a time—a time passed now—the effect of the insight that what seemed natural was constructed was so hypnotic that the questions that followed from it remained unasked.[4] Construction, Taussig writes, "deserves more respect" and should not be simply a conclusion. Judith Butler detaches the implicit adjective "mere" that often precedes the phrase "social construction." Of human bodies she writes:

> For surely our bodies live and die; eat and sleep; feel pain, pleasure; endure illness and violence; and these "facts," one might skeptically proclaim, cannot be dismissed as mere construction. Surely there must be some kind of necessity that accompanies these primary and irrefutable experiences. . . . [But] why is it that what is constructed is understood as an artificial and dispensable character? What are we to make of those constructions without which we would not be able to think, to live, to make sense at all, those which have acquired for us a kind of necessity?[5]

Indeed, discussion needs to move away from a dyadic debate over whether mental illness is real or constructed in an absolute sense into more depth about the ways it is produced in particular historical formations. Many, for example, take the relativity, and therefore the "constructedness," of mental disorders to be so axiomatic as to not require discussion, but the omission of history from cross-cultural psychiatry has had misleading results in authors taking vastly differing approaches.

Take, for example, Jane Murphy's article on psychiatric labeling—a classic, if controversial, article in ethnopsychiatry.[6] This article is perhaps the most influential exposition of the *anti*-relativist approach to mental illness.[7] The article aims to dislodge a cornerstone of labeling theory, namely, the belief that other cultures have radically different canons of deviance. Scheff and others argued that if very different cultures had radically different conceptions of mental illness, this would support the idea that "mental illness" was a social convention—and, by implication, not a "real" disease. For example, it might be shown that the behavior the West considers madness was construed as shamanism or special insight in other cultures, and we would therefore have to reconsider our own understanding, and treatment. Ruth Benedict and other ethnographers were cited to indicate that this was the case. Murphy, a participant in the Cornell/Aro project who had both anthropological and psychiatric training, conducted an empirical test.

Murphy's article was based on fieldwork among the Inuit and the Yoruba. She showed convincingly that among Inuit, where shamanism existed, the behavior of shamans was not identical to the mad, and that in fact those societies had *both* the categories of shamanism and madness—and that their categories of madness was not too dissimilar from Western ones. As for the Yoruba, Murphy argued that *were* was a fair translation of "madness," since it covered a similar range of behavioral abnormality.

Murphy's blow to labeling theory was far from decisive. Claims of cultural difference were never logically crucial to labeling theory. The most Murphy could claim to have proven was that similar labeling processes take place in different cultures.[8] But the problems with Murphy's article run deeper. She shared with the labeling theorists the assumption that the Yoruba could fairly be used as an "Archimedean point" from which to assess Western psychiatric practice. In order for the Yoruba to fulfill this function they would ideally exist in remote isolation from Western practice. From a scientific point of view, one would not want to choose a part of Africa that had had 80 years of British-style asylums. This history, and indeed the asylums and mental hospitals generally, were entirely omitted in the article. This was not from ignorance. On the contrary, Aro Mental Hospital was Murphy's point of entry into Nigerian society. In fact, Murphy would have been unlikely to have come to Nigeria in the first place without the Aro Hospital, which provided the site and partial rationale for the Cornell study.

A more historical approach would also enrich much epidemiological research. Take, for example, a paper on the genesis of schizophrenia by Oye Gureje and A. Adewunmi, which was based on research conducted at Aro in the 1980s.[9] The paper belongs to a genre of epidemiology that seeks to assess the role of life events in the etiology of mental disorders. The authors stress that such studies in developing countries were important in the light of World Health Organization data which suggest that the course of schizophrenia may be different in those countries.[10] After interviewing patients to see how many significant life events had occurred in the previous six months, Gureje and Adewunmi presented a negative conclusion: The patients had no more significant life events than a control group. They acknowledged, though, that they were not able to date the onset of the illness for the patients.

But in research on life events, accurate dating of onset is clearly essential; one cannot hope to discover whether life events had a role in triggering the illness if one does not know whether the events came before or after onset. But there seems to be a deeper problem. Gureje and Adewunmi write: "The possibility of a reduction in social interactions, and consequently, number of life events being due to the prodromal manifestations of the illness could not be discounted. Unfortunately, we cannot be sure of this, since what constitutes the prodromal syndrome of schizophrenia in the African is not known."[11] In general, while the paper seeks to use a standard, international category (schizophrenia), it invokes fundamental cultural difference—here expressed with the collective singular "the African"—whenever the results do not match those of the "developed" societies, which is where, of course, the universal instruments are forged.

Similar problems mar the World Health Organization's massive international studies of schizophrenia. One of the main findings of the WHO study was that schizophrenia (treated in the study as an unproblematic category) seems to have a more favorable course in less developed countries. The study thus set up a vast polar opposition between the developed and less developed world and assumed that the illnesses were essentially the same, even though the course may differ. I am not dogmatically opposed to either their assumptions or to their findings, but I do argue that such research will not advance unless it goes much farther in *specifying* what factors are different in which locales. Some recent writers have questioned the very operation of epidemiology, particularly psychiatric, arguing that it belongs to the wider apparatus of power which oppresses the mentally ill.[12] This seems to me extreme. Epidemiology, done carefully, is crucial to identifying the causes of affliction and their remedies. Variables, though, must be precisely formulated; abstractions such as "the African," or "the less-developed countries" obscure more than they reveal.

The flaws in the epidemiology can also be found in literature with a more "anti-psychiatric" inflection. Olayiwole Erinosho, for example, seeks to apply a Laingian framework to the cross-cultural study of mental illness. Erinosho cites in Laing's favor that he "undermines the widely shared individual-centred etiological explanation for the incidence of schizophrenia" and instead directs attention to the contradictions in people's social experience that leads them to assume the role of schizophrenic.[13] Erinosho further posits that Laing's theory may be more applicable to industrialized societies, which have high degree of division of labor, the nuclear family, and an emphasis on universalistic norms. These societies he opposes to "folk" societies, which would be relatively immunized from schizophrenia because the diffuseness of roles allows greater tolerance of deviance in a time of distress.

Although Erinosho concedes that folk and industrialized societies are "typological constructs" which may not exist *"in toto,"* his argument is entirely dependent on this opposition. In any event, any time we might try to confine Nigeria within these constructs, we would have to capture a moving target. The making of the mad in Nigeria has taken place not in a typological construct but in a context of change and conflict. In chapters 4 and 5, I laid great stress on the *content* of insanity—the *specifics* of the visions, voices, utterances, and transgressions of the mad. This content indicated unequivocally that the "stresses" of the asylums' denizens would be poorly understood as those of a "folk" society—or indeed, of an industrialized one. Rather, the content repeatedly referred to specifics of Nigerian colonial history: religious conversion, foreign domination, the changing justice system (including the development of the police force), and the struggle for independence.

The content of the expressions of insanity show specificity; so too does the content of colonialism. The growth of microstudies of colonial medical institutions suggests the hazards of incorporating these institutions into a grand theory of the nature of colonial power. I have argued that some concept of "social control" is indispensable to telling the story of Nigerian institutions but have also stressed that this control cannot be seen as a monolithic European force enacting a grand scheme of confinement, classification, or observation on Nigerians. What is more apparent is the contradictory, half-hearted nature of the institutions for most of the colonial period. Once designated as asylums, they could be perceived and used in a variety of ways. Within the government, there was continual debate over even whether the institutions ought to be medical ones. Nigerians perceived them as places to dread but also in some cases as a last resort for managing chronically distressing people. Colonial medical policy was mainly reactive, and given this fitfulness, generalizations about the nature of colonial medicine are risky. On the level of ideology, some patterns emerge—many studies have now shown how colonial thought rationalized its medical interventions (or lack of them) with reference to racist characterizations about the nature of Africans. But the existence of these patterns did not imply the enactment of anything like a coherent plan. One might say instead that the universals implied in modern psychiatry collided with colonial thinking's stress on incommensurate difference to produce a paralysis in policy.

And what of "social control's" more fashionable sibling term, "cultural hegemony"? As the study of colonial medicine has grown in the past decade, there has been a concurrent growth in interest in the cultural power of colonial institutions. It is not surprising then, that the power of colonial medicine to advance colonial hegemony has been a preoccupation of some major work in the field.[14] One premise that the literature on colonial medicine has worked with holds that medicine could have at least two "hegemonizing" effects: 1) it would, in its efficacy, persuade the colonized of the rightness of imperial rule, and 2) it would undermine the indigenous belief systems, helping to create a new cosmology, a new common sense, which would facilitate the development of colonial, capitalist social forms.

Vaughan has questioned the reach of such an approach, though,[15] and indeed, what is frequently much more striking is the limits of both hegemonic power and hegemonic aspirations in colonial medical institutions. Certainly this would seem to be one reasonable conclusion from the literature on medical "pluralism." Pier Larson has recently made a powerful case for the resilience of the world views of colonized peoples.[16] One could add that in many colonial situations, the cultural work done by colonial institutions was far too shifting and diffident to accomplish hegemonic domination. While the hegemonic power of colonial medicine may well be more evident in other contexts, for other medicines, in other colonies, some caution seems called for. This is not intended as a critique of the concept of hegemony; historians do need a vocabulary with which to describe the persuasive elements in power relations, as well as the more coercive ones. But Nigeria's colonial asylums were far more coercive than they were persuasive. It is not surprising that colonial asylums did little to promote changing idioms for understanding distress. Upon the opening of Aro, new idioms were promoted with some vigor, though they did not gain wide currency because older ones retained the full faith and credit of most medical consumers. The psychiatrists who modernized Aro recognized this in their use of traditional healers to induct patients into the alien world of the hospital. Even granting that hegemony is always partial and contested, the records presented here show how little Western medical understandings were internalized by patients. In a postcolonial period, when the global public health initiatives of cosmopolitan medicine must traverse a barrier of earned distrust, the historical significance of colonial medicine may lie less in its intention or ability to colonize the mind than in its tendency more simply to control or neglect the ailing person.

Such neglect followed from the basic premises of the colonial state. Indirect Rule sought an impossible goal—colonialism without "impositions"—and by the period between 1945 and 1955 the numbers of vagrant and incarcerated lunatics which no one was taking responsibility for was one visible sign of this contradiction. The imperial government abdicated, and Nigerians took responsibility for the institutions and their potential patients. This in turn changed the nature of social control, leading to a growing number of "harmless" patients in institutions; the range of behavior that warranted institutionalization widened as the institutions became less oppressive.

At each step, the content of madness reflected these changes. It would be crude to say colonialism *caused* madness, but we can say that it brought about specifically colonial pathologies. It is critical to avoid the fallacy of seeing the insane as emblematic of the colonial situation. While the representations of their problems did refract the particularities of their epoch, they were also clearly exceptional representations.

Diagnosis and theory were also "symptomatic" of the contradictory colonial situation. In the nineteenth century, madness was something Europeans and Africans could *recognize* in one another's culture. And during the twentieth century, the use of European psychiatric categories was considered unproblematic, indicating that even across the genuinely broad cultural frontier between Africans and Europeans, family resemblances could be seen in the presentation of symptoms. Yet the ideology of colonialism promoted the idea of incommensurable difference, and this idea was reflected in psychiatric theory that articulated the notion of a unique "African mind." While the confined insane in colonial Nigeria were people who clearly stood out in their communities, in colonial psychiatric theory, they were ironically made to stand in for Africa writ large.

Notes

Chapter 1.   Introduction

1. "What Is Mental Illness?" in Yaba Mental Hospital, *From Asylum to Hospital* (Lagos: Gabumo, 1987), 26.

2. See, for example, Oye Gureje and A. Adewunmi, "Life Events and Schizophrenia in Nigerians: A Controlled Investigation," *British Journal of Psychiatry* 153 (September 1988): 369.

3. Scholars have, of course, become increasingly aware of the ideological component of the term "traditional," of the ways it can be used to mask relatively recent cultural constructions and deployed to confer legitimacy and/or to stigmatize. A central text is Eric Hobsbawm and Terence Ranger, eds., *The Invention of Tradition* (Cambridge: Cambridge University Press, 1983).

4. There has been, with the development of postcolonial theory in recent years, an increase in scholarly interest in Fanon. See for example, Henry Louis Gates, Jr., "Critical Fanonism," *Critical Inquiry* 17 (Spring 1991): 457–70. For a critique of Gates, see Cedric Robinson, "The Appropriation of Frantz Fanon," *Race and Class* 15 (1993): 79–91. For an important appraisal of the continuing significance of Fanon (and the source, for me, of these citations), see Fred Cooper, "Conflict and Connection: Rethinking Colonial African History," American *Historical Review* 99, 5 (December 1994): 1516–45. Note as well that psychology has had a greater prominence in recent postcolonial theory than in anticolonial and nationalist writing of mid-century; see, for example, Ashis Nandy, *The Intimate Enemy: Loss and Recovery of Self Under Colonialism* (Delhi: Oxford University Press, 1983); and Anne McClintock, *Imperial Leather: Race, Gender, and Sexuality in the Colonial Contest* (New York: Routledge, 1995), especially ch. 4.

5. Frantz Fanon, *The Wretched of the Earth* (New York: Grove Press, 1963).

6. When I presented some of these ideas at the African Studies Association Meeting in Orlando in 1995, Martin Klein trenchantly remarked that this chapter may be neglected because it strongly undercuts the romantic valorization of

violence for which Fanon became best known, despite the fact that Fanon's remarks on violence were in fact a rather small and undeveloped part of his work.

7. See Irene Gendzier, *Frantz Fanon: A Critical Study* (New York: Pantheon, 1973), 114. The clinical origins of Fanon's work are receiving growing attention; see the special issue of *History of Psychiatry* (1996) devoted to Fanon.

8. Fanon, *Wretched of the Earth,* 250–51.

9. Megan Vaughan, "Idioms of Madness: Zomba Lunatic Asylum, Nyasaland, in the Colonial Period," *Journal of Southern African Studies* 9, 2 (1983): 218–38. See also chapter 5 of Vaughan's *Curing Their Ills: Colonial Power and African Illness* (Stanford: Stanford University Press, 1991); Saul Dubow, "Wulf Sachs's *Black Hamlet:* A Case of 'Psychic Vivisection'?" *African Affairs* 92, 369 (1993): 519–56; Saul Dubow and Jacqueline Rose, introduction to Wulf Sachs, *Black Hamlet* (Baltimore: Johns Hopkins University Press, 1996); Jock McCulloch, *Colonial Psychiatry and the African Mind* (Cambridge: Cambridge University Press, 1995); John Comaroff and Jean Comaroff, "The Madman and the Migrant: Work and Labor in the Consciousness of a South African People," *American Ethnologist* 14 (May 1987): 191–209; G. Allen German, "Mental Health in Africa: 1. The Extent of Mental Health Problems in Africa Today," *British Journal of Psychiatry* 151 (October 1987): 435–39; Leland Bell, *Mental and Social Disorder in Sub-Saharan Africa: The Case of Sierra Leone, 1781–1990* (New York: Greenwood Press, 1991); Harriet Deacon, "Racial Segregation and Medical Discourse in Nineteenth-Century Cape Town," *Journal of Southern African Studies* 22, 2 (June 1996): 287–308; Sally Swartz, "Changing Diagnoses in Valkenberg Asylum, Cape Colony, 1891–1920: A Longitudinal View," *History of Psychiatry* 6 (1995): 431–51.

10. Vaughan, "Idioms of Madness."

11. Vaughan, *Curing Their Ills,* ix; Michel Foucault, *Madness and Civilization,* trans. Richard Howard (New York: Vintage Books, 1965; originally published 1961).

12. For example, see Roy Porter, "The Patient's View: Doing Medical History from Below," *Theory and Society* 14 (1985): 175–98; and Sheila Rothman, *Living in the Shadow of Death: Tuberculosis and the Social Experience of Illness in American History* (New York: Basic Books, 1994). An example of a history of a psychiatric institution with close attention to the patients is Nancy Tomes, *A Generous Confidence: Thomas Story Kirkbride and the Art of Asylum-Keeping, 1840–1883* (Cambridge: Cambridge University Press, 1984), especially ch. 5. Also, see Geoffrey Reaume's excellent review essay, "Keep Your Labels off My Mind! or 'Now I Am Gong to Pretend I Am Craze but Dont Be a Bit Alarmed': Psychiatric History from the Patients' Perspectives," *Canadian Bulletin of the History of Medicine* 11 (1994): 397–424.

13. A superb overview can be found in the introduction to Andrew Scull, *The Most Solitary of Afflictions: Madness and Society in Britain, 1700–1900* (New Haven: Yale University Press, 1993). Edward Shorter, *A History of Psychiatry: From the Era of the Asylum to the Age of Prozac* (New York: Wiley, 1997), is a recent attempt to revive the progress narrative, seeing in the rise of biological psychiatry a happy ending, when psychiatry finally got things right.

14. It is a ritual practice I follow here. See also Vaughan, "Idioms of

Madness"; Comaroff and Comaroff, "The Madman and the Migrant"; David Rothman, *The Discovery of the Asylum: Social Order and Disorder in the New Republic*, rev. ed. (Boston: Little, Brown, 1990; originally published 1971); and Michael MacDonald, *Mystical Bedlam* (Cambridge: Cambridge University Press, 1981).

15. This historiography often allied itself with the anti-psychiatric theories made familiar by figures such as Thomas Szasz, R. D. Laing, and Erving Goffman. The ideas of these writers were far from identical, but they had a combined effect of defining an antipsychiatric turn of thought. Thomas Szasz, *The Myth of Mental Illness: Foundations of a Theory of Personal Conduct* (New York: Hoeber-Harper, 1961); R. D. Laing, *The Divided Self* (Middlesex: Viking: 1959); Erving Goffman, *Asylums* (New York: Anchor, 1961).

16. Andrew Scull, "Psychiatry and Social Control in the Nineteenth and Twentieth Centuries," *History of Psychiatry* 2, 2 (1991): 149–69.

17. See the revised edition of Rothman, *Discovery of the Asylum*, xxxv–xxxvi; and Constance M. McGovern, "The Myths of Social Control and Custodial Oppression: Patterns of Psychiatric Medicine in Late Nineteenth Century Institutions," *Journal of Social History* 20 (Fall 1986): 3–23.

18. Elizabeth Lunbeck, *The Psychiatric Persuasion: Knowledge, Gender, and Power in Modern America* (Princeton: Princeton University Press, 1994), 5–6, 47.

19. Waltraud Ernst, *Mad Tales from the Raj: The European Insane in British India* (London: Routledge, 1991), 168.

20. Allen Horwitz, *The Social Control of Mental Illness* (New York: Academic Press, 1982). Horwitz's book does, though, suffer from inattention to the detail of particular contexts. For example, an Africanist scholar cannot help but be alarmed when Horwitz refers to "the Yoruba of rural Ghana" (p. 43). In my conclusion, I will sketch some limitations to Horwitz's contribution.

21. Michel Foucault, *The Archaeology of Knowledge*, trans. A. M. Sheridan Smith (New York: Pantheon Books, 1972), 47.

22. See especially Thomas Scheff, *Being Mentally Ill: A Sociological Theory*, 2nd ed. (Chicago: Aldine de Gruyter, 1982).

23. Anonymous, in Yaba Mental Hospital, *From Asylum to Hospital*, 25.

24. In *Girls at War and Other Stories* (London: Heinemann, 1972). For a social scientific application of labeling theory, see the frequently-cited study by D. L. Rosenhan, "On Being Sane in Insane Places," *Science* 179, 70 (January 1973): 250–58.

25. Achebe, "The Madman," 11.

26. See Walter Gove, "The Current Status of the Labeling Theory of Mental Illness," in *Deviance and Mental Illness* (Beverly Hills: Sage, 1982). Psychiatrist Mark Warren noted in reading this that labeling theory has also tended to assume that being labeled mentally ill is an unfortunate outcome, whereas many of the labeled—whether sick or not—are people in trouble for whom the label provides access to support networks which might have been unavailable otherwise. Mark Warren, personal communication.

27. This is not to imply that the profession has been completely successful in this regard.

28. This literature is huge, but see I. I. Gottesman and J. Shields, *Schizophrenia and Genetics: A Twin Vantage Point* (New York: Academic Press, 1972); and A. Bertelsen, "A Danish Twin Study of Manic-Depressive Disorders," in *Origin, Prevention and Treatment of Affective Disorders,* eds. M. Schou and E. Stomgren (London: Academic Press, 1979).

29. R. C. Lewontin's work is helpful on this point; see, for example, his *Biology as Ideology: The Doctrine of DNA* (New York: Harper Collins, 1991).

30. This was borne out by several of my own interviews with healers and is discussed by Raymond Prince in "Indigenous Yoruba Psychiatry," in *Magic, Faith, and Healing,* ed. Ari Kiev (New York: Free Press of Glencoe, 1964).

31. I draw here on Bruce G. Link, et al., "A Modified Labeling Theory Approach to Mental Disorders: An Empirical Assessment," *American Sociological Review* 54 (June 1989): 400–23.

32. This point is developed at length in Arthur Kleinman, *Rethinking Psychiatry: From Cultural Category to Personal Experience* (New York: Free Press, 1988). One strength of Kleinman's argument is that he treats social analysis as complementary to biomedical approaches, not simply as a critique of them.

33. J. O., "The Psychiatric Hospital Yaba—As Seen by the Patient," in Yaba Mental Hospital, *From Asylum to Hospital,* 42.

34. See I. Sow, *Anthropological Structures of Madness in Black Africa* (New York: International Universities Press, 1980), ch. 1. Other discussions include the essays collected in Anthony J. Marsella and Geoffrey M. White, eds., *Cultural Conceptions of Mental Health and Therapy* (Dordrecht: Reidel, 1989; originally published 1982); and in Atwood Gaines, ed., *Ethnopsychiatry: The Cultural Construction of Professional and Folk Psychiatries* (Albany: State University of New York Press, 1992).

35. See, for example, the work of Atwood Gaines, "Cultural Definitions, Behavior and the Person in American Psychiatry," in Marsella and White, eds., *Cultural Conceptions,* and "From DSM-I to III-R: Voices of Self, Mastery, and the Other: A Cultural Constructivist Reading of U. S. Psychiatric Classification," *Social Science and Medicine* 35, 1 (1992): 3–24.

36. Vaughan, "Idioms of Madness."

37. Interview, Tolani Asuni, Lagos, March 13, 1990.

38. This can be seen by surveying David Westley, *Mental Health and Psychiatry in Africa: An Annotated Bibliography* (London: Hans Zell, 1993). See also Robert Edgerton, "Traditional Treatment for Mental Illness in Africa: A Review." *Culture, Medicine and Psychiatry* (1980): 179.

39. The question of the antiquity of Yoruba identity is a controversial one; I address it in the following chapter. On the division of Yoruba-peoples by colonial political boundaries, see A. I. Asiwaju, *Western Yorubaland Under European Rule, 1889–1945* (London: Longman, 1976).

40. Margaret Drewal, *Yoruba Ritual: Performers, Play, Agency* (Bloomington: Indiana University Press, 1992), 12, citing Rowland Abiodun, "The Future of African Art Studies: An African Perspective," in *African Art Studies: The State of the Discipline, Papers Presented at a Symposium Organized by the National Museum of Art, Smithsonian Institution, September 16, 1987* (Washington, DC: National Museum of African Art, 1990), 63–89.

41. See Robert Smith, *Kingdoms of the Yoruba*, 3rd ed. (Madison: University of Wisconsin Press, 1988), 9.

42. For a recent analysis of the political culture, see John Pemberton III and Funso S. Afolayan, *Yoruba Sacred Kingship: "A Power Like That of the Gods"* (Washington, DC: Smithsonian Institution, 1996).

43. Smith, *Kingdoms of the Yoruba*, 31.

44. Stephen Clingman, "Beyond the Limit: The Social Relations of Madness in Southern African Fiction," in *Bounds of Race: Perspectives on Hegemony and Resistance,* ed. Dominick LaCapra (Ithaca: Cornell University Press, 1991). See, for example, p. 231: "It turns out that the darkness at the heart of the colonial experience may be a certain history of madness."

45. A few prominent examples include Achebe, "The Madman"; Bayo Adebowale, *Out of His Mind* (Ibadan: Spectrum Books, 1987); Wole Soyinka, *Madmen and Specialists* (New York: Hill and Wang, 1971); and Gabriel Okara, *The Voice* (London: Heinemann, 1964).

46. Amos Tutuola, *My Life in the Bush of Ghosts* (New York: Grove, 1954), 50–51.

47. This criticism has dogged Tutuola's writing since it began to appear in the late colonial period. See, for example, James Booth, *Writers and Politics in Nigeria* (London: Hotter and Stoughton, 1981), 66–73.

48. Robert Darnton makes a similar point for folktales in "Peasants Tell Tales," in *The Great Cat Massacre and Other Episodes in French Cultural History* (New York: Basic Books, 1984).

Chapter 2.   The Nineteenth Century

1. Lagos *Weekly Record*, May 4, 1895.

2. In part, this attention grows out of the larger Africanist critique of the concept of "tribe." See Leroy Vail, ed., *The Creation of Tribalism in Southern Africa* (Berkeley: University of California Press, 1991), for representative approaches. This inquiry was given even wider significance by V. Y. Mudimbe's searching archaeology of African studies in *The Invention of Africa* (Bloomington: Indiana University Press, 1988). But while the problem has a special significance for Africa because of colonialism, the construction of identity and tradition has, of course, been a dominant preoccupation of scholarly life in recent years. Two landmark texts are Benedict Anderson, *Imagined Communities* (London: Verso, 1983), and Terence Ranger and Eric Hobsbawm, eds., *The Invention of Tradition* (Cambridge: Cambridge University Press, 1983).

3. J. D. Y. Peel, *Ijeshas and Nigerians: The Incorporation of a Yoruba Kingdom* (Cambridge: Cambridge University Press, 1983), and also Peel's "The Cultural Work of Yoruba Ethnogenesis," in *History and Ethnicity,* eds. Elizabeth Tonkin, Maryon MacDonald, and Malcolm Chapman (London: Routledge, 1989).

4. David Laitin, *Hegemony and Culture: Politics and Religious Change Among the Yoruba* (Chicago: University of Chicago Press, 1986). Laitin argues as well that forging of this pan-Yoruba identity mutes Christian-versus-Muslim religious conflict in the region. Regardless of the empirical merits of this argu-

ment, it is hard to see in what sense this is hegemony in the Gramscian sense Laitin claims; the Marxist dimension has completely dropped out.

5. A. I. Asiwaju, *Western Yorubaland Under European Rule, 1889–1945* (London: Longman, 1976), 9 and 19.

6. Smith, *Kingdoms of the Yoruba*, 9.

7. See S. O. Biobaku, *The Egba and Their Neighbours* (Oxford: Oxford University Press, 1957). See also Peel, "Cultural Work."

8. As Appiah has pointed out, the phrase "the invention of tradition" is a redundancy—invented traditions are the only ones there are—in Africa, or anywhere. Kwame Anthony Appiah, *In My Father's House: Africa in the Philosophy of Culture* (New York: Oxford University Press, 1992), 32.

9. See, for example, Hugh Trevor-Roper, "The Highland Tradition of Scotland," in Hobsbawm and Ranger, eds., *Invention of Tradition*.

10. Karin Barber, *I Could Speak Until Tomorrow: Oriki, Women and the Past in a Yoruba Town* (Washington, DC: Smithsonian Institution, 1991), 5–6.

11. This point has been made especially persuasively in B. Hallen and J. O. Sodipo, *Knowledge, Belief, and Witchcraft: Analytic Experiments in African Philosophy* (London: Ethnographica, 1986). See also Buckley, *Yoruba Medicine*, 161–62.

12. Wande Abimbola, *Ifa: An Exposition of Ifa Literary Corpus* (Ibadan: Caxton, 1976); Anthony Buckley, *Yoruba Medicine* (Oxford: Clarendon Press, 1985); William Bascom, *Ifa Divination: Communication Between Gods and Men in West Africa* (Bloomington: Indiana University Press, 1969); George E. Simpson, *Yoruba Religion and Medicine in Ibadan* (Ibadan: University of Ibadan, 1980). Buckley highlights the role of color symbolism in Yoruba healing, the importance of which is questioned in Roger O. A. Makanjuola, "Symbolic Features in the Management of Mental Disorders by Yoruba Traditional Healers," *Psychopathologie Africaine* 21, 2 (1986–87): 185–96.

13. Segun Gbadegesin, *African Philosophy: Traditional Yoruba Philosophy and Contemporary African Realities* (New York: Peter Lang, 1991), 127

14. See especially Prince, "Indigenous Yoruba Psychiatry." See also his "Curse, Invocation, and Mental Health Among the Yoruba," *Canadian Psychiatric Association Journal* 5, 2 (April 1960): 65–79; "The Use of Rauwolfia by Nigerian Native Doctors," *American Journal of Psychiatry* 118 (1960): 147–49; and "The Yoruba Image of the Witch," *Journal of Mental Science* 107 (1961): 795–805. See also the film by Prince and Francis Speed, *He Is a Madman*. (Ibadan: Institute of African Studies, University of Ibadan, 1963).

15. Gbadegesin, *African Philosophy*, 29.

16. Kristin Mann also notes that insanity, because it was considered hereditary, was an obstacle to marriage in the nineteenth century. *Marrying Well: Marriage, Status and Social Change Among the Educated Elite in Colonial Lagos* (Cambridge: Cambridge University Press, 1985), 37.

17. Prince, "Indigenous Yoruba Psychiatry," especially pp. 86–96. Soponna continues to be strongly associated with madness now that smallpox has been eradicated. See also Buckley, *Yoruba Medicine*, ch. 6. On diagnostic categories, see also William Bascom, "Social Status, Wealth and Individual Differences Among the Yoruba," *American Anthropologist* 53 (1951): 493.

18. Buckley, *Yoruba Medicine*, 26–27.

19. Olufemi Morakinyo, "The Yoruba *Ayanmo* Myth and Mental Health Care in West Africa," *Journal of Culture and Ideas* 1, 1 (1983): 61–92. A slightly different account is in Bascom, "Social Status," 492. I prefer the term "narrative" to "myth" because of the pejorative connotations of "myth." Also see Babatunde Lawal, "*Ori*: The Significance of the Head in Yoruba Sculpture," *Journal of Anthropological Research* 41 (Spring 1985): 91–103.

20. Morakinyo, "*Ayanmo* Myth," 69.

21. See Robert Edgerton, "Traditional Treatment for Mental Illness in Africa: A Review." *Culture, Medicine and Psychiatry* (1980): 167–89.

22. On the efficacy of traditional healers, see Z. A. Ademuwagun, J. A. A. Ayoade, I. Harrison, and D. M. Warren, eds., *African Therapeutic Systems.* (Waltham, MA: Crossroads Press, 1979). On greater social acceptance, see Nancy Waxler, "Is Mental Illness Cured in Traditional Societies? A Theoretical Analysis," *Culture, Medicine, and Psychiatry* 1 (1977): 233–254.

23. These associations are widespread in West Africa and appear in a number of fictional sources. See, for example, Chinua Achebe, *A Man of the People* (London: Heinemann, 1966), 132.

24. Kemi Morgan, *Akinyele's Outline History of Ibadan: Part One* (Ibadan: Caxton Press, n.d.), 28. For a valuable discussion of Morgan's account, see Toyin Falola, "Kemi Morgan and the Second Reconstruction of Ibadan History," *History in Africa* 18 (1991): 93–112.

25. An instance of this was noted by the missionary Joseph Smith in Ibadan in 1866: "About halfway through the town, I saw a man tied hands and feet to a tree & many spectators looking in from a distance. . . . On enquiry I was told that the man was mad, and had attempted to murder four persons, & on that account was arrested in the night and tied there." Church Missionary Society Archives (hereafter CMS) CA2/083/21.

26. For overviews and critiques of this belief, see Leo Srole et al., "The Midtown Manhattan Longitudinal Study versus the 'Mental Paradise Lost Doctrine': A Controversy Joined," *Archives of General Psychiatry* 37, 2 (February 1980): 209–21.

27. One important source on this point is Ruth Benedict's paper "Anthropology and the Abnormal," *Journal of General Psychology* 10 (1934): 59–82. See also Benedict's *Patterns of Culture* (Boston: Houghton Mifflin, 1934), 257–60.

28. The attack began as early as 1861, when Edward Jarvis showed that in rural Massachusetts mental disorder was just as common as in urban areas but was less visible. Edward Jarvis, *Insanity and Idiocy in Massachusetts* (Cambridge: Harvard University Press, 1971; originally published 1855). More recently, see Srole, "The Midtown Manhattan Study."

29. Peel, *Ijeshas and Nigerians*, 31.

30. See J. F. A. Ajayi and Robert Smith, *Yoruba Warfare in the Nineteenth Century* (Cambridge: Cambridge University Press, 1964). John Iliffe points out that the wars were a major cause of unemployment and conjunctural poverty; see his *The African Poor: A History* (Cambridge: Cambridge University Press, 1987), 85.

31. Clapperton wrote: "His madness took a very unhappy turn. In the midst

of a paroxysm, he would constantly shout that he should go to hell, for having put so many good mussulmen to death." Hugh Clapperton, *Journal of a Second Expedition Into the Interior of Africa from the Bight of Benin to Soccotoo* (London: John Murray, 1966; originally published 1820), 206.

32. Alexander Boroffka, "The History of Mental Hospitals in Nigeria," in Yaba Mental Hospital, *From Asylum to Hospital* (Lagos: Gabumo, 1987), 15. See also Alexander Boroffka, "Mental Illness in Lagos," *Psychopathologie africaine* 9 (1973): 407.

33. This theme is developed in J. D. Y. Peel, "The Pastor and the *Babalawo:* The Interaction of Religions in Nineteenth-Century Yorubaland," *Africa* 60 (1990): 338–69.

34. See, for example, Terence Ranger, "Godly Medicine: The Ambiguities of Medical Mission in Southeastern Tanzania," in *The Social Basis of Health and Healing in Africa,* eds. John Janzen and Steven Feierman (Berkeley: University of California Press, 1992). Vivien Ng reports that Catholic missionaries in eighteenth-century China made vigorous attempts to convince "pagans" that Christianity had special curative powers against madness. Vivien Ng, *Madness in Late Imperial China* (Norman: University of Oklahoma Press, 1990), ch. 2. The CMS efforts in Nigeria seem to have been less pro-active in comparison.

35. CMS CA/061/56.

36. CMS G3/A2/0/1881, 100. In his history of the Yoruba, Johnson also described "human sacrifices" among the Ijebu. Such a man would be "acted upon in some way or other unknown (by magic arts) that he always became demented, and left to wander about sheepishly in the Aha forest, until he perished there." Samuel Johnson, *The History of the Yorubas* (Norfolk: Lowe & Brydone, 1976; originally published 1921), 19.

37. CMS G3/A2/0/1880/130. See also CMS CA2/025/3.

38. CMS G3/A2/0/1880/130.

39. CMS CA2/019/15

40. CMS G3/A2/0/1893/132.

41. Peel, "The Pastor and the *Babalawo.*"

42. CMS G3/A2/0/1893/132.

43. CMS G3/A2/0/1892/38, emphasis added. Note that being clothed is a key element of Jonah's return to sanity.

44. CMS CA2/066, 95.

45. CMS CA2/066, 95. Peel claims that *the missionaries regarded ifá priests* with more respect as both interlocutors and competitors than other religious authorities. The latter they referred to derisively as "fetish priests." Peel, "The Pastor and the *Babalawo.*"

46. CMS CA2/066, 104.

47. Lagos *Weekly Record,* October 31, 1891. For a discussion of the *Weekly Record* and its milieu, see Fred Omu, *Press and Politics in Nigeria, 1880–1937* (Atlantic Highlands, NJ: Humanities Press, 1978), 33–36.

48. Lagos *Weekly Record,* May 4, 1895, emphasis in original.

49. Ibid.

50. Ibid., February 3, 1900.

51. Ibid., April 6, 1907.

52. Lagos *Weekly Times,* May 10, 1890.

53. Lagos *Times,* September 12, 1883.

54. Lagos *Weekly Record,* April 22, 1905.

55. Nigerian National Archives, Ibadan [hereafter NAI], *Special List of Records on the Origins and Development of Nigerian Medical Aid and Sanitary Services 1861–1960,* 100–2. Many of these themes are developed in Adell Patton, Jr., *Physicians, Colonial Racism, and Diaspora in West Africa* (Gainesville: University of Florida Press, 1996).

56. NAI, *Special List,* 100–2.

57. Lagos *Observer,* July 14–21, 1888.

58. Boroffka, "History of Mental Hospitals," 15.

59. See Robert July, *The Origins of Modern African Thought* (New York: Praeger, 1967), ch. 14, for an overview of Johnson's career. For more on Johnson's contributions to health reform, see Spencer H. Brown, "Public Health in Lagos, 1850–1900: Perceptions, Patterns, and Perspectives," *International Journal of African Historical Studies* 25, 2 (1992): 337–60.

60. For a more complete account of the Adeola scandal, see Adelola Adeloye, *African Pioneers of Modern Medicine: Nigerian Doctors of the Nineteenth Century* (Ibadan: University of Ibadan, 1985), 60–72.

61. All female and some male lunatics were housed in the Lagos prison; the reasons for the different treatment are unclear. Lunatics left in Lagos were kept in the prison kitchen and an attached enclosure. Public Record Office, London [hereafter PRO], CO 96 150.

62. Boroffka, "Mental Illness in Lagos," 408.

63. Lagos *Weekly Record,* May 14, 1904.

64. PRO CO 147 70.

65. PRO CO 147 71.

66. Ibid.

67. PRO CO 147 77.

68. See Toyin Falola, *Development Planning and Decolonization in Nigeria* (Gainesville: University Press of Florida, 1996), 9–14.

69. In epidemiology, incidence refers to the rate by which new cases appear over a given period of time, and prevalence to the total number of afflicted as a proportion of the population. See Judith S. Mausner and Shira Kramer, *Epidemiology: An Introductory Text* (Philadelphia: Harcourt Brace Jovanovich, 1985), 44–54, for a good overview.

70. See, for example, Kristin Mann, "The Rise of Taiwo Olowo: Law, Accumulation, and Mobility in Early Colonial Lagos," in *Law in Colonial Africa,* eds. Kristin Mann and Richard Roberts (Portsmouth: Heinemann, 1991), 85–89.

71. See Leland Bell, *Mental and Social Disorder in Sub-Saharan Africa: The Case of Sierra Leone, 1781–1990* (New York: Greenwood Press, 1991). In Sierra Leone, colonial medical observers believed asylums were unnecessary because Africans had low incidence rates for mental illness.

Chapter 3.   Material Conditions and the Politics of Care

1. Forbes Winslow, ed., *An Act for the Regulation of the Care and Treatment of Lunatics* (London: W. Benning, 1845), 1. Winslow may well have exaggerated the depravity of pre-Victorian institutions.

2. Midlefort suggests that asylums were not a European innovation but were developed by Arab societies and imported to Christian Europe by way of Spain. Erik C. Midlefort, "Madness and Civilization in Early Modern Europe: A Reappraisal of Michel Foucault," in *After the Reformation: Essays in Honor of J. H. Hexter,* ed. Barbara Malament (Philadelphia: University of Pennsylvania Press, 1980).

3. Michel Foucault, *Madness and Civilization,* trans. Richard Howard (New York: Vintage Books, 1965; originally published 1961).

4. Midlefort, "Madness and Civilization in Early Modern Europe." Foucault's "Gallocentrism" is also stressed in a number of the articles in German Berrios and Hugh Freeman, eds., *150 Years of British Psychiatry, 1842–1991* (London: Gaskell, 1991).

5. Roy Porter, *Mind Forg'd Manacles: A History of Madness in England from the Restoration to the Regency* (London: Penguin, 1987), 2.

6. See Waltraud Ernst, "The European Insane in British India 1800–1858," in *Imperial Medicine and Indigenous Societies,* ed. David Arnold (Manchester: Manchester University Press, 1988); and Waltraud Ernst, *Mad Tales from the Raj: The European Insane in British India* (London: Routledge, 1991).

7. John Iliffe, *The African Poor: A History* (Cambridge: Cambridge University Press, 1987), 100; Harriet Jane Deacon, "Madness, Race and Moral Treatment: Robben Island Lunatic Asylum, Cape Colony, 1846–1890," *History of Psychiatry* 7 (1996): 287–97. Institutions would also later be used in Nyasaland and Kenya. On Nyasaland, see Megan Vaughan, "Idioms of Madness: Zomba Lunatic Asylum, Nyasaland, in the Colonial Period," *Journal of Southern African Studies* 9, 2 (1983): 218–38.

8. Bruce F. Home, "Insanity in Nigeria," Manuscript, Lagos, 1928, 10.

9. Government of Southern Nigeria, *Government Gazette,* November 7, 1906. With the amalgamation of Nigeria in 1916, a colony-wide ordinance was enacted with much the same language.

10. The number of people confined in colonial asylums was always much smaller than the number in prisons; for example, in 1935 the prison population totaled 33,005, down from 38,259 the previous year. Several studies do exist of the police and of the judicial and penal systems, e.g., Omoniyi Adewoye, *The Judicial System in Southern Nigeria, 1854–1954* (Atlantic Highlands, NJ: Humanities Press, 1977), and Philip Terdoo Ahire, *Imperial Policing: The Emergence and Role of the Police in Colonial Nigeria* (Philadelphia: Open University Press, 1991), but little work has been done on the prisons themselves. Some attention is paid to prisons in Toyin Falola, *Politics and Economy in Ibadan, 1893–1945* (Lagos: Modelor, 1989), 41, 48, 120, 190. Also see Elisabeth Isichei, *A History of West Africa Since 1800* (London: MacMillan, 1977), 228.

11. In the Gold Coast, in fact, lunatics were generally placed in prisons until the 1940s. Robert Cunyngham Brown, *Report III on the Care and Treatment*

of the Mentally Ill in British West African Colonies (London: Garden City Press, 1938).

12. Alexander Boroffka, "The History of Mental Hospitals in Nigeria," *Psychiatry* 8 (1985): 15.

13. NAI CSO N1210/1916. These were cells that had previously housed European convicts.

14. Tolani Asuni, "Aro Hospital in Perspective," *American Journal of Psychiatry* 124, 6 (December 1967): 763–70.

15. In 1936, Brown wrote that the Yaba Asylum was "becoming increasingly surrounded by new buildings in this rapidly developing area." Brown, *Report III*, 52.

16. For more on Adeniyi-Jones, see Adell Patton, Jr., *Physicians, Colonial Racism, and Diaspora in West Africa* (Gainesville: University of Florida Press, 1996), 192–93.

17. Yaba Lunatic Asylum, Monthly Report for November 1907, from personal collection of Dr. Alexander Boroffka.

18. Alexander Boroffka, "Mental Illness in Lagos," *Psychopathologie africaine* 9 (1973): 408.

19. Adeniyi-Jones's letters are available at the Contemporary Medical Archives Centre, Wellcome Institute for the History of Medicine, GC/146/1.

20. Alexander Boroffka, "A History of Psychiatry in Nigeria," Paper presented to the World Psychiatric Congress, Vienna, 1983, 2.

21. NAI CSO N.3605/1915.

22. Important studies of the perception, and reality, of European ill health in tropical colonies include Philip Curtin, *Death by Migration: Europe's Encounter with the Tropical World in the Nineteenth Century* (Cambridge: Cambridge University Press, 1991); Warwick Anderson, "Disease, Race and Empire" *Bulletin of the History of Medicine* 70, 1 (Spring 1996): 62–67; Mark Harrison, "'The Tender Frame of Man': Disease Climate, and Racial Difference in India and the West Indies, 1760–1860," *Bulletin of the History of Medicine* 70, 1 (Spring 1996): 68–93; and Warwick Anderson, "Immunities of Empire: Race, Disease, and the New Tropical Medicine, 1900–1920," *Bulletin of the History of Medicine* 70, 1 (Spring 1996): 94–118.

23. This was in contradistinction to organic mental diseases.

24. NAI Oyo Prof. 2/3 C69, "Incidence of Functional Nervous Diseases Amongst European Officials," 2.

25. Ibid. Helen Callaway has shown how, especially in the later colonial period, the presence of officers' wives was thought desirable, though the notion of Nigeria as a "man's country" endured. See especially p. 19: "The presence of wives was . . . justified as *instrumental* to the better health of men." Helen Callaway, *Gender, Culture, and Empire: European Women in Colonial Nigeria* (Urbana: University of Illinois Press, 1987), emphasis in original.

26. NAI Oyo Prof. 2/3 C69, "Incidence of Functional Nervous Diseases Amongst European Officials," 2.

27. NAI Comcol 1 735 Vol. I, "Lunatic Asylum," 2. For some anecdotal data on individual European lunatics, see NAI CSO. 1. 32. 69, and NAI Comcol 1 51/S.40.

28. Home, "Insanity," 5.

29. NAI New File MH (Fed) 1/1 3313, 69–70.

30. NAI New File MH (Fed) 1/1 3313, "Lunatics, Care of," 31, inspection notes by J. G. C. Allen, Senior Resident, July 18, 1955. See also MH (Fed) 1/2 MH 59 Vol. II, 54.

31. Brown, *Report III*, 40.

32. See, for example, NAI CSO 26 26793, "Abeokuta Mental Hospital," Vol. I, 7.

33. NAI Oyo Prof. 1 4113, "Crime and Its Treatment," a report by Alexander Paterson, 14. The Director of Medical and Sanitary Services expressed willingness to substitute restraint jackets for chains in the early 1940s, but chains were still in use a decade later. See also NAI New File MH (Fed) 1/1 3313, "Lunatics: Care of," 4.

34. NAI Oyo Prof. 1 4113, "Crime and Its Treatment," 4.

35. Home, "Insanity," 6.

36. Brown, *Report III*, 62.

37. J C. Carothers, "On the Psychiatric Services of Nigeria," Manuscript, 1955, 4.

38. NAI MH (Fed) 1/1 3420, 95, Chief Medical Adviser F. O. Campbell to Director of Public Works, June 11, 1956.

39. PRO CO 657 20, 419. In 1936, Brown also reported that the physical health of inmates was "quite satisfactory," even finding that the asylum patients in the south were generally more robust than their counterparts in the small Native Administration asylums in the north; see Brown, *Report III*, 28, 35.

40. PRO CO 657 24, 466–67.

41. NAI MH (Fed) 1/1 3420, "Lunatic Asylum, Yaba," 3–5.

42. NAI CSO 01507/ S.2, "Yaba Asylum," 11–13.

43. PRO CO 657 24, 467; PRO CO 657 69, 27. Traditional healers in the region also sometimes employed patients in farm work, but this was more typically as payment *after* treatment, not for any possible curative effect.

44. According to Asuni, the only medications dispensed in Yaba's early days were paraldehyde and potassium bromide. Asuni, "Aro Hospital in Perspective."

45. Home, "Insanity," appendix, 2.

46. Ibid., 3.

47. See, for example, PRO CO 657 47, 231.

48. Kathleen Jones, "The Culture of the Mental Hospital," in *150 Years of British Psychiatry, 1842–1991*, eds. German Berrios and Hugh Freeman (London: Gaskell, 1991), 23–24.

49. Toyin Falola, *Development Planning and Decolonization in Nigeria* (Gainesville: University Press of Florida, 1996), 17–23.

50. NAI CSO 26 1507/S.1/T.1

51. Ibid.

52. Ibid.

53. NAI CSO 01507, Vol. IV, 412c.

54. Anne Phillips, *The Enigma of Colonialism: British Policy in West Africa* (London: James Currey, 1989), 3. It may not yet go without saying that this "African way of life" was frequently imagined and constructed according to colonial convenience.

55. The political organizations of Indirect Rule did not so much "preserve" existing forms as transform them and even substantially create them in many places. This is a very well documented aspect of colonial history, but for one treatment, see Martin Chanock, "Making Customary Law: Men, Women, and Courts in Colonial Northern Rhodesia," in *African Women and the Law: Historical Perspectives,* eds. Margaret Jean Hay and Marcia Wright (Boston: African Studies Center, 1982).

56. My discussion here draws on James Coleman, *Nigeria: Background to Nationalism* (Berkeley: University of California Press, 1968), 53.

57. Bill Freund, *The Making of Contemporary Africa* (London: MacMillan, 1984), 79.

58. NAI Ondo Prof. 1/1 662, "Lunatics: Matters Arising," 52.

59. G. St. J. Orde Browne, "Witchcraft and British Colonial Law," *Africa* 8, 4 (October 1935): 483.

60. See T. O. Beidelman, "Towards More Open Theoretical Interpretations," in *Witchcraft Accusations and Confessions,* ed. Mary Douglas (London: Tavistock, 1970).

61. NAI Oyo Prof. 1150, "Witchcraft or Juju Cases, Trial of by Native Courts Forbidden Except in Minor Cases," 14.

62. See, for example, J. C. Carothers, "Frontal Lobe Function and the African," *Journal of Mental Science* 97, 406 (January 1951): 13.

63. E. E. Evans Pritchard, *Witchcraft, Oracles and Magic Among the Azande,* abridged ed. (Oxford: Clarendon, 1976; originally published 1937), 27, emphasis added, see also p. 24. The catalogue of the Southern Provinces Anthropological Library can be found at NAI Oyo Prof. 1 4225, "Anthropology—All Matters Relating To."

64. NAI Oyo Prof. 1150, Witchcraft or Juju Cases, Trial of by Native Courts Forbidden Except in Minor Cases," 41.

65. Anthony Appiah, "Madmen and Specialists," *London Review of Books* 17, 17 (September 7, 1995): 16–17.

66. NAI CSO 26 41987/ S.2, "Studies in Mental Illness in the Gold Coast," 16.

67. NAI Comcol 1 735 Vol. I, "Lunatic Asylum," 130.

68. Brown, *Report III,* 60.

69. NAI CSO 26 01507, Vol. IV, 496.

70. NAI CSO 52898, "Mental Hospital (Aro Site) Abeokuta," 5 19.

71. Several thousand Nigerian soldiers, most of them from the south of the colony, served with Allied forces in the Second World War. The majority served in Burma, some in the Middle East, and a small number in the European theater. See also PRO 657/56, 934. Wars have frequently provided stimulus for reform of psychiatric practice; see, for example, Elaine Showalter, *The Female Malady* (New York: Viking, 1985), ch. 7.

72. NAI Oyo Prof. 2/3 C.311, "Resettlement of Ex-Soldiers After the War."

73. Geoffrey Tooth, a psychiatrist working in the Gold Coast, noted that in Accra, an "unduly large" proportion of lunatic asylum admissions in the postwar period were ex-soldiers. NAI MH (Fed) 1/1 2nd Accession 5280B, "Research in Mental Illness and Juvenile Delinquency," A1. See also NAI Oyo Prof. 2/3 C.311, "Resettlement of Ex-soldiers After the War," Vol. I, 90.

74. J. C. Carothers, *The African Mind in Health and Disease* (Geneva: World Health Organization, 1953), 138.

75. See, for example, NAI Comcol 1 735/ S. 1, Vol. I, "Lunatics: General Matters Affecting," 73, and NAI Comcol 1 735/ S, Vol. III, "Discharge and Release on Trial of Lunatics," 481–82.

76. NAI Oyo Prof. 1. 2188, "Unification and Staffing of the Colonial Prisons Service, Ibadan Native Authority System," 9. "Lunatic soldiers" were transferred to Lantoro from Yaba; see NAI MH (Fed) 1/1 3420, 23.

77. NAI CSO 52898/S. 1, "Lantoro Lunatic Asylum (Abeokuta)," 1.

78. Asuni, "Aro Hospital in Perspective," 769.

79. Tolani Asuni, "Development in Mental Health Care in Africa with Special Reference to Western Nigeria," *Proceedings of the IV World Congress of Psychiatry,* Madrid, September 1966, 1067–68.

80. Asuni, "Aro Hospital in Perspective," 769.

81. Boroffka, "History of Psychiatry in Nigeria," 3.

82. See Showalter, *The Female Malady,* 2–3.

83. Aro Mental Hospital, *40th Anniversary of the Establishment of Aro Neuro-Psychiatric Hospital Complex* (Ibadan: Sketch Press, 1984), 9.

84. Asuni, "Aro Hospital in Perspective."

85. According to Boroffka, "Two psychiatrists were working with him for one year each (Cameron 1955 and Campbell Young 1958) but did not contribute much to this task, lacking Mr. Ordia's optimism and zest." Boroffka, "History of Psychiatry in Nigeria," 5.

86. Interview, A. A. Marinho, Lagos, November 20, 1990.

87. Interview, Tolani Asuni, Lagos, March 13, 1990.

88. Ibid.

89. Freud himself was skeptical about the utility of psychoanalysis for psychotic patients, as opposed to neurotics.

90. The career trajectories of Lambo and Asuni, in particular, show some interesting similarities to Sigmund Freud's. Freud's early interests were humanistic, leaning to philosophy, literature, and art history, and his first career plan was law school. Freud chose medicine instead after concluding that it would provide a relatively secure route for an ambitious young man. After he completed his medical training, psychiatry provided Freud with a bridge back to the humanities, most clearly reflected in his attempts to apply theory based on clinical observations to metahistorical cultural speculations. Lambo and Asuni also recall choosing medicine for practical reasons and finding psychiatry a link to broader humanistic concerns. In naming a model for his interests, Lambo, who is very well versed in medical history, named not a psychiatrist or a doctor but the anthropologist Margaret Mead, with whom he was well acquainted. Interview, T. A. Lambo, Lagos, April 7, 1990. In the interview, I did not actively solicit a model; Lambo offered it without prompting.

91. J. F. A. Ajayi, *Christian Missions in Nigeria 1841–1891: The Making of a New Elite* (Essex, UK: Longman, 1965), 272. See also Elizabeth Isichei, *A History of Nigeria* (London: Longman, 1983), 340. Asuni in fact lacked sufficient funds for medical school when he left Nigeria and claimed he was going to study engineering.

92. See T. A. Lambo, "Patterns of Psychiatric Care in Developing African

Countries: The Nigerian Village Program," in *International Trends in Mental Health,* ed. Henry David (New York: McGraw Hill, 1966), 149.

93. Aro Mental Hospital, *40th Anniversary,* 11.

94. Ben Park, *The Healers of Aro,* 16 mm. film (New York: United Nations, 1960).

95. Alexander Leighton, et al., *Psychiatric Disorder Among the Yoruba* (Ithaca: Cornell University Press, 1963), 2.

96. Asuni, "Aro Hospital in Perspective," 765. Insulin therapy was abandoned early on, being considered risky and no more efficacious than other treatments.

97. Park, "The Healers of Aro."

98. See Leighton et al., *Psychiatric Disorder,* 2.

99. Cited in Asuni, "Aro Hospital in Perspective," 765.

100. Tolani Asuni, "Community Development and Public Health: By-Product of Social Psychiatry in Nigeria," *West African Medical Journal* 13, 4 (1964). One disadvantage of the village plan was that it excluded some urban patients because doctors thought it was inappropriate to make them work on farms. They were treated as in-patients at the hospital as space allowed.

101. Interview, Tolani Asuni, March 26, 1990.

102. Senior Medical Officer E. N. O. Sodeinde documented a visit to the residence of Abudu Onileyan Olori, a healer on Afiko Street in Lagos. NAI MH (Fed) 1/2 195 S.1, "Private Asylums: Closure Of." The government warned Olori to register in the future; Olori replied: "I don't know that I ought to take permission before I treat people."

103. NAI MH (Fed) MH 59 1/2 S. 4, "Lunacy: Repatriation of Lunatics to Nigeria." These included six lunatics who would need to be certified locally before they could be admitted to a Nigerian asylum; their admission would be avoided if kin could be located.

104. For one critique of celebratory nationalist historiography, see Caroline Neale, *Writing "Independent" History: African Historiography, 1960–1980* (Westport, CT: Greenwood Press, 1985). See also Freund, *The Making of Contemporary Africa,* introduction.

105. Crawford Young, *The African Colonial State in Comparative Perspective* (New Haven: Yale University Press, 1994), 242.

106. William Ll. Parry-Jones, "The Model of the Geel Lunatic Colony and Its Influence on the Nineteenth-Century Asylum System in Britain," in *Madhouses, Mad-Doctors, and Madmen: The Social History of Psychiatry in the Victorian Era,* ed. Andrew Scull (Philadelphia: University of Pennsylvania Press, 1981).

107. See Patricia Allridge, "The Foundation of Maudsley Hospital," in *150 Years of British Psychiatry, 1842–1991,* eds. German Berrios and Hugh Freeman (London: Gaskell, 1991). See also Douglas Bennett, "The Drive Towards the Community" in the same volume.

108. New York *Herald Tribune,* December 27, 1942. See the Alan Mason Chesney Medical Archives, The Johns Hopkins University, biographical file on Alexander Leighton.

109. See Ann Braden Johnson, *Out of Bedlam: The Truth About De-institutionalization* (Boston: Basic Books, 1990).

110. For a scathing indictment of de-institutionalization, published before

such critiques became common, see Andrew Scull, *Decarceration: Community Treatment and the Deviant: A Radical View* (Englewood Cliffs, NJ: Prentice Hall, 1977).

111. From the 1970s onward, other areas near the hospital have taken part in the housing of patients.

112. In 1932, for example, the number in prison was 89, up from 75 the previous year. PRO CO 657 34.

Chapter 4.   "Proper Subjects for Confinement"

1. "Contribution by the Patients," in Yaba Mental Hospital, *From Asylum to Hospital* (Lagos: Gabumo, 1987), 26.

2. For one discussion, see Ronald Bayer, *Homosexuality and American Psychiatry* (Princeton: Princeton University Press, 1987), 184–85.

3. Anonymous, "Who Is a Madman," in Yaba Mental Hospital, *From Asylum to Hospital.*

4. Lorna Amarasingam Rhodes, "The Subject of Power in Medical/Psychiatric Anthropology," in *Ethnopsychiatry: The Cultural Construction of Professional and Folk Psychiatries,* ed. Atwood Gaines (Albany: State University of New York Press, 1992). 52.

5. I am also drawing here on Joan Scott's directive to unpack the very categories through which "experience" is formed. See Joan Scott, "The Evidence of Experience," in *Questions of Evidence: Proof, Practice, and Persuasion Across the Disciplines,* eds. James Chandler, Arnold I. Davidson, and Harry Harootunian (Chicago: University of Chicago Press, 1994).

6. *Irapada* is Yoruba for "redemption."

7. Unnumbered Aro Case File. In the interests of protecting the privacy of patients and their families, I will not be using patients' surnames; I will thus use first names or initials; no disrespect is intended.

8. Ann Braden Johnson, *Out of Bedlam: The Truth About De-institutionalization* (Boston: Basic Books, 1990), 112.

9. I am influenced here by Janis Hunter Jenkins, "Emotion and Mental Disorder," in *Handbook of Psychological Anthropology,* ed. Philip K. Bock (Westport, CT: Greenwood Press, 1994). See especially Jenkins's discussion of Harry Stack Sullivan, pp. 104–6.

10. See, for example, Thomas Szasz, *The Myth of Mental Illness: Foundations of a Theory of Personal Conduct* (New York: Hoeber-Harper, 1961).

11. Robert Cunyngham Brown, *Report III on the Care and Treatment of the Mentally Ill in British West African Colonies* (London: Garden City Press, 1938), 15.

12. Alexander Leighton et al., *Psychiatric Disorder Among the Yoruba* (Ithaca: Cornell University Press, 1963), 139.

13. For an idea of how small the proportion of wage earners was in 1936, see Michael Crowder, *Colonial West Africa* (London: Frank Cass, 1978), 123. Wage laborers were, of course, more significant in Lagos. See Arnold Hughes and Robin Cohen, "An Emerging Nigerian Working Class," in *African Labor His-*

tory, eds. Peter C. W. Gutkind, Robin Cohen, and Jean Copans (Beverly Hills: Sage, 1978).

14. Margaret Field, *Search for Security: An Ethnopsychiatric Study of Rural Ghana* (London: Faber & Faber, 1960).

15. On this point, Phyllis Chesler's *Women and Madness* (New York: Avon, 1973) has the ambiguous status of a much-criticized classic. I refer frequently to Showalter's *The Female Malady,* which handles the political questions involved in psychiatric history especially adroitly, but note that Waltraud Ernst has questioned whether Showalter's focus on the gendered identities in the construction of insanity in Europe is warranted in "European Madness and Gender in Nineteenth-century British India," *Social History of Medicine* 9, 3 (1996): 357–82. Leland Bell, *Mental and Social Disorder in Sub-Saharan Africa: The Case of Sierra Leone, 1781–1990* (New York: Greenwood Press, 1991).

16. See Susan Nolan-Hoeksema, *Sex Differences in Depression* (Stanford: Stanford University Press, 1990), for a strong overview of the problem from within the field of psychology. Dorothy Smith, *The Conceptual Practices of Power: A Feminist Sociology of Knowledge* (Boston: Northeastern University Press, 1990), ch. 5, is a useful, but not entirely convincing, critique of the processes by which the epidemiological data are formed. Smith relies on labeling theory but ignores the critiques that have been made of it.

17. More research on the colonial articulation of gender, and the consequent transformations in gender identity and experience in Nigeria, is badly needed. For one useful treatment see Lisa Lindsay, "Shunting Between Manly Ideals: Nigerian Railway Men, 1935–65," Paper presented at the Thirty-Eighth Annual Meeting of the African Studies Association, Orlando, Florida, November 3–6, 1995, ASA 1995: 72.

18. Raymond Prince, "Indigenous Yoruba Psychiatry," in *Magic, Faith, and Healing,* ed. Ari Kiev (New York: Free Press of Glencoe, 1964); Henry John Drewal and Margaret Drewal, *Gelede: Art and Female Power Among the Yoruba* (Bloomington: Indiana University Press, 1983).

19. NAI Oyo Prof. 1015, "Lunatics, Oyo Province," Vol. II, 147. Pottinger thus claimed a "secondary gain" which inhibited recovery. As for the regularity of food, there was at least one recorded case of a patient starving to death while under detention; Elizabeth A. was confined in Osogbo prison, due to lack of asylum space, and died in May 1956, due to "chronic starvation, self-neglect, and cardiac failure." Her starvation may have been a form of protest, but this can only be speculated. NAI Oshun Div. 1/1 86/13, 15.

20. NAI Oyo Prof. 1 1015, "Lunatics, Oyo Province," Vol. II, 144–46.

21. Starting in the 1970s a number of important studies have stressed the importance of the complex social processes by which patients and their families determine their therapeutic options in pluralistic medical settings. Landmark treatments include John Janzen, *The Quest for Therapy in Lower Zaire* (Berkeley: University of California Press, 1978); Steven Feierman, "Struggles for Control: The Social Roots of Health and Healing in Modern Africa," *African Studies Review* 28, 2–3 (1985): 73–147; and Leith Mullings, *Therapy, Ideology, and Social Change: Mental Healing in Urban Ghana* (Berkeley: University of California Press, 1984).

22. I compiled these numbers based on letters I found in the NAI Comcol 1 735/S. 1, Vols. I–III. While it is likely that many letters have not survived, I do not see signs that a systematic bias was built into the ones that remain.

23. By the 1950s, the system had become more formalized, requiring the relative to sign a certificate taking responsibility for the patient. See NAI Comcol 1 735/S.1, Vol. I, "Lunatics: General Matters Affecting," 355, for a sample certificate.

24. See NAI Comcol 1 735/S. 1 Vol. I, "Lunatics, General Matters Affecting," 406.

25. Ulli Beier, *Luckless Heads: Paintings by Deranged Nigerians* (Bremen: CON Medien-und Vertriebsgesellschaft, 1982). 84.

26. NAI Ije Prof 1 655, "Lunatics in Ijebu Province," Vol. I, 72–73. The Acting Resident for Ijebu Province wrote to the provincial office, Ijebu-Ode, that if Debule could indeed be cured, he would be released.

27. The letter may also show a canny awareness of the organic bias of British psychiatric thinking at that time—that is, Debule was not a madman because the source of his trouble was preternatural, and therefore not organic. Or, the petitioners may have been alert to the unwillingness of many in the government to get involved with witchcraft cases.

28. See NAI Comcol 1. 735/S.1, "Lunatics: General Matters Affecting," Vol. I, 18–20.

29. Ibid., 131.

30. Ibid., 139. The allusion to mermaids most likely refers to the "Mami Wata" female water spirits that are worshipped in many parts of West Africa. See Henry John Drewal, "Interpretation, Invention, and Re-presentation in the Worship of Mami Wata," *Journal of Folklore Research* 25, 1–2 (1988): 101–39, for one account.

31. NAI Comcol 735/ S. 1, "Lunatics: General Matters Affecting," Vol. II, 615–27.

32. A classic source on this point is D. L. Rosenhan, "On Being Sane in Insane Places," *Science* 179, 70 (January 1973): 250–58. The methods and some of the findings of this study have been controversial, but the point that it can be difficult to be "unlabelled" mentally ill has received support, as in Bruce G. Link, et al, "A Modified Labeling Theory Approach to Mental Disorders: An Empirical Assessment," *American Sociological Review* 54 (June 1989): 400–23.

33. NAI Ekiti Div. 1/1 56, Vol. I, "The Lunacy Ordinance, Cap. 51," 121.

34. Ibid., 122–23.

35. "Onishan" is the title of the traditional ruler of Ishan.

36. NAI Ekiti Div. 1/1 56, Vol. I, 125. The Onishan's letter was backed by another letter from the District Officer.

37. Aro Case File [number illegible], 1948.

38. Escapees raised a question of responsibility. After the escape of one patient from Lantoro in late 1955, A. N. Cohen, Acting Permanent Secretary for the Ministry of Public Health, noted that the escape was reported to the Superintendent of Lantoro Asylum and to the Superintendent of Police, Akure, both of whom claimed he was the other's responsibility. The next month, the Ministry of Home Affairs declared that escapees were the responsibility of the police. NAI Ondo Prof. 1/1 662, "Lunatics: Matters Arising," 282, 230.

39. The basis of the prostitution charge is unclear. NAI Comcol 197/63, 10–11.

40. NAI Comcol 197/63.

41. NAI CSO 26 52898/ S.1, "Lantoro Lunatic Asylum (Abeokuta)," 29. Carothers also observed that many Nigerian mental patients in the 1950s were strangers to the areas in which they were confined; see J. C. Carothers, "On the Psychiatric Services of Nigeria," Manuscript, 1955, 37.

42. NAI Ije Prof. 1 655, "Lunatics in Ijebu Province," Vol. I, 80.

43. There were attempts to confine lunatics in their region of origin, on the grounds that it would be easier to provide them with the food to which they were accustomed, and that this would facilitate remission. See NAI Comcol 1 735 Vol. I, "Lunatic Asylum," 24.

44. NAI Comcol 1 2366/3.

45. NAI CSO 22097, "Criminal Lunatics," Vol. I, 47.

46. NAI Ekiti Div. 1/1 56, Vol. I, "The Lunacy Ordinance, Cap. 51."

47. NAI Ondo Prof 1/1 662, "Lunatics: Matters Arising," 52.

48. Ibid., 55.

49. A 1950 letter requesting someone's incarceration came from a compound in Ibadan with 57 signatures and several thumb prints. The man, the petitioners complained, wielded cutlasses against pedestrians. NAI Oyo Prof. 1 1015, Vol. II, "Lunatics—Oyo Province," 129. For another example, see NAI Oshun Div. 1/1 86/10, 1.

50. See, for example, NAI MH (Fed) 1/1 13522, "Lepers and Lunatics—Petitions for Admission into the Asylums."

51. NAI Comcol 735/S.1, Vol. II, "Lunatics: General Matters Affecting," 463.

52. NAI MH (Fed) 1/1 135/22, "Lepers and Lunatics—Petitions for Admission into the Asylums," 23.

53. T. A. Lambo, "The Role of Cultural Factors in Paranoid Psychoses Among the Yoruba Tribe of Nigeria," *Journal of Mental Science* 101, 423 (April 1955): 247.

54. For one introduction to this literature, see Peter O. Ebigbo, "The Nigerian Worker and Somatisation," in Pita N. O. Ejiofor and Vincent A. Aniagoh, *Managing the Nigerian Worker* (Ikeja: Longman, 1984). Ebigbo found that in all the subjects of his study, psychiatric problems were somatised to some degree.

55. Olufemi Morakinyo, "Phobic States Presenting as Somatic Complaints Syndromes in Nigeria: Socio-cultural Factors Associated with Diagnosis and Psychotherapy," *Acta Psychiatrica Scandinavia* 71, 4 (April 1985): 356–65.

56. Raymond Prince, "The Concept of Culture-Bound Syndromes: Anorexia Nervosa and Brain-Fag," *Social Science and Medicine* 21, 2 (1985): 202.

57. See the discussion in Arthur Kleinman, *The Illness Narratives: Suffering, Healing, and the Human Condition* (New York: Harper Collins, 1988), 57–60. Oyeronke Oyewume has recently called attention to Western "somatocentrism," a tendency based on the epistemological privileging of vision. Oyeronke Oyewume, *The Invention of Women: Making an African Sense of Western Gender Discourses* (Minneapolis: University of Minnesota Press, 1997), 2–3.

58. Largactil, a sedative used to treat mania and schizophrenia, was one of the main medications used in the new mental hospitals in Nigeria, along with

insulin. It had been used in continental European hospitals since the early 1950s, and was undergoing trials in Britain at this time. See A. A. Baker, "Observations on the Effect of Largactil in Psychiatric Illness," *Journal of Mental Science* 101, 422 (April 1955): 175–82.

59. Aro Case File Pt. Opd. 68, 1955.

60. Prince, "Indigenous Yoruba Psychiatry," 87.

61. Aro Case File Pt. Opd. 102, 1956.

62. Aro Case File 337.

63. Kleinman, *Illness Narratives,* 195.

64. Thomas J. Csordas, "The Affliction of Martin: Religious, Clinical, and Phenomenological Meaning in a Case of Demonic Oppression," in *Ethnopsychiatry: The Cultural Construction of Professional and Folk Psychiatries,* ed. Atwood Gaines (Albany: State University of New York Press, 1992).

65. Tolani Asuni, "Socio-Medical Problems of Religious Converts," *Psychopathologie africaine* 9, 2 (1973): 229.

66. E. Bolaji Idowu, Olodumare: God in Yoruba Belief (Singapore: Longman, 1962), 169; Olufemi Morakinyo and Akinsola Akiwowo, "The Yoruba Ontology of Personality and Motivation: A Multidisciplinary Approach," Journal of Social and Biological Structures 4 (1981): 19–38. See also Segun Gbadegesin, African *Philosophy: Traditional Yoruba Philosophy and Contemporary African Realities* (New York: Peter Lang, 1991), 33. Gbadegesin sees ẹ̀mí as that which activates the lifeless body—but distinguished from eémí (breath), which is physically identifiable.

67. Asuni, "Socio-Medical Problems of Religious Converts," 227.

68. Aro Case File 123, 1959.

69. This phrase is inspired by Jenkins's concept of the "state construction of affect" in the anthropology of emotions. See Janis Hunter Jenkins, "The State Construction of Affect: Political Ethos and Mental Health Among Salvadoran Refugees," *Culture, Medicine, and Psychiatry* 15 (1991): 139–65.

70. NAI CSO 19/9 N.290 (1921).

71. Prince relates an instance of a Nigerian healer traveling to England to treat a patient at about the same time, but does not provide a citation. It seems likely that it is the same incident. Raymond Prince, "The Use of Rauwolfia by Nigerian Native Doctors," *American Journal of Psychiatry* 118 (1960): 148.

72. NAI Ije Prof. 1 655, "Lunatics in Ijebu Province," 225.

73. NAI CSO 19/9 N.290 (1921).

74. Compare, for example, a letter from the Acting Governor from the Balogun of Ibadan, regarding a conflict between Ibadan and Abeokuta: "You are not on the same footing as the Egba. . . . The English government is the father of the Egbas and of the Ibadans." In a conciliatory speech, the Balogun said contritely, "You are our father, and we are your children." Quoted in Toyin Falola, *Politics and Economy in Ibadan, 1893–1945* (Lagos: Modelor, 1989), 60–61.

75. Ian Nicolson, *The Administration of Nigeria, 1900–1960* (Oxford: Clarendon Press, 1969), 182.

76. Shula Marks, *The Ambiguities of Dependence in South Africa* (Johannesburg: Ravan, 1986).

77. Roy Porter, *Mind Forg'd Manacles: A History of Madness in England*

from the Restoration to the Regency (London: Penguin, 1987), 235.

78. J. C. Carothers, "Frontal Lobe Function and the African," *Journal of Mental Science* 97, 406 (January 1951): 12–48.

79. They also seem to have been a common theme in mid-century British psychiatry, due in part to the influence of Melanie Klein. See Phyllis Grosskurth, *Melanie Klein: Her World and Her Work* (Cambridge: Harvard University Press, 1986), 102–17.

80. NAI Comcol I 51/ S. 43, "(Mental Patient): Repatriation of." For another example of this kind, see NAI CSO 19/4 N. 1104 (1916) "Accused Lunatic."

81. NAI Ekiti Div. 1/1 56/1, "Lunatic Rufus A., Arrest of," 20. "Oloye" is the title of the traditional ruler of Oye.

82. Ibid., 2.

83. Ibid., 13. Oswald John Vanderpuye, the physician who wrote the certificate, added: "He is not at present violent, neither does he at present sing and dance." Note also that Rufus saw snakes in his cell. Isaac O., the subject of the following chapter, also had this experience. The apparent commonness of this hallucination in mental patients—cross-culturally—invites more investigation.

84. Aro Case File NA/31591.

85. Kwame Anthony Appiah, *In My Father's House: Africa in the Philosophy of Culture* (New York: Oxford University Press, 1992), 7.

86. Comparative data also encourage this consideration. In the United States, black men tend disproportionately to be labeled paranoid upon entry to a mental hospital. Explanations for this have included the suggestion that paranoia is a healthy reaction to racism in American society, as well as subjective bias or projection on the part of the clinicians. See Marti Loring and Brian Powell, "Gender, Race, and DSM-III: A Study of the Objectivity of Psychiatric Behavior," *Journal of Health and Social Behavior* 29, 1 (March 1988): 1–22. Loring and Powell found that although all clinicians tended to favor the description of paranoia in black males, black male clinicians were least likely to.

87. Aro Case File M46, 1946.

88. See, for example, Karen Fields, *Revival and Rebellion in Central Africa* (Princeton: Princeton University Press, 1985); and Robert Edgar, *Because They Chose the Plan of God: The Story of the Bulhoek Massacre* (Johannesburg: Ravan, 1988).

89. NAI Comcol 1 735/S Vol. III, "Discharge and Release on Trial of Lunatic."

90. NAI MH (Fed) 1/1 62421, "Lunatics and Lepers: Transfer to Yaba Asylum," 550–57.

91. NAI Comcol 1 735/S Vol. III, "Discharge and Release on Trial of Lunatic."

92. Aro Case File M46, 1946.

93. This way of putting it I have taken from Stephen Black's film *Witchdoctor* (British Broadcasting Corporation, 1969), about traditional healers among the Yoruba; the film is hardly a model of a respectful representation of the healers, but Black does speak aptly of the colonial "delusion of racial grandeur."

94. Brown, *Report III,* 62–63, emphasis added.

95. See, for example, Karl Abraham, "Notes on the Treatment of Manic-Depressive Psychosis," in *Essential Papers on Depression,* ed. James Coyne (New York: New York University Press, 1986).

96. Jane Murphy, in "Psychiatric Labeling in Cross-Cultural Perspective," *Science* 191, 4231 (March 1976): 1019–28, criticizes this myth.

97. For a political application of this reasoning, see Shula Marks, *The Ambiguities of Dependence in South Africa* (Johannesburg: Ravan, 1986), ch. 1.

98. Nikolai Gogol, *Diary of a Madman,* trans. Ronald Wilks (Middlesex: Viking Penguin, 1972; originally published 1834).

99. James Glass, *Delusion: Internal Dimensions of Political Life* (Chicago: University of Chicago Press, 1985), 79.

100. NAI Ije Prof. 1 655, "Lunatics in Ijebu Province," Vol. II.

101. Helen H. Tartakoff, "The Normal Personality in Our Culture and the Nobel Prize Complex," in *Psychoanalysis: A General Psychology,* eds. Rudolph M. Loewenstein, et al. (New York: International Universities Press, 1966), 236.

102. Tartakoff, "Normal Personality," 239.

103. See David Abernethy, *The Political Dilemma of Popular Education* (Stanford: Stanford University Press, 1969), especially 284–85. Abernethy stresses that the problem was acute in the 1950s. Murphy, in fact, found that while Western education was not in itself a risk factor for psychiatric symptoms, inability to translate that education into jobs in the "modern" sector was. Jane M. Murphy, "Sociocultural Change and Psychiatric Disorder Among Rural Yorubas in Nigeria," *Ethos* (1972).

104. NAI Comcol 1 735 Vol. I, "Lunatic Asylum."

105. Aro Case File 167, 1947.

106. Leon Wurmser, *The Mask of Shame* (Baltimore: Johns Hopkins University Press, 1981), 7–8, emphasis in original.

107. Jean Comaroff and John Comaroff, *Of Revelation and Revolution: Christianity, Colonialism, and Consciousness in South Africa,* vol. 1 (Chicago: University of Chicago Press, 1991), 29.

108. This model was demolished by the "articulation of modes of production" thesis, which contained reifications of its own but advanced discussion of apartheid political economy in irreversible ways. See Harold Wolpe, "Capitalism and Cheap Labour-Power in South Africa: From Segregation to Apartheid," in *The Articulation of Modes of Production* (London: Routledge and Kegan Paul, 1980).

109. Gananath Obeyesekere, "Buddhism, Depression, and the Work of Culture in Sri Lanka," in *Culture and Depression,* eds. Arthur Kleinman and Byron Good (Berkeley: University of California Press, 1985), 134–52.

110. Catherine Lutz also wonders whether the ideal of "happiness" might not be a particularly Western one, in "Depression and the Translation of Emotional Worlds," in *Culture and Depression,* eds. Arthur Kleinman and Byron Good (Berkeley: University of California Press, 1985).

111. Obeyesekere, "Buddhism, Depression," 136.

112. Tsung-Li Lin, "Neurasthenia Revisited: Its Place in Modern Psychiatry," *Culture, Medicine and Psychiatry* 13, 2 (June 1989): 105–29. See also Kleinman, *The Illness Narratives,* ch. 6.

113. Edward Shorter has developed the idea of "symptom repertoires" in

the history of psychiatry. See, for example, Shorter, "Paralysis: The Rise and Fall of a 'Hysterical' Symptom," *Journal of Social History* 19, 4 (Summer 1986): 549–82.

114. This is not meant as a criticism of what is really a very short article; Obeyesekere develops some very rich symbolic analysis. See also his *Medusa's Hair: An Essay on Personal Symbols and Religious Experience* (Chicago: University of Chicago Press, 1981).

115. Andrew Apter, *Black Critics and Kings: The Hermeneutics of Power in Yoruba Society* (Chicago: University of Chicago Press, 1992), 7.

116. For all the universalizations psychoanalysis has been justly criticized for, it did initiate a tradition of close attention to the specific associations articulated in patient discourse. One *locus classicus* for the cultural relativist critique of psychoanalysis is Bronislaw Malinowski, *Sex and Repression in Savage Society* (London: Routledge and Kegan Paul, 1927). For the psychoanalytic emphasis on the specificity of content, see Sigmund Freud, *The Interpretation of Dreams*, trans. James Strachey (New York: Avon Books, 1965; originally published 1900), especially 137.

117. This point is made on more clinical grounds in Arthur Kleinman and Alex Cohen, "Psychiatry's Global Challenge," *Scientific American* (March 1997): 86–89.

118. Frantz Fanon, *The Wretched of the Earth* (New York: Grove Press, 1963), 250–51.

Chapter 5.   The Confinements of Isaac O.

1. NAI Ekiti Div. 1/1, 56, Vol I.

2. These are instances I can document on the basis of archival documents; there may well have been other instances.

3. NAI Ekiti Div. 1/1 56, Vol. I.

4. Ibid.

5. Ibid.

6. Ibid.

7. Ibid.

8. Ibid.

9. See Raymond Prince, "Indigenous Yoruba Psychiatry," in *Magic Faith, and Healing*, ed. Ari Kiev (New York: Free Press of Glencoe, 1964), 87.

10. NAI Ekiti Div. 1/1 56, Vol. I.

11. Ibid.

12. Ibid., emphasis added. The Boy's Brigade is a Nigerian Christian organization for male children.

13. Ibid.

14. Ibid.

15. It is possible that the clerk tampered in some way with the testimonies, but I see no evidence for this, or reason to assume it.

16. Church Missionary Society.

17. The clerk wrote "road" in several instances where the context indicates Isaac meant "load."

18. *Iborun* is Yoruba for "shawl."

19. NAI Comcol 1 735/s.1 Vol. I, "Lunatics: Matters Affecting," 126.

20. Ibid., 185.

21. Ibid.,126.

22. I am not necessarily convinced by Tayo's testimony that Isaac was stark naked when arrested. No one else mentions it, and Tayo seems to have tried to portray Isaac as being as crazy as possible. But it does appear that Isaac had at least partially disrobed.

23. Also compare Mark Vonnegut's account of his schizophrenia: "At some point I gave up clothing. It was just too sticky and confining, almost like drowning. No clothes would have been ok if I hadn't taken it into my head to make a break for it." Mark Vonnegut, *The Eden Express* (New York: Praeger, 1975).

24. Elizabeth Isichei, *A History of Nigeria* (London: Longman, 1983), 389.

25. See Raymond Prince, "Curse, Invocation, and Mental Health Among the Yoruba." *Canadian Psychiatric Association Journal* 5, 2 (April 1960): 65–79.

26. E. A. Ayandele, *The Missionary Impact on Modern Nigeria* (London: Longman, 1966), 30.

27. Ibid., 162.

28. See, for example, Margery Perham's remarks on the famous "women's riots" in Aba, quoted in Sylvia Leith-Ross, *African Women,* 2nd ed. (London: Routledge and Kegan Paul, 1965), 36–37. Another example, the Mau Mau uprisings in Kenya, will be discussed in the following chapter.

29. "Mania" is still used, as a symptom cluster, to describe disorders which involve manic episodes, but neither "mania" nor "acute mania" is used now to refer to a discrete disorder. See Robert Belmaker and H. M. van Praag, *Mania: An Evolving Concept* (New York: Luce, 1980).

30. Howard C. Warren, *Dictionary of Psychology* (Boston: Houghton Mifflin, 1934).

31. D. K. Henderson and R. D. Gillespie, *A Textbook of Psychiatry* (London: Oxford University Press, 1930), 118, emphasis added.

32. Bruce F. Home, "Insanity in Nigeria," Manuscript, Lagos, 1928, 3.

33. Robert Cunyngham Brown, *Report III on the Care and Treatment of the Mentally Ill in British West African Colonies* (London: Garden City Press, 1938), 39.

34. Joop T. V. M. De Jong, *A Descent Into African Psychiatry* (Amsterdam: Royal Tropical Institute, 1987), 44.

35. Allen Horwitz, *The Social Control of Mental Illness* (New York: Academic Press, 1982).

36. Thomas Szasz, *The Myth of Mental Illness: Foundations of a Theory of Personal Conduct* (New York: Hoeber-Harper, 1961); R. D. Laing, *The Divided Self* (Middlesex: Viking, 1959); and Thomas Scheff, *Being Mentally Ill: A Sociological Theory,* 2nd ed. (Chicago: Aldine de Gruyter, 1982). In this edition of *Being Mentally Ill,* Scheff concedes that there may be nonsociological (i.e., biochemical) factors that may be as important in the etiology of mental disorders.

37. In this respect, Horwitz's approach resembles the "symbolic interactionist" view of mental illness. See Morris Rosenberg, "A Symbolic Interactionist View of Psychosis," *Journal of Health and Social Behavior* 25, 3 (September 1984): 289–302.

38. Cullen was not a psychiatrist.

39. See Paulin Hountondji, *African Philosophy: Myth and Reality* (Bloomington: Indiana University Press, 1976); and V. Y. Mudimbe, *The Invention of Africa* (Bloomington: Indiana University Press, 1988).

40. American Psychiatric Association, *Diagnostic and Statistical Manual of Mental Disorders*. 4th ed. (Washington, DC: American Psychiatric Association, 1994), 328–30.

41. A. Bertelsen, "A Danish Twin Study of Manic-Depressive Disorders," in *Origin, Prevention and Treatment of Affective Disorders*, eds. M. Schou and E. Stomgren. (London: Academic Press, 1979).

42. See John M. Davis, "Overview: Maintenance Therapy in Psychiatry: II. Affective Disorders," *American Journal of Psychiatry* 133, 1 (1976): 1–13.

Chapter 6.   Psychiatry and Colonial Ideology

1. T. A. Lambo, "The Role of Cultural Factors in Paranoid Psychoses Among the Yoruba Tribe of Nigeria." *Journal of Mental Science* 101, 423 (April 1955): 241.

2. Frantz Fanon, *The Wretched of the Earth* (New York: Grove Press, 1963), 77.

3. This is a major theme in Megan Vaughan, *Curing Their Ills: Colonial Power and African Illness* (Stanford: Stanford University Press, 1991); and Randall M. Packard, "The 'Healthy Reserve' and the 'Dressed Native': Discourses on Black Health and the Language of Legitimation in South Africa," *American Ethnologist* 16, 4 (November 1989): 686–703. For historical epidemiologies which treat this theme, John Ford's *The Role of Trypanosomiasis in African Ecology* (Oxford: Clarendon Press, 1971) is a classic, and Randall Packard's *White Plague, Black Labor: Tuberculosis and the Political Economy of Health and Disease in South Africa* (Berkeley: University of California Press, 1989) is another fine example of the strengths of this literature. Gwyn Prins, "But What Was the Disease? The Present State of Health and Healing in African Studies," *Past and Present* 124 (August 1989): 159–79, is a useful survey.

4. See, for example, Jock McCulloch, *Colonial Psychiatry and the African Mind* (Cambridge: Cambridge University Press, 1995), 105.

5. I use Karl Mannheim's definition of ideology, which refers to a set of doctrines presented as having universal value, but which reflect the social position and interests of the group which formulates them. Such a position neither requires nor precludes ideology having hegemonic force in the Gramscian sense. It also retains a specifically political meaning, unlike Clifford Geertz's usage, which seems to refer to little more than "values." See Mannheim, *Ideology and Utopia* (New York: Harcourt Brace Jovanovich, 1936), and Geertz, "Ideology as a Cultural System," in *The Interpretation of Cultures* (New York: Basic Books, 1973).

6. This approach is influenced by the synthetic discussion of recent philosophy of science in Helen Longino, *Science as Social Knowledge* (Princeton: Princeton University Press, 1990), as well as by historical studies using similar approaches, including Stephen Jay Gould, *The Mismeasure of Man* (New York: Norton, 1981); Londa Schiebinger, "Skeletons in the Closet: The First Illustrations of the Female Skeleton in Eighteenth-Century Anatomy," in *The Making*

of the Modern Body, eds. Thomas Laqueur and Catherine Gallagher (Berkeley: University of California Press, 1987), and "Why Mammals Are Called Mammals: Gender Politics in Eighteenth-Century Natural History," *American Historical Review* 98, 2 (April 1993): 383–411; and Sandra Harding, ed., *The "Racial" Economy of Science* (Bloomington: Indiana University Press, 1993).

7. As Sander Gilman writes, "It is within texts that we can best examine our representations of the world through . . . the rigid structures of the stereotype." Sander Gilman, *Difference and Pathology* (Ithaca: Cornell University Press, 1985), 16. This follows a discussion in which Gilman shows how the term "stereotype" was itself derived from the manufacture of texts.

8. See, for example, Packard, "The 'Healthy Reserve.' "

9. NAI MH (Fed) 1/2 59, "Home, B. F., *Insanity in Nigeria,*" 4.

10. J. F. A. Ajayi, *Christian Missions in Nigeria 1841–1891: The Making of a New Elite* (Essex, UK: Longman, 1965), 261.

11. See, for example, Philip D. Curtin, *The Image of Africa: British Ideas and Action, 1780–1850* (Madison: University of Wisconsin Press, 1964); Michel-Rolph Trouillot, "Anthropology and the Savage Slot: The Poetics and Politics of Otherness," in *Recapturing Anthropology: Working in the Present,* ed. Richard G. Fox (Santa Fe: School of American Research, 1991); Nancy Stepan, *The Idea of Race in Science: Great Britain, 1800–1960* (London: Archon Books, 1982); and Sander Gilman, "On the Nexus of Blackness and Madness" in *Difference and Pathology.*

12. One early text in this genre was R. E. Dennett, *At the Back of the Black Man's Mind* (London: Frank Cass, 1968; originally published 1906).

13. Bruce F. Home, "Insanity in Nigeria," Manuscript, Lagos, 1928, 2. After his report on Nigeria, Home continued his far-flung promotion of British mental science by directing a mental hospital in Singapore.

14. Ibid., 1.

15. Ibid., 2.

16. Ibid.

17. Gilman, *Difference and Pathology,* 21.

18. Robert Cunyngham Brown, *Report III on the Care and Treatment of the Mentally Ill in British West African Colonies* (London: Garden City Press, 1938), 36.

19. Ibid., 7–8.

20. Ibid.

21. Ibid.,, 14.

22. On this point, see also Margaret Field, *Search for Security: An Ethnopsychiatric Study of Rural Ghana* (London: Faber & Faber, 1960).

23. Brown, *Report III,* 22.

24. Anxious disdain for the "town" African was a widespread feature of late colonial culture throughout Africa; see Packard, "The 'Healthy Reserve.' "

25. A classic, subversive representation of this theory in fiction is Charlotte Perkins Gilman, "The Yellow Wallpaper," in *The Charlotte Perkins Gilman Reader* (New York: Pantheon, 1980; originally published 1892).

26. Brown, *Report III,* 13.

27. J. C. Carothers, *The African Mind in Health and Disease* (Geneva: World Health Organization, 1953), 85.

28. J. C. Carothers, "On the Psychiatric Services of Nigeria," Manuscript, 1955.

29. Gilman, *Difference and Pathology*, 147.

30. See Morris Rosenberg, "A Symbolic Interactionist View of Psychosis," *Journal of Health and Social Behavior* 25, 3 (September 1984): 289–302.

31. J. C. Carothers, *The Psychology of Mau Mau* (Nairobi: Government Printer, 1954).

32. Brown, *Report III*, 36.

33. A. S. Cleary, "The Myth of *Mau Mau* in Its International Context," *African Affairs* 89, 355 (April 1990): 228, emphasis added. For a more complete account of the context of Mau Mau, see Bruce Berman and John Lonsdale, *Unhappy Valley: Conflict in Kenya and Africa*, 2 vols. (London: James Currey, 1992).

34. Carothers, *Psychology of Mau Mau*, 2.

35. Ibid., 3.

36. Ibid., 6.

37. Carothers, *African Mind*, 8, emphasis added.

38. See also Carothers, *Psychology of Mau Mau*, 5.

39. Carothers, *African Mind*, 91.

40. Ibid., 96–107.

41. Ibid., 96.

42. Ibid., 107.

43. Ibid., 119.

44. Ibid., 142.

45. Ibid., 139. One wonders how much tautology was contained in this statement, i.e., that the diagnosis was given to all those who seemed chronically insane.

46. Ibid., 147.

47. J. C. Carothers, "Frontal Lobe Function and the African." *Journal of Mental Science* 97, 406 (January 1951): 12–48. The paper actually responded to a request for a screening test for employees from a laboratory director in Kenya!

48. G. Allen German, "Mental Health in Africa: 1. The Extent of Mental Health Problems in Africa Today," *British Journal of Psychiatry* 151 (October 1987): 435.

49. Lambo, "The Role of Cultural Factors."

50. Carothers, "Frontal Lobe Function," 37. "Leucotomy" and "lobotomy" are synonyms.

51. Carothers did visit Nigeria at least one more time; he attended the First Pan-African Psychiatric Conference in 1961.

52. Lambo, "The Role of Cultural Factors."

53. Ibid., 241

54. On this point, see also Jock McCullough, "The Empire's New Clothes: Ethnopsychiatry in Colonial Africa," *History of the Human Sciences* 6, 2 (1993): 35–52.

55. See Stefan Kuhl, *The Nazi Connection: Eugenics, American Racism and German National Socialism* (Oxford: Oxford University Press, 1994), ch. 3, for a powerful discussion of the revival of scientific racism in the 1980s and 1990s.

As if to underscore the importance of Kuhl's discussion, Charles Murray and Richard Herrnstein's *The Bell Curve: Intelligence and Class Structure in American Life* (New York: Free Press, 1994) was published with much publicity the same year, bringing these ongoing debates under renewed public scrutiny. Though this is not the place for an extended critique of *The Bell Curve*, it is worth noting that Murray and Herrnstein make many of the same rhetorical moves as Carothers, such as the conflation of analytically distinct categories such as race, ethnicity, and culture. See *The Bell Curve*, 296–97, for an egregious example.

56. See, for example, Arthur Kleinman, "Anthropology and Psychiatry: The Role of Culture in Cross-Cultural Research on Illness," *British Journal of Psychiatry* 151 (October 1987): 447–54.

Chapter 7.   Conclusion

1. David William Cohen, "Doing Social History from Pim's Doorway," in *Reliving the Past: The Worlds of Social History,* ed. Olivier Zunz (Chapel Hill: University of North Carolina Press, 1985), 209.

2. Charles Rosenberg, "Framing Disease," in *Explaining Epidemics and Other Studies in the History of Medicine* (Cambridge: Cambridge University Press, 1992), 307.

3. For a useful example of such a treatment, see Robert A. Aronowitz, "Lyme Disease: The Social Construction of a New Disease and Its Social Consequences," *Milbank Quarterly* 69, 1 (1991): 79–111.

4. Michael Taussig, *Mimesis and Alterity: A Particular History of the Senses* (New York: Routledge, 1993), xvi.

5. Judith Butler, *Bodies That Matter: On the Discursive Limits of "Sex"* (New York: Routledge, 1995), x–xi.

6. Jane Murphy, "Psychiatric Labeling in Cross-Cultural Perspective," *Science* 191, 4231 (March 1976): 1019–28.

7. It is cited, to give just one example, in virtually every article in Anthony J. Marsella and Geoffrey M. White, eds., *Cultural Conceptions of Mental Health and Therapy* (Dordrecht: Reidel, 1989; originally published 1982).

8. Nell Boyce clarified this point for me.

9. Gureje and Adewunmi, "Life Events and Schizophrenia."

10. Sartorius et al, *Schizophrenia.*

11. Oye Gureje and A. Adewunmi, "Life Events and Schizophrenia in Nigerians: A Controlled Investigation." *British Journal of Psychiatry* 153 (September 1988): 3/4.

12. Dorothy Smith, The *Conceptual Practices of Power: A Feminist Sociology of Knowledge* (Boston: Northeastern University Press, 1990), ch. 5.

13. Olayiwole Erinosho, "Laing's 'Conspiratorial' Theory of Mental Illness and 'Folk' Societies." *African Notes* 10, 1 (1986): 45.

14. David Arnold, for example, has centered his interpretation of colonial medicine in India on the concept of cultural hegemony. David Arnold, *Colonizing the Body: State Medicine and Epidemic Disease in Nineteenth Century India* (Berkeley: University of California Press, 1993), and "Public Health and

Public Power: Medicine and Hegemony in Colonial India," in *Contesting Colonial Hegemony*, eds. Dagmar Engels and Shula Marks (London: British Academic Press; German Historical Institute, 1994). Another major example is Jean Comaroff and John Comaroff, *Of Revelation and Revolution: Christianity, Colonialism and Consciousness in South Africa* (Chicago: University of Chicago Press, 1991), especially ch. 6. Shula Marks has recently and aptly noted that the emphasis on the cultural powers of colonial medicine, while an important subject in its own right, has tended to background questions of political economy and health. See her "What Is Colonial About Colonial Medicine? And What Has Happened to Imperialism and Health?" *Social History of Medicine* 10, 2 (1997): 205–19.

15. Megan Vaughan, "Healing and Curing Issues in the Social History and Anthropology of Medicine in Africa," *Social History of Medicine* 7, 2 (1994): 288.

16. Pier Larson, "'Capacities and Modes of Thinking': Intellectual Engagements and Subaltern Hegemony in the Early History of Malagasy Christianity," *American Historical Review* 102, 4 (October 1997): 969–1002. Larson's handling of empirical material is admirable, and his argument is congruent with mine, but he lumps quite a bit of very disparate scholarship into what he calls "a Neo-Foucaldian school." On page 998, in ff. 110, for example, he names Comaroff and Comaroff, Megan Vaughan, Sander Gilman, and Gayatri Chakravorty Spivak, among others. Gilman's framework is expressly psychoanalytic, Spivak's famous testimony to the muteness of the subaltern is based partly on her preference for Derrida over Foucault, and Vaughan explicitly disavows the utility of Foucault for many colonial contexts. Sander Gilman, *Difference and Pathology: Stereotypes of Sexuality, Race, and Madness* (Ithaca: Cornell University Press, 1985); Gayatri Chakravorty Spivak, "Can the Subaltern Speak?" in *Marxism and the Interpretation of Culture*, eds. Cary Nelson and Lawrence Grossberg (Urbana: University of Illinois Press, 1988); Megan Vaughan, *Curing Their Ills: Colonial Power and African Illness* (Stanford: Stanford University Press, 1991). On Vaughan, see also Ann Laura Stoler, *Race and the Education of Desire: Foucault's History of Sexuality and the Colonial Order of Things* (Durham: Duke University Press, 1995), 33, ff. 39.

Bibliography

Archives and Document Collections

Alan Mason Chesney Archives, The Johns Hopkins University, United States.
Aro Mental Hospital Case Files, Abeokuta, Nigeria.
Church Missionary Society Archives, Birmingham, United Kingdom.
Contemporary Medical Archives Centre, Wellcome Institute for the History of Medicine, London, United Kingdom.
Nigerian National Archives, Ibadan, Nigeria.
Personal Collection of Dr. Alexander Boroffka, Kiel, Germany (by correspondence).
Public Record Office, London, United Kingdom.

Nigerian Newspapers

Daily Service
Nigerian Life Mirror
Observer
Sunday Punch
Times
Vanguard
Weekly Record
Weekly Times
West African Pilot

Hospital and Government Publications

Aro Mental Hospital. *40th Anniversary of the Establishment of Aro Neuro-Psychiatric Hospital Complex.* Ibadan: Sketch Press, 1984.

Brown, Robert Cunyngham. *Report on Mission to the British Colonies of the West Coast of Africa on the Care and Treatment of Lunatics.* Colonial Office West Africa Pamphlet 238A, 1937.
———. *Report III on the Care and Treatment of the Mentally Ill in British West African Colonies.* London: Garden City Press, 1938.
Carothers, J. C. "On the Psychiatric Services of Nigeria." Manuscript, 1955.
———. *The Psychology of Mau Mau.* Nairobi: Government Printer, 1954.
Home, Bruce F. "Insanity in Nigeria." Manuscript, Lagos, 1928.
Southern Nigeria, Government of. *Government Gazette.* November 7, 1906.
Yaba Mental Hospital. *From Asylum to Hospital.* Lagos: Gabumo, 1987.

Interviews Conducted by the Author

Professor Tolani Asuni, Lagos, March 13, 1990.
Professor Tolani Asuni, Lagos, March 26, 1990.
Professor T. A. Lambo, Lagos, April 7, 1990.
Professor A. A. Marinho, Lagos, November 20, 1990.

Interviews Conducted by the Author with Dr. Samuel Osunwole

Chief Olusole Ayodabo, Ibadan, February 7, 1990.
Chief Waidi Omo-oso, Ibadan, February 8, 1990.
Fatumbi Famoriyo, Ife, February 17, 1990.
Chief Joshua Obidahunsi, Ife, February 17, 1990.
Chief Odugbemi, Ikire, February 21, 1990.
Alhaji Ajana Anigbajumo Oogun, Ife, February 21, 1990.
Akanbi Elero, Abeokuta, March 21, 1990.
Matthew Owojori, Ife, April 1, 1990.
Alhaja Taibatu Monilola, Ibadan, May 25, 1990.
Alhaja Motemibola Akee, Oyo, June 1, 1990.
Muniratu Omkehinde Iyasango, Ibadan, June 4, 1990.
J. L. E. Sodunke, Abeokuta, June 18, 1990.
Chief Alayande Amoo, Iwo, July 28, 1990.

Films

Black, Stephen. *Witch Doctor,* British Broadcasting Corporation, 1969.
Park, Ben. *The Healers of Aro.* 16 mm. film New York: United Nations, 1960.
Prince, Raymond, and Francis Speed. *He Is a Madman.* Ibadan: Institute of African Studies, University of Ibadan, 1963.

Books and Journal Articles

Abernethy, David. *The Political Dilemma of Popular Education.* Stanford: Stanford University Press, 1969.

Abimbola, Wande. *Ifa: An Exposition of Ifa Literary Corpus*. Ibadan: Caxton, 1976.

Abraham, Karl. "Notes on the Treatment of Manic-Depressive Psychosis." In *Essential Papers on Depression*. Edited by James Coyne. New York: New York University Press, 1986.

Abraham, William E. *The Mind of Africa*. Chicago: University of Chicago Press, 1962.

Achebe, Chinua. "The Madman." In *Girls at War and Other Stories*. London: Heinemann, 1972.

———. *A Man of the People*. London: Heinemann, 1966.

Adebimpe, Victor R. "Overview: White Norms and Psychiatric Diagnosis of Black Patients." *American Journal of Psychiatry* 138, 3 (March 1981) 279–89.

Adebowale, Bayo. *Out of His Mind*. Ibadan: Spectrum Books, 1987.

Adeloye, Adelola. *African Pioneers of Modern Medicine: Nigerian Doctors of the Nineteenth Century*. Ibadan: University of Ibadan, 1985.

Ademuwagun, Z. A., J. A. A. Ayoade, I. Harrison, and D. M. Warren, eds. *African Therapeutic Systems*. Waltham, MA: Crossroads Press, 1979.

Adewoye, Omoniyi. *The Judicial System in Southern Nigeria, 1854–1954*. Atlantic Highlands, NJ: Humanities Press, 1977.

Ahire, Philip Terdoo. *Imperial Policing: The Emergence and Role of the Police in Colonial Nigeria*. Philadelphia: Open University Press, 1991.

Ajayi, J. F. A. *Christian Missions in Nigeria 1841–1891: The Making of a New Elite*. Essex, UK: Longman, 1965.

Ajayi, J. F. A., and Robert Smith. *Yoruba Warfare in the Nineteenth Century*. Cambridge: Cambridge University Press, 1964.

Akintoye, S. A. *Revolution and Power Politics in Yorubaland, 1840–1893*. London: Longman, 1971.

Alcoff, Linda. "The Problem of Speaking for Others." *Cultural Critique* 20 (Winter 1991–92): 5–32.

Allridge, Patricia. "The Foundation of Maudsley Hospital." In *150 Years of British Psychiatry, 1842–1991*. Edited by German Berrios and Hugh Freeman. London: Gaskell, 1991.

American Psychiatric Association. *Diagnostic and Statistical Manual of Mental Disorders*. 4th ed. Washington, DC: American Psychiatric Association, 1994.

Anderson, Benedict. *Imagined Communities*. London: Verso, 1983.

Anderson, Warwick. "Disease, Race and Empire." *Bulletin of the History of Medicine* 70, 1 (Spring 1996): 62–67.

———. "Immunities of Empire: Race, Disease, and the New Tropical Medicine, 1900–1920." *Bulletin of the History of Medicine* 70, 1 (Spring 1996): 94–118.

Appiah, Kwame Anthony. *In My Father's House: Africa in the Philosophy of Culture*. New York: Oxford University Press, 1992.

———. "Madmen and Specialists." *London Review of Books* 17, 17 (September 7, 1995): 16–17.

Apter, Andrew. *Black Critics and Kings: The Hermeneutics of Power in Yoruba Society*. Chicago: University of Chicago Press, 1992.

Arnold, David. *Colonizing the Body: State Medicine and Epidemic Disease in Nineteenth Century India*. Berkeley: University of California Press, 1993.

————. "Public Health and Public Power: Medicine and Hegemony in Colonial India." In *Contesting Colonial Hegemony*. Edited by Dagmar Engels and Shula Marks. London : British Academic Press; German Historical Institute, 1994.

Arnold, David, ed. *Imperial Medicine and Indigenous Societies.* Manchester: Manchester University Press, 1988.

Aronowitz, Robert A. "Lyme Disease: The Social Construction of a New Disease and Its Social Consequences." *Milbank Quarterly* 69, 1 (1991): 79–111.

Asiwaju, A. I. *Western Yorubaland Under European Rule, 1889–1945.* London: Longman, 1976.

Asuni, Tolani. "Aro Hospital in Perspective." *American Journal of Psychiatry* 124, 6 (December 1967): 763–70.

————. "Community Development and Public Health: By-Product of Social Psychiatry in Nigeria." *West African Medical Journal* 13, 4 (1964).

————. "Development in Mental Health Care in Africa with Special Reference to Western Nigeria." *Proceedings of the IV World Congress of Psychiatry.* Madrid (September 1966): 1067–68.

————. "Psychiatry in Nigeria over the Years." *Nigerian Medical Journal* 2, 2 (April 1972): 54–58.

————. "Socio-Medical Problems of Religious Converts." *Psychopathologie africaine* 9, 2 (1973): 223–36.

————. "Therapeutic Communities of the Hospital and Villages in Aro Hospital." *African Journal of Psychiatry* 5 (1979): 35–42.

Atanda, J. A. *The New Oyo Empire: Indirect Rule and Change in Western Nigeria 1894–1936.* London: Longman, 1973.

Ayandele, E. A. *The Missionary Impact on Modern Nigeria.* London: Longman, 1966.

Baker, A. A. "Observations on the Effect of Largactil in Psychiatric Illness." *Journal of Mental Science* 101, 422 (April 1955): 175–82.

Barber, Karin. *I Could Speak Until Tomorrow: Oriki, Women and the Past in a Yoruba Town.* Washington, DC: Smithsonian Institution, 1991.

Barnes, Sandra. "The Urban Frontier in West Africa: Mushin, Nigeria." In *The African Frontier.* Edited by Igor Kopytoff. Bloomington: Indiana University Press, 1983.

Bascom, William. *Ifa Divination: Communication Between Gods and Men in West Africa.* Bloomington: Indiana University Press, 1969.

————. "Social Status, Wealth and Individual Differences Among the Yoruba." *American Anthropologist* 53 (1951): 490–505.

Bateson, Gregory. *Steps to an Ecology of Mind.* San Francisco: Chandler, 1972.

Bayer, Ronald. *Homosexuality and American Psychiatry.* Princeton: Princeton University Press, 1987.

Beidelman, T. O. "Towards More Open Theoretical Interpretations." In *Witchcraft Accusations and Confessions.* Edited by Mary Douglas. London: Tavistock, 1970.

Beier, Ulli. *Luckless Heads: Paintings by Deranged Nigerians.* Bremen: CON Medien-und Vertriebsgesellschaft, 1982.

Bell, Leland. *Mental and Social Disorder in Sub-Saharan Africa: The Case of Sierra Leone, 1781–1990.* New York: Greenwood Press, 1991.

Belmaker, Robert, and H. M. van Praag. *Mania: An Evolving Concept*. New York: Luce, 1980.

Benedict, Ruth. "Anthropology and the Abnormal." *Journal of General Psychology* 10 (1934): 59–82.

———. *Patterns of Culture*. Boston: Houghton Mifflin, 1934.

Bennett, Douglas. "The Drive Towards the Community." In *150 Years of British Psychiatry, 1842–1991*. Edited by German Berrios and Hugh Freeman. London: Gaskell, 1991.

Berman, Bruce, and John Lonsdale. *Unhappy Valley: Conflict in Kenya and Africa*. 2 vols. London: James Currey, 1992.

Berrios, German, and Hugh Freeman, eds. *150 Years of British Psychiatry, 1842–1991*. London: Gaskell, 1991.

Bertelsen, A. "A Danish Twin Study of Manic-Depressive Disorders." In *Origin, Prevention and Treatment of Affective Disorders*. Edited by M. Schou and E. Stomgren. London: Academic Press, 1979.

Binitie, Ayo. "Outstanding Contributions to Nigerian Psychiatry." *Nigerian Journal of Psychiatry* 1, 3 (December 1988): 145–54.

Biobaku, S. O. *The Egba and Their Neighbours*. Oxford: Oxford University Press, 1957.

Boahen, A. Adu. *African Perspectives on Colonialism*. Baltimore: Johns Hopkins University Press, 1987.

Booth, James. *Writers and Politics in Nigeria*. London: Hodder and Stoughton, 1981.

Boroffka, Alexander. "Brief History of the Association of Psychiatrists in Nigeria and Introduction of Patron and Chairman." Secretary's Address Presented at Launching of Association of Psychiatrists in Nigeria, 1970.

———. "Concepts of Schizophrenia: The African Point of View." Paper presented to the World Psychiatric Association, Seminar on Concepts of Schizophrenia, Cologne, 1981.

———. "Different Ways of Starting Mental Health Care." *Psychopathologie africaine* 6 (1970): 181–99.

———. "Editorial," *Nigerian Medical Journal* 2, 2 (April 1972): 53.

———. "The History of Mental Hospitals in Nigeria." *Psychiatry* 8 (1985): 37–43.

———. "A History of Psychiatry in Nigeria." Paper presented to the World Psychiatric Congress, Vienna, 1983.

———. "A History of Psychiatry in Nigeria." *Psychiatry* 8 (1985): 709–14.

———. "Just a Dozen Years: Review of Psychiatric Experiences in Nigeria, 1961–1973." Address to the Annual Meeting of the Association of Psychiatrists in Nigeria, Benin City, 1973.

———. "Mental Illness in Lagos." *Psychopathologie africaine* 9 (1973): 405–17.

———. "Provision of Psychiatric Services in Developing Countries; Nigeria; An Example." *African Journal of Psychiatry* 1, 2 (October 1975): 117–32.

———. "A Psychiatry in Ascent: Nigeria Revisited." *Bulletin of the Royal College of Psychiatrists* 9 (July 1985): 141.

———. "Psychiatry Tomorrow—Continuation or New Beginning?" Paper presented to the Nigerian Medical Association Annual Meeting, Enugu, 1974.

Boroffka, Alexander, and Benjamin O. Osuntokun. "Hysteria in Nigerians." *Nigerian Medical Journal* 5, 1 (1974): 6–13.

Bowlby, John. *Attachment and Loss*. New York: Basic Books, 1969.

Brown, Spencer H. "Public Health in Lagos, 1850–1900: Perceptions, Patterns, and Perspectives." *International Journal of African Historical Studies* 25, 2 (1992): 337–60.

Buckley, Anthony. *Yoruba Medicine*. Oxford: Clarendon Press, 1985.

Butler, Judith. *Bodies That Matter: On the Discursive Limits of "Sex."* New York: Routledge, 1995.

Callaway, Helen. *Gender, Culture, and Empire: European Women in Colonial Nigeria*. Urbana: University of Illinois Press, 1987.

Carothers, J. C. *The African Mind in Health and Disease*. Geneva: World Health Organization, 1953.

————. "Frontal Lobe Function and the African." *Journal of Mental Science* 97, 406 (January 1951): 12–48.

Chanock, Martin. "Making Customary Law: Men, Women, and Courts in Colonial Northern Rhodesia." In *African Women and the Law: Historical Perspectives*. Edited by Margaret Jean Hay and Marcia Wright. Boston: African Studies Center, 1982.

Chesler, Phyllis. *Women and Madness*. New York: Avon Books, 1973.

Clapperton, Hugh. *Journal of a Second Expedition into the Interior of Africa from the Bight of Benin to Soccotoo*. London: John Murray, 1966; originally published 1820.

Cleary, A. S. "The Myth of *Mau Mau* in Its International Context." *African Affairs* 89, 355 (April 1990): 227–45.

Clingman, Stephen. "Beyond the Limit: The Social Relations of Madness in Southern African Fiction." In *Bounds of Race: Perspectives on Hegemony and Resistance*. Edited by Dominick LaCapra. Ithaca: Cornell University Press, 1991.

Cohen, David William. "Doing Social History from Pim's Doorway." In *Reliving the Past: The Worlds of Social History*. Edited by Olivier Zunz. Chapel Hill: University of North Carolina Press, 1985.

Coleman, James. *Nigeria: Background to Nationalism*. Berkeley: University of California Press, 1968.

Comaroff, Jean, and John Comaroff. "The Madman and the Migrant: Work and Labor in the Consciousness of a South African People." *American Ethnologist* 14 (May 1987): 191–209.

————. *Of Revelation and Revolution: Christianity, Colonialism, and Consciousness in South Africa*. Vol. 1. Chicago: University of Chicago Press, 1991.

Cooper, Fred. "Conflict and Connection: Rethinking Colonial African History." *American Historical Review* 99, 5 (December 1994): 1516–45.

Crowder, Michael. *Colonial West Africa*. London: Frank Cass, 1978.

Csordas, Thomas J. "The Affliction of Martin: Religious, Clinical, and Phenomenological Meaning in a Case of Demonic Oppression." In *Ethnopsychiatry: The Cultural Construction of Professional and Folk Psychiatries*. Edited by Atwood Gaines. Albany: State University of New York Press, 1992.

Curtin, Philip D. *Death by Migration: Europe's Encounter with the Tropical World in the Nineteenth Century*. Cambridge: Cambridge University Press, 1991.

————, *The Image of Africa: British Ideas and Action, 1780–1850*. Madison: University of Wisconsin Press, 1964.

Darnton, Robert. "Peasants Tell Tales." In *The Great Cat Massacre and Other Episodes in French Cultural History*. New York: Basic Books, 1984.

Davis, John M. "Overview: Maintenance Therapy in Psychiatry: II. Affective Disorders." *American Journal of Psychiatry* 133, 1 (1976): 1–13.

Deacon, Harriet. "Racial Segregation and Medical Discourse in Nineteenth-Century Cape Town." *Journal of Southern African Studies* 22, 2 (June 1996): 287–308.

Dembovitz, Captain N. "Psychiatry Amongst West African Troops." *Journal of the Royal Army Medical Corps* 84 (1944): 70–74.

Dennett, R. E. *At the Back of the Black Man's Mind*. London: Frank Cass, 1968; originally published 1906.

De Jong, Joop T. V. M. *A Descent Into African Psychiatry*. Amsterdam: Royal Tropical Institute, 1987.

De Reuck, A. V S., and Ruth Porter, eds. *CIBA Foundation Symposium on Transcultural Psychiatry*. London: J. & A. Churchill, 1965.

Devereux, George. *From Anxiety to Method in the Behavioral Sciences*. New York: Humanities Press, 1967.

Dohrenwend, Bruce P. "Sociocultural and Social-Psychological Factors in the Genesis of Mental Disorders." *Journal of Health and Social Behavior* 16, 4 (1974): 365–92.

Drewal, Henry John, and Margaret Drewal. *Gelede: Art and Female Power Among the Yoruba*. Bloomington: Indiana University Press, 1983.

Drewal, Henry John, and John Mason. "Ogun and Body / Mind Potentiality: Yoruba Scarification and Painting Traditions in Africa and the Americas." In *Africa's Ogun*. Edited by Sandra Barnes. Rev. ed. Bloomington: Indiana University Press, 1997.

Drewal, Margaret. *Yoruba Ritual: Performers, Play, Agency*. Bloomington: Indiana University Press, 1992.

Dubow, Saul. "Wulf Sachs's *Black Hamlet*: A Case of 'Psychic Vivisection'?" *African Affairs* 92, 369 (1993): 519–56.

Ebigbo, Peter O. "The Nigerian Worker and Somatisation." In *Managing the Nigerian Worker*. Edited by Pita N. O. Ejiofor and Vincent A. Aniagoh. Ikeja: Longman, 1984.

Edgar, Robert. *Because They Chose the Plan of God: The Story of the Bulhoek Massacre*. Johannesburg: Ravan, 1988.

Edgerton, Robert. "Conceptions of Psychosis in Four East African Societies." *American Anthropologist* 66: 1288–99.

————. "Traditional Treatment for Mental Illness in Africa: A Review." *Culture, Medicine and Psychiatry* (1980): 167–89.

Enekwechi, Emmanuel Ebelechukwu. "Culture and Mental Illness: A Study of the Ibos of West Africa." Doctor of Psychology Dissertation, Rutgers University, 1981.

Erinosho, Olayiwole. "Laing's 'Conspiratorial' Theory of Mental Illness and 'Folk' Societies." *African Notes* 10, 1 (1986): 45–49.

Erinosho, Olayiwole, and Norman Bell, eds. *Mental Health in Africa*. Ibadan: University of Ibadan Press, 1982.

Ernst, Waltraud. "The European Insane in British India 1800–1858." In *Imperial Medicine and Indigenous Societies*. Edited by David Arnold. Manchester: Manchester University Press, 1988.

———. "European Madness and Gender in Nineteenth-century British India." *Social History of Medicine* 9, 3 (1996) 357–82.

———. *Mad Tales from the Raj: The European Insane in British India*. London: Routledge, 1991.

Estroff, Sue. *Making It Crazy: An Ethnography of Psychiatric Clients in an American Community*. Berkeley: University of California Press, 1981.

Evans Pritchard, E. E. *Witchcraft, Oracles and Magic Among the Azande*. Abridged ed. Oxford: Clarendon Press, 1976; originally published 1937.

Falola, Toyin. *Development Planning and Decolonization in Nigeria*. Gainesville: University Press of Florida, 1996.

———. "Kemi Morgan and the Second Reconstruction of Ibadan History." *History in Africa* 18 (1991): 93–112.

———. *Politics and Economy in Ibadan, 1893–1945*. Lagos: Modelor, 1989.

Fanon, Frantz. *The Wretched of the Earth*. New York: Grove Press, 1963.

Farley, John. *Bilharzia: A History of Imperial Tropical Medicine*. Cambridge: Cambridge University Press, 1991.

Feierman, Steven. "Struggles for Control: The Social Roots of Health and Healing in Modern Africa." *African Studies Review* 28, 2–3 (1985): 73–147.

Felman, Shoshana. "Women and Madness: The Critical Phallacy." *Diacritics* 5, 4 (Winter 1975): 2–10.

Field, Margaret. *Search for Security: An Ethnopsychiatric Study of Rural Ghana*. London: Faber & Faber, 1960.

Fields, Karen. *Revival and Rebellion in Central Africa*. Princeton: Princeton University Press, 1985.

Fisher, Lawrence. *Colonial Madness*. New Brunswick, NJ: Rutgers University Press, 1985.

Ford, John. *The Role of Trypanosomiasis in African Ecology*. Oxford: Clarendon Press, 1971.

Foucault, Michel. *The Archaeology of Knowledge*. Translated by A. M. Sheridan Smith. New York: Pantheon Books, 1972.Vintage Books

———. *The History of Sexuality*. Vol. 1. Translated by Robert Hurley. New York: Vintage Books, 1980.

———. *Madness and Civilization*. Translated by Richard Howard. New York: Vintage Books, 1965; originally published 1961.

———. "What Is an Author?" In *Language, Counter-Memory, Practice*. Edited by Donald F. Bouchard. Ithaca: Cornell University Press, 1977.Vintage Books

Freud, Sigmund. *Civilization and Its Discontents*. Translated by James Strachey. New York: Norton, 1961; originally published 1930.

———. *The Interpretation of Dreams,* Translated by James Strachey. New York: Avon Books, 1965; originally published 1900.

———. "Mourning and Melancholia." In *Standard Edition of the Collected Works of Sigmund Freud*. Vol. 9. Translated by James Strachey. London: Hogarth, 1953–1974; originally published 1917.

Freund, Bill. *The Making of Contemporary Africa*. London: MacMillan, 1984.

Gaines, Atwood. "From DSM-I to III-R: Voices of Self, Mastery, and the

Other: A Cultural Constructivist Reading of U.S. Psychiatric Classification." *Social Science and Medicine* 35, 1 (1992): 3–24.

———. "Cultural Definitions, Behavior and the Person in American Psychiatry." In *Cultural Conceptions of Mental Health and Therapy*. Edited by Anthony J. Marsella and Geoffrey M. White. Dordrecht: Reidel, 1989; originally published 1982.

Gaines, Atwood, ed. *Ethnopsychiatry: The Cultural Construction of Professional and Folk Psychiatries*. Albany: State University of New York Press, 1992.

Gates, Henry Louis, Jr. "Critical Fanonism." *Critical Inquiry* 17 (Spring 1991): 457–70.

Gay, Peter. *Freud: A Life for Our Times*. New York: Norton, 1988.

Gbadegesin, Segun. *African Philosophy: Traditional Yoruba Philosophy and Contemporary African Realities*. New York: Peter Lang, 1991.

Geertz, Clifford. "Ideology as a Cultural System." In *The Interpretation of Cultures*. New York: Basic Books, 1973.

Gendzier, Irene. *Frantz Fanon: A Critical Study*. New York: Pantheon, 1973.

German, G. Allen. "Mental Health in Africa: 1. The Extent of Mental Health Problems in Africa Today." *British Journal of Psychiatry* 151 (October 1987): 435–39.

Gilman, Charlotte Perkins. "The Yellow Wallpaper." In *The Charlotte Perkins Gilman Reader*. New York: Pantheon, 1980; originally published, 1892.

Gilman, Sander. *Difference and Pathology*. Ithaca: Cornell University Press, 1985.

Ginzburg, Carlo. *The Cheese and the Worms*. Translated by John and Anne Tedeschi. New York: Penguin Books, 1982.

Glass, James. *Delusion: Internal Dimensions of Political Life*. Chicago: University of Chicago Press, 1985.

Goffman, Erving. *Asylums*. New York: Anchor, 1961.

Gogol, Nikolai. *Diary of a Madman*. Translated by Ronald Wilks. Middlesex: Viking Penguin, 1972; originally published 1834.

Goldstein, Jan. *Console and Classify: The French Psychiatric Profession in the Nineteenth Century*. Cambridge: Cambridge University Press, 1987.

Gottesman, I. I. and J. Shields. *Schizophrenia and Genetics: A Twin Vantage Point*. New York: Academic Press, 1972.

Gould, Stephen Jay. *The Mismeasure of Man*. New York: Norton, 1981.

Gove, Walter. "The Current Status of the Labeling Theory of Mental Illness." In *Deviance and Mental Illness*. Beverly Hills: Sage, 1982.

Grob, Gerald. *Mental Institutions in America: Social Policy to 1875*. New York: Free Press, 1973.

Grosskurth, Phyllis. *Melanie Klein: Her World and Her Work*. Cambridge: Harvard University Press, 1986.

Gureje, Oye, and A. Adewunmi. "Life Events and Schizophrenia in Nigerians: A Controlled Investigation." *British Journal of Psychiatry* 153 (September 1988): 367–75.

Hallen, B., and J. O. Sodipo. *Knowledge, Belief, and Witchcraft: Analytic Experiments in African Philosophy*. London: Ethnographica, 1986.

Harding, Sandra, ed. *The "Racial" Economy of Science*. Bloomington: Indiana University Press, 1993.

Harrison, Mark. "'The Tender Frame of Man': Disease Climate, and Racial Difference in India and the West Indies, 1760–1860." *Bulletin of the History of Medicine* 70, 1 (Spring 1996): 68–93.

Henderson, D. K. and R. D. Gillespie. *A Textbook of Psychiatry.* London: Oxford University Press, 1930.

Hobsbawm, Eric, and Terence Ranger, eds. *The Invention of Tradition.* Cambridge: Cambridge University Press, 1983.

Horton, Robin. "On the Rationality of Conversion." *Africa* 45, 3 and 4 (1975): 219–35, 373–99.

Horwitz, Allen. *The Social Control of Mental Illness.* New York: Academic Press, 1982.

Hountondji, Paulin. *African Philosophy: Myth and Reality.* Bloomington: Indiana University Press, 1976.

Hughes, Arnold, and Robin Cohen. "An Emerging Nigerian Working Class." In *African Labor History.* Edited by Peter C. W. Gutkind, Robin Cohen, and Jean Copans. Beverly Hills: Sage, 1978.

Idowu, E. Bolaji. *Olodumare: God in Yoruba Belief.* Singapore: Longman, 1962.

Ilechukwu, Sunny T. C. "Approaches to Psychotherapy in Africans: Do They Have to Be Non-Medical?" *Culture, Medicine and Psychiatry* 13, 4 (December 1989): 419–35.

Iliffe, John. *The African Poor: A History.* Cambridge: Cambridge University Press, 1987.

Isichei, Elizabeth. *A History of Nigeria.* London: Longman, 1983.

———. *A History of West Africa Since 1800.* London: MacMillan, 1977.

Janzen, John. *The Quest for Therapy in Lower Zaire.* Berkeley: University of California Press, 1978.

Jarvis, Edward. *Insanity and Idiocy in Massachusetts.* Cambridge: Harvard University Press, 1971; originally published 1855.

Jegede, Olukayode R., A. O. Williams, and A. O. Sijuwola. "Recent Developments in the Care, Treatment, and Rehabilitation of the Chronic Mentally Ill in Nigeria." *Hospital and Community Psychiatry* 36: 6 (June 1985): 658–61.

Jenkins, Janis Hunter. "The Psychocultural Study of Emotion and Mental Disorder." In *Handbook of Psychological Anthropology.* Edited by Philip K. Bock. Westport, CT: Greenwood, 1994.

———. "The State Construction of Affect: Political Ethos and Mental Health Among Salvadoran Refugees." *Culture, Medicine, and Psychiatry* 15 (1991): 139–65.

Johnson, Ann Braden. *Out of Bedlam: The Truth About De-institutionalization.* Boston: Basic Books, 1990.

Johnson, Samuel. *The History of the Yorubas.* Norfolk: Lowe & Brydone, 1976; originally published 1921.

Jones, Kathleen. "The Culture of the Mental Hospital." In *150 Years of British Psychiatry, 1842–1991.* Edited by German Berrios and Hugh Freeman. London: Gaskell, 1991.

July, Robert. *The Origins of Modern African Thought.* New York: Praeger, 1967.

Karp, Ivan. "Deconstructing Culture-Bound Syndromes." *Social Science and Medicine* 21, 2 (1985): 221–28.

Katz, P., and F. R. Kirkland. "Traditional Thought and Modern Western Surgery." *Social Science and Medicine* 26, 12 (1988): 1175–81.

Keller, Evelyn Fox. *Secrets of Life, Secrets of Death.* New York: Routledge, 1992.

Kennedy, Dane. "Constructing the Colonial Myth of Mau Mau." *International Journal of African Historical Studies* 25, 2 (1992): 241–60.

Kleinman, Arthur. "Anthropology and Psychiatry: The Role of Culture in Cross-Cultural Research on Illness." *British Journal of Psychiatry* 151 (October 1987): 447–54.

———. *The Illness Narratives: Suffering, Healing, and the Human Condition.* New York: Harper Collins, 1988.

———. *Rethinking Psychiatry: From Cultural Category to Personal Experience.* New York: Free Press, 1988.

Kleinman, Arthur, and Alex Cohen. "Psychiatry's Global Challenge." *Scientific American* (March 1997): 86–89.

Kleinman, Arthur, and Byron Good, eds. *Culture and Depression.* Berkeley: University of California Press, 1985.

Kuhl, Stefan. *The Nazi Connection: Eugenics, American Racism and German National Socialism.* Oxford: Oxford University Press, 1994.

Laing, R. D. *The Divided Self.* Middlesex: Viking, 1959.

Laitin, David. *Hegemony and Culture: Politics and Religious Change Among the Yoruba.* Chicago: University of Chicago Press, 1986.

Lambo, T. A. *African Traditional Beliefs: Concepts of Health and Medical Practice.* Ibadan: University of Ibadan, 1963.

———. "Akufo and Ibarapa." *Lancet* 1 (1965).

———. "Patterns of Psychiatric Care in Developing African Countries: The Nigerian Village Program." In *International Trends in Mental Health.* Edited by Henry P. David. New York: McGraw-Hill, 1966.

———. "Patterns of Psychiatric Care in Developing Countries." In *Magic, Faith, and Healing.* Edited by Ari Kiev. New York: Basic Books, 1964.

———. "Socioeconomic Changes in Africa and Their Implications for Mental Health." In *Man and Africa.* Edited by Gordon Wolsteholme and Maeve O'Connor. Boston: Little, Brown,, 1965.

———. "The Village of Aro." *Lancet* 2 (1964): 513–14.

Lambo, T. A. "The Role of Cultural Factors in Paranoid Psychoses Among the Yoruba Tribe of Nigeria." *Journal of Mental Science* 101, 423 (April 1955): 239–66.

Lambo, T. A, ed. *First Pan-African Psychiatric Conference, Abeokuta, Nigeria.* Ibadan: Government Printer, 1961.

Lawal, Babatunde. "*Ori:* The Significance of the Head in Yoruba Sculpture." *Journal of Anthropological Research* 41 (Spring 1985): 91–103.

Leighton, Alexander, et al. *Psychiatric Disorder Among the Yoruba.* Ithaca: Cornell University Press, 1963.

Leith-Ross, Sylvia. *African Women.* 2nd ed. London: Routledge & Kegan Paul, 1965.

Lewontin, R. C. *Biology as Ideology: The Doctrine of DNA.* New York: Harper Collins, 1991.

Lin, Tsung-Li. "Neurasthenia Revisited: Its Place in Modern Psychiatry." *Culture, Medicine and Psychiatry* 13, 2 (June 1989): 105–29.

Lindsay, Lisa. "Shunting Between Manly Ideals: Nigerian Railway Men, 1935–65." Paper presented at the Thirty-Eighth Annual Meeting of the African Studies Association, Orlando, Florida, November 3–6, 1995. ASA 1195: 72.

Link, Bruce G., et al. "A Modified Labeling Theory Approach to Mental Disorders: An Empirical Assessment." *American Sociological Review* 54 (June 1989): 400–23.

Longino, Helen. *Science as Social Knowledge.* Princeton: Princeton University Press, 1990.

Loring, Marti, and Brian Powell. "Gender, Race, and DSM-III: A Study of the Objectivity of Psychiatric Behavior." *Journal of Health and Social Behavior* 29, 1 (March 1988): 1–22.

Lunbeck, Elizabeth. *The Psychiatric Persuasion: Knowledge, Gender, and Power in Modern America.* Princeton: Princeton University Press, 1994.

Lutz, Catherine. "Depression and the Translation of Emotional Worlds." In *Culture and Depression.* Edited by Arthur Kleinman and Byron Good. Berkeley: University of California Press, 1985.

Lyons, Maryinez. *A Colonial Disease: A Social History of Sleeping Sickness in Northern Zaire, 1900–1940.* Cambridge: Cambridge University Press, 1992.

MacDonald, Michael. *Mystical Bedlam.* Cambridge: Cambridge University Press, 1981.

MacLean, Una. *Magical Medicine: A Nigerian Case Study.* London: Allen Lane, 1971.

Makanjuola, J. D. A., A. O. Odejide, and O. A. Erinosho. *The Integration of Mental Health Into Primary Health Care in Nigeria.* Lagos: Federal Ministry of Health, 1990.

Makanjuola, Roger O. A. "Symbolic Features in the Management of Mental Disorders by Yoruba Traditional Healers." *Psychopathologie africaine* 21, 2 (1986–87): 185–96.

Malinowski, Bronislaw. *Sex and Repression in Savage Society.* London: Routledge and Kegan Paul, 1927.

Mann, Kristin. *Marrying Well: Marriage, Status and Social Change Among the Educated Elite in Colonial Lagos.* Cambridge: Cambridge University Press, 1985.

———. "The Rise of Taiwo Olowo: Law, Accumulation, and Mobility in Early Colonial Lagos." In *Law in Colonial Africa.* Edited by Kristin Mann and Richard Roberts. Portsmouth, NH: Heinemann, 1991.

Mannheim, Karl. *Ideology and Utopia.* New York: Harcourt Brace Jovanovich, 1936.

Marks, Shula. *The Ambiguities of Dependence in South Africa.* Johannesburg: Ravan, 1986.

Marks, Shula, ed. *Not Either an Experimental Doll: The Separate Worlds of Three South African Women.* Bloomington: Indiana University Press, 1987.

Marsella, Anthony J., and Geoffrey M. White, eds. *Cultural Conceptions of Mental Health and Therapy.* Dordrecht: Reidel, 1989; originally published 1982.

Mausner, Judith S., and Shira Kramer. *Epidemiology: An Introductory Text.* Philadelphia: Harcourt Brace Jovanovich, 1985.

McClintock, Anne. *Imperial Leather: Race, Gender, and Sexuality in the Colonial Contest.* New York: Routledge, 1995.

McCulloch, Jock. *Colonial Psychiatry and the African Mind.* Cambridge: Cambridge University Press, 1995.

———. "The Empire's New Clothes: Ethnopsychiatry in Colonial Africa." *History of the Human Sciences* 6, 2 (1993): 35–52.

McGovern, Constance M. "The Myths of Social Control and Custodial Oppression: Patterns of Psychiatric Medicine in Late Nineteenth Century Institutions." *Journal of Social History* 20 (Fall 1986): 3–23.

McKenzie, Peter. "Dreams and Visions from Nineteenth Century Yoruba Religion." In *Dreaming, Religion and Society in Africa.* Edited by M. C. Jedrej and Rosalind Shaw. New York: Brill, 1992.

Micale, Mark. "Hysteria and Its Historiography: A Review of Past and Present Writings." *History of Science* 27, 3 and 4 (1989): 223–61, 319–51.

Midlefort, Erik C. "Madness and Civilization in Early Modern Europe: A Reappraisal of Michel Foucault." In *After the Reformation: Essays in Honor of J. H. Hexter.* Edited by Barbara Malament. Philadelphia: University of Pennsylvania Press, 1980.

Morakinyo, Olufemi. "Phobic States Presenting as Somatic Complaints Syndromes in Nigeria: Socio-cultural Factors Associated with Diagnosis and Psychotherapy." *Acta Psychiatrica Scandinavia* 71, 4 (April 1985): 356–65.

———. "The Yoruba *Ayanmo* Myth and Mental Health Care in West Africa." *Journal of Culture and Ideas* 1, 1 (1983): 61–92.

Morakinyo, Olufemi, and Akinsola Akiwowo. "The Yoruba Ontology of Personality and Motivation: A Multidisciplinary Approach." *Journal of Social and Biological Structures* 4 (1981): 19–38.

Morgan, Kemi. *Akinyele's Outline History of Ibadan: Part One.* Ibadan: Caxton Press, n.d.

Mudimbe, V. Y. *The Invention of Africa.* Bloomington: Indiana University Press, 1988.

Mullings, Leith. *Therapy, Ideology, and Social Change: Mental Healing in Urban Ghana.* Berkeley: University of California Press, 1984.

Murphy, Jane. "Psychiatric Labeling in Cross-Cultural Perspective." *Science* 191, 4231 (March 1976): 1019–28.

Murray, Charles, and Richard Herrnstein. *The Bell Curve: Intelligence and Class Structure in American Life.* New York: Free Press, 1994.

Nandy, Ashis. *The Intimate Enemy: Loss and Recovery of Self Under Colonialism.* Delhi: Oxford University Press, 1983.

Neale, Caroline. *Writing "Independent" History: African Historiography, 1960 – 1980.* Westport, CT.: Greenwood, 1985.

Ng, Vivien. *Madness in Late Imperial China.* Norman: University of Oklahoma Press, 1990.

Nicolson, Ian. *The Administration of Nigeria, 1900 –1960.* Oxford: Clarendon Press, 1969.

Nolan-Hoeksema, Susan. *Sex Differences in Depression.* Stanford: Stanford University Press, 1990.

Obembe, Ayodele. "Nigerian Psychiatry—Past, Present, Future." In *Psychiatry in Developing Countries.* Edited by Stephen Brown. London: Gaskell, 1983.

Obeyesekere, Gananath. "Buddhism, Depression, and the Work of Culture in

Sri Lanka." In *Culture and Depression*. Edited by Arthur Kleinman and Byron Good. Berkeley: University of California Press, 1985.

———. *Medusa's Hair: An Essay on Personal Symbols and Religious Experience*. Chicago: University of Chicago Press, 1981.

Odejide, A. O., Lamidi Kolawole Oyeminmi, and Jude Uzoma Ohaeri. "Psychiatry in Africa: An Overview." *American Journal of Psychiatry* 146, 6 (1989): 708–16.

Okara, Gabriel. *The Voice*. London: Heinemann, 1964.

Omu, Fred. *Press and Politics in Nigeria, 1880–1937*. Atlantic Highlands, NJ: Humanities Press, 1978.

Orde Browne, G. St. J. "Witchcraft and British Colonial Law." *Africa* 8, 4 (October 1935).

Ordia, Abraham. "A Brief Outline of the History and Development of Mental Health Service and Facilities in Nigeria for the Care and Treatment of Mentally Ill Patients." In *Mental Disorders and Mental Health in Africa South of the Sahara*. Bukavu: Scientific Council for Africa South of the Sahara publication #35, 1958.

Orley, John H. *Culture and Mental Illness: A Study from Uganda*. Nairobi: East African Publishing House, 1970.

Packard, Randall M. "The 'Healthy Reserve' and the 'Dressed Native': Discourses on Black Health and the Language of Legitimation in South Africa." *American Ethnologist* 16, 4 (November 1989): 686–703.

———. *White Plague, Black Labor: Tuberculosis and the Political Economy of Health and Disease in South Africa*. Berkeley: University of California Press, 1989.

Parry-Jones, William L. "The Model of the Geel Lunatic Colony and Its Influence on the Nineteenth-Century Asylum System in Britain." In *Madhouses, Mad-Doctors, and Madmen: The Social History of Psychiatry in the Victorian Era*. Edited by Andrew Scull. Philadelphia: University of Pennsylvania Press, 1981.

Patton, Adell, Jr. *Physicians, Colonial Racism, and Diaspora in West Africa*. Gainesville: University of Florida Press, 1996.

Peel, J. D. Y. *Aladura: A Religious Movement Among the Yoruba*. Suffolk: University of Oxford, 1968.

———. "The Cultural Work of Yoruba Ethnogenesis." In *History and Ethnicity*. Edited by Elizabeth Tonkin, Maryon MacDonald, and Malcolm Chapman. London: Routledge, 1989.

———. *Ijeshas and Nigerians: The Incorporation of a Yoruba Kingdom*. Cambridge: Cambridge University Press, 1983.

———. "The Pastor and the *Babalawo*: The Interaction of Religions in Nineteenth-Century Yorubaland." *Africa* 60 (1990): 338–69.

Pemberton, John, III, and Funso S. Afolayan. *Yoruba Sacred Kingship: "A Power Like That of the Gods"* Washington, DC: Smithsonian Institution Press, 1996.

Phillips, Anne. *The Enigma of Colonialism: British Policy in West Africa*. London: James Currey, 1989.

Porter, Roy. *Mind Forg'd Manacles: A History of Madness in England from the Restoration to the Regency*. London: Penguin, 1987.

————. "The Patient's View: Doing Medical History from Below." *Theory and Society* 14 (1985): 175–98.

Prince, Raymond. "The 'Brain Fag' Syndrome in Nigerian Students." *Journal of Mental Science* 116 (1960): 559–70.

————. "The Changing Picture of Depressive Syndromes in Africa: Is It Fact or Diagnostic Fashion?" *Canadian Journal of African Studies* 1, 2 (November 1967): 177–92.

————. "The Concept of Culture-Bound Syndromes: Anorexia Nervosa and Brain-Fag." *Social Science and Medicine* 21, 2 (1985): 197–203.

————. "Curse, Invocation, and Mental Health Among the Yoruba." *Canadian Psychiatric Association Journal* 5, 2 (April 1960): 65–79.

————. "Indigenous Yoruba Psychiatry." In *Magic Faith, and Healing.* Edited by Ari Kiev. New York: Free Press of Glencoe, 1964.

————. "The Use of Rauwolfia by Nigerian Native Doctors." *American Journal of Psychiatry* 118 (1960): 147–49.

————. "The Yoruba Image of the Witch." *Journal of Mental Science* 107 (1961): 795–805.

Prins, Gwyn. "But What Was the Disease? The Present State of Health and Healing in African Studies." *Past and Present* 124 (August 1989): 159–79.

Ranger, Terence. "Godly Medicine: The Ambiguities of Medical Mission in Southeastern Tanzania." In *The Social Basis of Health and Healing in Africa.* Edited by John Janzen and Steven Feierman. Berkeley: University of California Press, 1992.

Ranger, Terence, and Eric Hobsbawm. *The Invention of Tradition.* Cambridge: Cambridge University Press, 1983.

Reaume, Geoffrey. "Keep Your Labels off My Mind! or 'Now I Am Gong to Pretend I Am Craze but Dont Be a Bit Alarmed': Psychiatric History from the Patients' Perspectives." *Canadian Bulletin of the History of Medicine* 11 (1994): 397–424.

Rhodes, Lorna Amarasingam. "The Subject of Power in Medical / Psychiatric Anthropology." In *Ethnopsychiatry: The Cultural Construction of Professional and Folk Psychiatries.* Edited by Atwood Gaines. Albany: State University of New York Press, 1992.

Robinson, Cedric. "The Appropriation of Frantz Fanon." *Race and Class* 15 (1993): 79–91.

Rosenberg, Charles. "Framing Disease." In *Explaining Epidemics and Other Essays in the History of Medicine.* Cambridge: Cambridge University Press, 1992.

Rosenberg, Morris. "A Symbolic Interactionist View of Psychosis." *Journal of Health and Social Behavior* 25, 3 (September 1984): 289–302.

Rosenfield, Sarah. "Race Differences in Involuntary Hospitalization: Psychiatric vs. Labeling Perspectives." *Journal of Health and Social Behavior* 25 (March 1984): 14–23.

Rosenhan, D. L. "On Being Sane in Insane Places." *Science* 179, 70 (January 1973): 250–58.

Rothman, David. *The Discovery of the Asylum: Social Order and Disorder in the New Republic.* Rev. ed. Boston: Little, Brown, 1990; originally published 1971.

Rothman, Sheila. *Living in the Shadow of Death: Tuberculosis and the Social Experience of Illness in American History*. New York: Basic Books, 1994.

Rotimi, Ola. *Our Husband Has Gone Mad Again*. Ibadan: University of Ibadan, 1977.

Sachs, Wulf. *Black Hamlet*. Edited by Saul Dubow and Jacqueline Rose. Baltimore: Johns Hopkins University Press, 1996; originally published 1937.

Sadowsky, Jonathan. "The Confinements of Isaac O.: A Case of 'Acute Mania' in Colonial Nigeria." *History of Psychiatry* 7 (1996): 91–112.

———. "Psychiatry and Colonial Ideology in Nigeria." *Bulletin of the History of Medicine* 71, 1 (Spring 1997): 94–111.

Sartorius, Norman, et al. *Schizophrenia: An International Follow-up Study*. Chichester: Wiley, 1979.

Scheff, Thomas. *Being Mentally Ill: A Sociological Theory*. 2nd ed. Chicago: Aldine de Gruyter, 1982.

Scheibinger, Londa. "Skeletons in the Closet: The First Illustrations of the Female Skeleton in Eighteenth-Century Anatomy." In *The Making of the Modern Body*. Edited by Thomas Laqueur and Catherine Gallagher. Berkeley: University of California Press, 1987.

———. "Why Mammals Are Called Mammals: Gender Politics in Eighteenth-Century Natural History." *American Historical Review* 98, 2 (April 1993): 383–411.

Scheper-Hughes, Nancy, and Margaret M. Lock. "The Mindful Body: A Prolegomenon to Future Work in Medical Anthropology." *Medical Anthropology Quarterly* 1, 1 (1987): 6–41.

Schram, Ronald. *A History of the Nigerian Health Services*. Ibadan: University of Ibadan, 1971.

Scott, James. *Domination and the Arts of Resistance*. New Haven: Yale University Press, 1990.

Scott, Joan. "The Evidence of Experience." In *Questions of Evidence: Proof, Practice, and Persuasion Across the Disciplines*. Edited by James Chandler, Arnold I. Davidson, and Harry Harootunian. Chicago: University of Chicago Press, 1994.

Scull, Andrew. *Decarceration: Community Treatment and the Deviant: A Radical View*. Englewood Cliffs, NJ: Prentice Hall, 1977.

———. *The Most Solitary of Afflictions: Madness and Society in Britain, 1700–1900*. New Haven: Yale University Press, 1993.

———. "Psychiatry and Social Control in the Nineteenth and Twentieth Centuries." *History of Psychiatry* 2, 2 (1991): 149–69.

Shorter, Edward. *A History of Psychiatry: From the Era of the Asylum to the Age of Prozac*. New York: Wiley, 1997.

———. "Paralysis: The Rise and Fall of a 'Hysterical' Symptom." *Journal of Social History* 19, 4 (Summer 1986): 549–82.

Showalter, Elaine. *The Female Malady*. New York: Viking, 1985.

Simpson, George E. *Yoruba Religion and Medicine in Ibadan*. Ibadan: University of Ibadan, 1980.

Smith, Dorothy. *The Conceptual Practices of Power: A Feminist Sociology of Knowledge*. Boston: Northeastern University Press, 1990.

Smith, Robert. *Kingdoms of the Yoruba.* 3rd ed. Madison: University of Wisconsin Press, 1988.

Sodipo, J. O., and Barry Hallen, *Knowledge, Belief, and Witchcraft: Analytic Experiments in African Philosophy.* London: Ethnographica, 1986.

Sow, Ibrahim. *Anthropological Structures of Madness in Black Africa.* New York: International Universities Press, 1980.

Soyinka, Wole. *Madmen and Specialists.* New York: Hill and Wang, 1971.

———. *Myth, Literature, and the African World.* Cambridge: Cambridge University Press, 1976.

Spence, Jonathan. *The Question of Hu.* New York: Knopf, 1988.

Srole, Leo, et al. "The Midtown Manhattan Longitudinal Study versus the 'Mental Paradise Lost Doctrine': A Controversy Joined." *Archives of General Psychiatry* 37, 2 (February 1980): 209–21.

Stepan, Nancy. *The Idea of Race in Science: Great Britain, 1800–1960.* London: Archon Books, 1982.

Stowe, Steven. "Seeing Themselves at Work: Physicians and the Case Narrative in the Mid-Nineteenth-Century American South." *American Historical Review* 101,1 (February 1996): 41–79.

Swartz, Sally. "Changing Diagnoses in Valkenberg Asylum, Cape Colony, 1891–1920: A Longitudinal View." *History of Psychiatry* 6 (1995): 431–51.

Szasz, Thomas. *The Myth of Mental Illness*

Tartakoff, Helen H. "The Normal Personality in Our Culture and the Nobel Prize Complex." In *Psychoanalysis: A General Psychology.* Edited by Rudolph M. Loewenstein, et al. New York: International Universities Press, 1966.

Taussig, Michael. *Mimesis and Alterity: A Particular History of the Senses.* New York: Routledge, 1993.

Tomes, Nancy. *A Generous Confidence: Thomas Story Kirkbride and the Art of Asylum-Keeping, 1840–1883.* Cambridge: Cambridge University Press, 1984.

Trouillot, Michel-Rolph. "Anthropology and the Savage Slot: The Poetics and Politics of Otherness." In *Recapturing Anthropology: Working in the Present.* Edited by Richard G. Fox. Santa Fe: School of American Research, 1991.

Tutuola, Amos. *My Life in the Bush of Ghosts.* New York: Grove, 1954.

Vail, Leroy, ed. *The Creation of Tribalism in Southern Africa.* Berkeley: University of California Press, 1991.

Vaughan, Megan. *Curing Their Ills: Colonial Power and African Illness.* Stanford: Stanford University Press, 1991.

———. "Healing and Curing: Issues in the Social History and Anthropology of Medicine in Africa." *Social History of Medicine* 7, 2 (1994): 283–95.

———. "Idioms of Madness: Zomba Lunatic Asylum, Nyasaland, in the Colonial Period." *Journal of Southern African Studies* 9, 2 (1983): 218–38.

Vonnegut, Mark. *The Eden Express.* New York: Praeger, 1975.

Warren, Howard C. *Dictionary of Psychology.* Boston: Houghton Mifflin, 1934.

Waxler, Nancy. "Is Mental Illness Cured in Traditional Societies? A Theoretical Analysis." *Culture, Medicine, and Psychiatry* 1 (1977): 233–54.

Westley, David. *Mental Health and Psychiatry in Africa: An Annotated Bibliography.* London: Hans Zell, 1993.

Winslow, Forbes, ed. *An Act for the Regulation of the Care and Treatment of Lunatics.* London: W. Benning, 1845.

Wober, Mallory. *Psychology in Africa.* London: International African Institute, 1975.

Wolf, Eric. *Europe and the People Without History.* Berkeley: University of California Press, 1982.

Wolpe, Harold. "Capitalism and Cheap Labour-Power in South Africa: From Segregation to Apartheid." In *The Articulation of Modes of Production.* London: Routledge and Kegan Paul, 1980.

Wurmser, Leon. *The Mask of Shame.* Baltimore: Johns Hopkins University Press, 1981.

Young, Crawford. *The African Colonial State in Comparative Perspective.* New Haven: Yale University Press, 1994.

INDEX

My Life in the Bush of Ghosts (Tutuola), 11

nakedness, as symptom of madness, 15, 75, 90
Nandy, Ashis, 119n4
Nigerian National Archives, vii, 49, 55

Obeyesekere, Gananath, 74, 75
objectivity, 97, 109
Of Revelation and Revolution (Comaroff and Comaroff), 73
Oloye of Oye, 68, 139n81
Onisegun, 14
Onishan of Ishan, 57
Ordia, Abraham, 42
Ori Ode, 62
Orisa, 14, 15
Osunwole, Samuel, viii
Oye, 68

paranoia, 54, 58, 69
patients' perspectives, 3, 7–8, 48–52
Peel, J. D. Y., 12
phenoziathines, 14
Phillips, C., 19, 20
Pinel, Philippe, 41
police, 72, 90
Pottinger, J. H., 54
prisons, 29
Prince, Raymond, 14, 61, 62
Psychiatric Disorder Among the Yoruba (Leighton, et al.), 9, 46
psychiatry, vii
historiography of , 3–5, 26
psychoanalysis, 71, 72, 73, 107
Psychology of Mau Mau (Carothers), 106, 109
Psychopharmacology, 110. See also under particular medications

Rattray, R. S., 38
Rauwolfia, 14
resistance, 76, 89, 90–92, 105
Rhodes, Lorna, 49

Rosenberg, Charles, 111

Scheff, Thomas, 6, 7, 93, 112, 121n22
schizophrenia, 15, 108, 111, 114
Smith, Robert, 13
social control, vii, 4, 27, 47, 92–96, 115
soldiers, 40–41
somatization, 60–65
Sri Lanka, 74
stereotypes, 80, 98, 105–10
stigma, 6, 7, 23, 33, 39, 41, 44, 59
Swarts, Sally, 120n9
Szasz, Thomas, 93

Tartakoff, Helen, 72
Taussig, Michael, 111, 112
Tayo, Michael, 81
Times (Lagos), 23
Tutuola, Amos, 11
twin studies, 7

Vaughan, Megan, vii, 3, 8, 74, 116

Weekly Record (Lagos), 12, 22, 24
Weekly Times (Lagos), 23
witchcraft, 37, 38
Witchcraft, Oracles, and Magic Among the Azande (Evans-Pritchard), 38
Winslow, Forbes, 26
World Health Organization, 9, 105, 113, 114
World War II, 27, 36, 40–41
Wretched of the Earth (Fanon), 3, 76, 77

Yaba Lunatic Asylum (later, Yaba Mental Hospital), 1, 10, 28, 29, 40, 41, 42, 59, 78, 79, 89, 94
Yoruba identity, 10, 12–13, 111
Yoruba medicine, 13–15
Young, Crawford, 45

Zaria, 32
Zomba Lunatic Asylum (Nyasaland), vii

Text:	10/13 Galliard
Display:	Galliard
Composition:	G & S Typesetters, Inc.
Printing and binding:	Thomson-Shore, Inc.